The Sense of Wonder

For Phil, who cannot stop wondering, which is more than worrying.
With love,

The Sense of Wonder

Robert E. Neale

One Part of the *Trilogy of Magic*

Published by Theory and Art of Magic Press

The Sense of Wonder
Robert E. Neale

First Edition, 2014

Published by Theory and Art of Magic Press:
www.TheoryandArtofMagic.com

Lawrence Hass, publisher and editor,
Lawrence@LawrenceHass.com

George Parker, layout, interior design, and cover:
www.GeorgeParker.tv

Kiva Singh, illustrator: www.kivasingh.com

Marja Lingsma, cover art: www.marjalingsma.nl

Jane Kenyon, "Otherwise" from Collected Poems. Copyright © 2005 by The Estate of Jane Kenyon. Reprinted with the permission of The Permissions Company, Inc. on behalf of Graywolf Press, Minneapolis, Minnesota, www.graywolfpress.org.

This book is available as a paperback from Theory and Art of Magic Press, www.TheoryandArtofMagic.com. (Dealers please contact Murphy's Magic Supplies.) It is also available as a downloadable PDF only from Theory and Art of Magic Press, www.TheoryandArtofMagic.com.

Paperback: ISBN-10: 0985532653; ISBN-13: 978-0-9855326-5-9
PDF: ISBN-10: 0985532661; ISBN-13: 978-09855326-6-6

© Copyright 2014 by Robert E. Neale and Lawrence Hass. All rights reserved. No part of this publication may be reproduced, stored in retrieval systems, or transmitted in any form or by any means—electronic, mechanical, photocopying, recording, or otherwise—without the prior written permission of the publisher at: Lawrence@LawrenceHass.com.

For my publishers:

Jeff Busby

Karl Fulves

Larry Hass

Richard Hatch

Todd Karr

Richard Kaufman

Jay Marshall

Stephen Minch

Charlie Randall

Allan Slaight

Man is a small thing,
and the night is very large
and full of wonders.

>   Lord Dunsany
>   *The Laughter of the Gods*

Table of Contents

Introduction, Lawrence Hass, Publisher and Editor..........13

Preface, Robert E. Neale 31

Chapter 1: The Many Worlds of Wonder........................37
    A. Credulous World..38
    B. Ironic World 42
    C. Occult World...47
    D. Sentimental World 51
    E. Word World 53

Performances for Chapter 1 67
    1.1. Rexile 70
    1.2. The Line Between 76
    1.3. The Magic of Patriotism 81
    1.4. On the Romantic Card Trick.........................86
    1.5. The Affair 93
    1.6. Go to the Devil 96
    1.7. Ultimate Sheep and Goats 102
    1.8. You Can't Beat the Devil 106
    1.9. Two Stories I Carry with Me 115

Chapter 2: Will Wonders Never Cease 117
    A. What Wonder Is..121
    B. Where Wonder is Directed 134
    C. Stages of Wonder..148

Performances for Chapter 2 163
    2.1. Toy Ball 165
    2.2. Framed 174
    2.3. Through the Eye of a Needle 184
    2.4. The Tortured Bill 187
    2.5. A King's Mourning 198

Chapter 3: The Mystery of Enchantment 207
    A. Enchantment and Disenchantment 207
    B. Traditional Enchantment 210
    C. Contemporary Enchantment 214
    D. Mystery 218
    E. Wonder 224
    F. Epiphany 228

Performances for Chapter 3 245
    3.1. Prometheus's Box 247
    3.2. Arrow of Good Fortune 252
    3.3. Open Book 257
    3.4. Easy Reader 260
    3.5. Saint of Cardicians 266

Chapter 4: Wonderwork 269
    A. Magic as Trivial 269
    B. Magic as Re-enchantment 271
    C. Magic as Education 277
    D. Wonder Performance 285
    E. A Cautionary Wonder 297

Performances for Chapter 4 302
    4.1. Satan's Solitaire 304
    4.2. Bizarre Impact 309

4.3. Your Mistakes Were Not Made 317
4.4. Kiddy Trinity 324
4.5. Money Purse 329
4.6. Only a Paper Doll 338
4.7. The Risk Trick 343
4.8. Synchronicity Schtick 349
4.9. Aching Heart Illusion 354
4.10. Upside Down Man 360
4.11. Jack's Veto 366
4.12. Twin Towers 371

Bibliography 377

About the Author 391

About Theory and Art of Magic Press 393

Introduction
Lawrence Hass, Publisher and Editor

The Sense of Wonder is the second installment in Robert E. Neale's *Trilogy of Magic*—a triad of books that seeks to explore and understand three foundational themes of magic: illusion, wonder, and magic itself. As the title of this book conveys, you are about to plunge into his careful study and exploration of the second of these themes, the human capacity to *wonder*.

The first installment of the *Trilogy* was *The Magic of Celebrating Illusion* (2013). The third installment will be *An Essay on Magic* (2015); it will feature the original version of Bob's landmark essay on the nature of magic and magic performance that was edited for inclusion in *The Magic Mirror* (Seattle: Hermetic Press, 2002). In addition to the more philosophical chapters on its respective theme, each book in the *Trilogy* includes a whole slate of new, unpublished tricks from Bob Neale's exceptionally creative mind and hands.

In my introduction to *The Magic of Celebrating Illusion*, I explained the history and genesis of Bob's *Trilogy*, so I will not rehash those details here. What I will say again is that it is not a linear or developmental trilogy so there is no need to read the books in order. On the contrary, you can jump in anywhere, and each book can be understood entirely on its own. Even so, readers who continue on to the other books will discover that each one has important areas of overlap with the other two. These overlaps connect the books and help us grasp the inter-relationship between these three elements of our magical lives. All this is why I believe that the *Trilogy* is best modeled in terms of a classical Venn diagram (see figure 1).

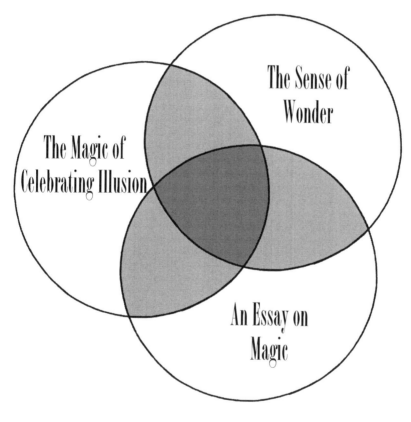

Figure 1

Introduction

The other claim I will repeat here is my firm, continued belief that Bob Neale's *Trilogy of Magic* is the key to understanding his entire body of work as a magician—both as a thinker and as a prolific creator of tricks and presentations. The analogy I previously used still seems correct: the *Trilogy* forms the central hub of ideas, views, and commitments from which radiate all the various spokes of his life-long creative output. To read it is to better understand the man, the extraordinary things he has created, and the extent of his contribution to the art of magic.

In other words, there is *a lot going on* in this book and its two companion volumes, and there is always more going on than it might appear. In general, I would say that this "more going on" thing is a distinctive characteristic of the way Bob thinks and writes. Thus, I want to offer two friendly suggestions to assist your reading—insights that I, myself, have learned from nearly twenty years of reading, editing, and teaching Bob's work. Of course you are free to read these books any way you choose, but I believe keeping these two things in mind will help you get the very most out of your time with them.

First, I suggest that you not assume, the first time through, that you fully understand the *content* of what you are reading. In one sense, Bob Neale is "easy to read"; he uses relatively simple words, avoids jargon, and offers many examples. Thus, it is tempting to assume you are getting it all, and it is tempting to consume his sentences in your rush to finish a chapter or get on to the tricks. However, experience has taught me the cost of this approach: at best, a superficial understanding of his view, or at worst, a mistaken one. In other words, my friendly advice is to *slow down*. Read one paragraph or trick at a time and then stop to think about it, explore it, and test it. Come up with your own examples of what he is discussing; try to extend his ideas to experiences he didn't mention. If you savor Bob's writings rather than swilling them, you will start seeing and getting the "more going on" all over.

To illustrate this, I want to share two specific places (of many) in *The Sense of Wonder* where this slowing down practice paid off for me—one is a passage, the other a trick. The passage is a section at the end of chapter 2 titled "Stages of Wonder." Here, Bob provides a list of what he sees as the three stages of wonder, each with three elements and different outcomes. The first few times I read this section—with its analytic apparatus of *list*, *stages*, *elements*, and *outcomes*—I rather consumed it. But recently, as I was carrying out my most vigilant edit of the chapters, I made myself slow down and think about each stage and their different elements. I made myself think of times in my life when I experienced those stages and aspects. I also thought about times when I failed to do so because I was too bored, busy, hurried, or stuck in a habit. Having done this extra thinking, I now

Introduction

realize how superficial my previous understanding of the section had been, and I saw for the first time that the fairly common view of wonder (discussed below) is, for Bob, only one element of one stage. Wow!

My other example of "seeing more going on" relates to performance piece 4.1, "Satan's Solitaire." I had read this piece several times over the past few years and had perceived its quality, but a few weeks ago I worked through the routine with cards in hand. Another wow! As words on the page, the cutting, dealing, and shuffling used in the routine reads as a procedural description, but in practice the process feels totally free and fair, and thus the pay-off is quite astonishing. Again, it wasn't possible for me to recognize this "more going on" until I made myself slow down and, in this case, pick up the props. Generalizing from my own experiences, I think this slower approach will serve you, too.

My second suggestion is to not assume that you fully understand the *significance* of what you are reading. At the risk of embarrassing Bob, let me say that he is a gentle soul and a humble man. In person and in writing, he is quick to acknowledge the limits of his thinking and the things he doesn't understand. Like Socrates (in *The Apology*), Bob knows that there is a lot he doesn't know. He prefers to offer claims with caution. And he always shares his views with an unstated coda, "until further reflection or evidence shows otherwise." In my view, this intellectual humility is a highly admirable attitude of mind, and you find it in the best thinkers in every field. But it doesn't do much for PR, driving sales, and sweeping claims.

My point is that Bob writes his humility into every page. He is not going to tell you that what you are reading is important or unprecedented. But here is the thing I have learned over twenty years: *with Bob Neale it so often is.* Looking closely, you will discover, time and again, that Bob creates methods and presentations for tricks that are ahead of his time. You will discover entirely new applications for old methods. You will encounter his uncanny talent for connecting tricks and props with literary themes and stories. You will realize that Bob has been a true pioneer in using magic to explore the full range of human life and emotions. (This is something other art forms easily do, but which magic has struggled to do.) And if you read this *Trilogy* thoughtfully, I believe you will come to appreciate that no other magician has seen or said *these* things about illusion, wonder, and magic itself. Bob's accounts of them are exceptionally original; I believe they achieve a new level of insight on these phenomena with which any further discussion of them must come to terms.

Recognizing the significance of Bob Neale's creations, ideas, and views is not to say that you necessarily will "like" every trick, "agree" with every claim, or always feel "comfortable." As a philosopher and an educator, I can tell you that "liking," "agreeing," and "feeing comfortable" are fine attitudes, and they are nice when they happen. But they aren't essential for *learning*. What is essential is that we explore new thoughts and innovations that push our envelope, and thus make it possible to achieve our own new insights and practices. And Bob Neale's *Trilogy of Magic* will do this for you in spades.

It is my own recognition of the larger significance of Bob Neale's work that helps explain why I have committed myself to publishing his *Trilogy*. Because again, I believe the heart and core of his whole approach to magic is laid out in these books, but also because I know that they have the potential to expand your thinking and practice of magic, just as they have done for me.

The Sense of Wonder

So let's turn our attention to the book you hold in your hands, *The Sense of Wonder*. What is going on in this part of the *Trilogy?* Actually, quite a lot; it is probably the most ambitious book of the three. On my reading of it, Bob Neale's primary goal is to expand our understanding of wonder so that we magicians can better strive for it in our performances. (That last sentence is pretty important, so you might want to read it again.) You might ask, why is this expansion necessary? Aren't we already in great shape on wonder? On the contrary, I suspect Bob would say that we are in rather poor shape. He would say, I think, that it is easy to lose a feeling for wonder in our lives, and it is easy to lose sight of how multi-faceted and important our wonders really are.

To help you better understand his concerns, I want to discuss what I have come to see as two primary sources of confusion about wonder. I suspect that Bob would agree, but I am not certain of it. In any event, these are insights I have had after studying *The Sense of Wonder*, and I think they might help you see why the book is worth your time.

The first kind of confusion has to do with how tempting it is to "think about" wonder by settling for a quotation. As Bob will discuss in the chapters below, there is something about wonder itself that resists our carefully studying it. Somehow, when wonder comes up, it *feels better* to offer a quote, and this actively gets in the way of understanding it.

To help you see what I mean, please consider one of today's most popular quotes about wonder, Einstein's oft-cited sentence, "He who can no longer pause to wonder . . . is as good as dead." This is a powerful metaphor and, like all effective metaphors, it generates strong feelings: wonder equals life and that *feels good*. But this quote does not articulate what wonder is and is not, and it does not offer clear examples or consider whether there are different kinds of wonder.

Introduction

Many other familiar quotes scarcely do better when it comes to offering careful thinking about wonder. Here are a small few found in every webpage of quotes on the topic:

> Plato: "Wonder is the beginning of wisdom."
> Aristotle: "Philosophy was born in wonder."
> Ralph Waldo Emerson: "Men love to wonder and that is the seed of science."
> Lao Tzu: "Existence opens from wonder to wonder."
> Abraham Joshua Heschel: "Wonder is the source of all knowledge."
> Ray Bradbury: "If you enjoy living it is not hard to keep your sense of wonder."

And so on and on. My point is *not* that metaphors are bad. They are not bad; metaphors play an extremely important, widespread function in life and art. But that doesn't mean such quotes offer careful, precise understanding of their subject. They don't; that's not their function. And again, there seems to be something about wonder that makes it tempting to settle for a pithy quote.

We can see this problem again in one of the primary references magicians have on the topic of wonder: Sam Sharpe's booklet *Words on Wonder* (1984, reprinted in his *Art and Magic,* The Miracle Factory,

The Sense of Wonder

2003). After a few short chapters in which Sharpe draws the distinction between "illusion" and "wonder" and tells us that "wonder is the most divine of human emotions,"[1] the rest of the book consists of various and sundry quotes about wonder from a wide variety of people—philosophers, scientists, poets, magicians, religious writers, mystics, and Sam Sharpe himself. Again, there is nothing wrong with this, and many of the quotes are thought provoking, but none of it adds up to a clear and coherent view. Indeed, if our thinking remains satisfied with a quote—even a whole book of quotes—we will remain quite unclear about wonder. And this will be a big problem if creating wonder is one of the things we magicians are supposed to be doing.

The other confusion that interferes with wonder is that many magicians assume they already know what it is. In my view, in my experience, when magicians hear or say the word, they think of it as something like an "oooo ahhh, mouth hanging open, feel good moment," perhaps even a "return to childhood." Some magicians today love this idea of wonder and embrace it; others dislike it and reject it. Wherever they land, they still seem to have the same view of wonder in mind—the view bequeathed to us by *Doug Henning*.

Most readers of this book will know that Doug Henning embraced wonder as the whole theme and purpose of his magic. His tremendous and much-deserved success shows how fully this theme spoke to the tie-dyed, peace-and-love, post-Vietnam ethos of his time —the early 1970s. But also it pretty clearly spoke to Henning. Writing about wonder in 1984, he defines wonder as "a beautiful feeling" that "actually transcends the intellect." He continues, "[Wonder] is completely uplifting and elevating in every aspect of the human spirit . . . . It is a true emotion, like love." And so, "The art of a magician is to create wonder, and if we live with a sense of wonder, our lives will be filled with joy."²

All this sounds pretty groovy, and it was. (Hey, I was there!) My point here is that somewhere along the line, and no doubt because of his great celebrity, Doug Henning's particular "oooo ahhh, feel good" view of wonder somehow became the whole of wonder. For magicians of an entire generation—and for many magicians still today—the word "wonder" automatically calls up something like Doug's view. The problem is, as Bob Neale will quickly show (chapter 1), this default view of wonder is totally insufficient. To be precise, Bob argues that we certainly do experience oooo ahhh, feel good, childlike wonder, but it is *only one type or style of wonder*, and a fairly limited one at that. In other words, there is a lot more going on with wonder than magicians themselves might realize.

With this in place, I can now elucidate the overall character of *The Sense of Wonder*. At the outset of this section, I stated that Bob Neale sets out to "expand" our understanding of wonder, and this word is literally true.

He seeks to show that instead of there being one, simple, single thing "Wonder," there are, in fact, *several different styles or flavors of wonder that belong to different spheres or domains of life*. Here are the details:

In chapter 1, Bob lays out five common, yet limited "worlds" (he calls them), in which we experience different wonders: in our credulity, in our irony, in our sentimentality, in our flirtations with the occult, and in our wonder words.

In chapter 2, Bob sets out to take us to another "world of wonder," a deeper and richer one: the psychological and ethical one in which we learn to greet and respect things, events, and other people in their arresting complexity. (If there is anything in this book that can be called "Bob Neale's preferred world of wonder," it probably would be this one.)

In chapter 3, Bob rolls up his sleeves and bares his soul to separate his psychological-ethical view of wonder from currently popular notions of "mystery" and "enchantment." (I'll give you a preview: he is finished with mystery, and happy to be rid of it.)

Then in the final chapter 4—a chapter of exhilarating significance to magic performers—he elaborates how magicians can draw upon these insights to create more, better, and more different wonders for their audiences.

I realize that what I have just laid out might appear to be a bit overwhelming. In actual reading and practice it is far less so. Everything in this book unfolds one step at a time. Also, as I mentioned earlier, Bob's language is not jargon-y, and he gives many examples—it is no problem if you proceed slowly and thoughtfully. If one feels a bit blown away by the prospect of what lies ahead, it might be because one hasn't thought quite this expansively about wonder before. This is exactly why thoughtful magicians need to read *The Sense of Wonder*, and for me, it is one of the great pleasures of doing so: Bob Neale is way out ahead of me on this subject, showing me that there is a lot "more going on" than I had realized. And so I *learn*.

In this section, I have tried to elucidate what is in store as you read *The Sense of Wonder*. I have done so by highlighting two common confusions when it comes to wonder—resting content with quotations and already assuming the Doug Henning view of it. If you are like me, over the course of this book you will see that wonder is so much more than most people think and that magicians ought to do much better on its behalf. Wherever you land at the end of your journey with this book, I am sure you won't think of wonder the same way again.

The Wonder Performances

In my introduction to *The Magic of Celebrating Illusion*, I explained in detail how Bob and I worked together to select the performance pieces that would go along with each chapter of the first two installments (*Illusion* and *Wonder*). Again briefly, I had well over a hundred and fifty previously unpublished routines from which to select. I studied them all and made suggestions to Bob about which ones might be especially good and appropriate in relation to the specific themes of each chapter in these two books. In addition to thematic fit, I was also looking for routines that featured: 1) particularly interesting or deceptive methods, 2) a wide variety of props, and 3) a wide variety of presentation themes and tones. Bob and I worked through my suggestions, and we arrived at the twenty-one performance pieces that appeared in *The Magic of Celebrating Illusion* and the thirty-one pieces you will find in *The Sense of Wonder*.

Speaking for myself, I believe that there is incredible performing material in this book, including one piece that made me cry, one that tickles me to laughter, one that is sitting on my fireplace mantel, one that continues to astonish me even though I know the secret, and one that hit me so hard I immediately put the manuscript down and started working on it. (A version of it is now in my professional repertoire.) How many magic trick books can generate such a wide variety of responses? Not all that many, and I think you would find that Bob Neale would have authored more than one of them.

Introduction

At the time of this writing, Bob and I have decided upon most of the unpublished routines that will be included in *An Essay on Magic*. These selections were made from two additional, large manuscripts of unpublished materials, and we will be including *a lot* of them. So please do come back for the third installment of the *Trilogy* in 2015. In addition to Bob's original version of his landmark essay on magic, many extraordinary routines will await you there.

Concluding Words

In these pages I have tried to welcome readers who are jumping into Bob Neale's *Trilogy of Magic* by providing some context and information about the project. I have also shared some suggestions about how to approach *The Sense of Wonder* and what lies in store for you. Personally, I have been incredibly stimulated by this book, and I am honored to be a part of bringing this book to magicians and scholars of magic everywhere.

I have some important thanks to give people who have supported my work on this book. These acknowledgments will resemble but not duplicate those made in *The Magic of Celebrating Illusion*:

To Bob Neale for being a wise teacher, dear friend, and great partner in this project. And to Gail Neale for much love and kindness.

Once again to Stephen Minch for granting permission for me to publish this *Trilogy*, for his kind words of appreciation and support, and for indispensable help with some of the references.

To my exceptional team of artists: George Parker (layout, interior design, and cover), Marja Lingsma (front cover still life), and Kiva Singh (the interior illustrations). Thank you for your talents and generosity!

To Craig Conley and Mike Henkel for, again, copy-editing the manuscript with their super-sharp eyes. Also to Mike Warwick for assistance in this regard.

To Max Maven for his generous assistance with references and proper crediting, and for his support of this project.

To Bill Goodwin and Lisa Cousins, Librarians of the William W. Larsen, Sr., Memorial Library at the Magic Castle, who helped me track down references between my shows during Magic & Mystery School Week (January 2014).

To the extraordinary community of the Magic and Meaning Conference—a community of magicians, scholars, teachers, friends, and thinkers who come together every October in Las Vegas to celebrate and explore the art of magic. Thank you all for your support of my thinking and presentations over the years and for your tremendous reception last year of *The Magic of Celebrating Illusion*.

Introduction

To the Faculty of the Magic & Mystery School, dear friends and colleagues: Jeff McBride (without whose vision, energy, and resources there would be no School), Eugene Burger, Bryce Kuhlman, Tobias Beckwith, Abigail McBride, and George Parker. Also to our other teachers and close friends: Ross Johnson, Kenton Knepper, Marja Lingsma, Jenny Pauls, Ricardo Rosenkranz, Tim Wise, and Jordan Wright.

Also to my loving family: Cameron Hass, Jessica Hass, and my wife Marjorie Hass. Marjorie: thank you for everything you do that allows me to pursue my bliss—to be a performer, teacher, and publisher of magic, all day and every day.

And finally, once again, to my many friends and mentors in magic whom I mentioned by name in *The Magic of Celebrating Illusion*. You know who you are and my appreciation is ongoing, deep, and sincere. There is, however, one dear friend whose name was inadvertently left off that list: Tom Meseroll. Thank you, Tom, and thank you for understanding.

My work on this book is dedicated to the memory of Jill Meseroll, who passed away, much too soon, on December 13, 2013.

—Lawrence Hass
Sherman, Texas

February 24, 2014

Notes

1. S. H. Sharpe, *Words on Wonder*, included in *Art and Magic*, edited by Todd Karr and Vito Lupo (no city: The Miracle Factory, 2003), pages 179-226. This quote is from page 184. The book was originally published by Wonder Publications in 1984.

2. Doug Henning, "Introduction" to S. H. Sharpe's *Words on Wonder*, included in *Art and Magic*, pages 181-182.

Preface
Robert E. Neale

Wonder is a subject that must be explored but about which almost nothing can be said. So a great many thinkers mention it and then leave it alone.

For a few examples: Sam Sharpe tackled the subject on behalf of magicians. His valuable text *Words on Wonder* discusses magic as the "evocation of wonder" and offers an important reminder on the distinction between wonder and illusion and also the relationship between them.[1] Doug Henning, who wrote the introduction to Sharpe's book, illuminated the spirit of wonder in his performances. He embodied what he defined as the purpose of magic—"to create mystery to be experienced with wonder"—and he communicated what he proclaimed, "if we live with a sense of wonder, our lives will be filled with joy."[2] Paul Harris titled his three-volume work on close-up magic *The Art of Astonishment* (Rancho Cordova, CA: A-1 Multimedia, 1996), and in an epigraph at the end of Book 1, he observes, "We play together, the audience and me, until only astonishment remains."[3] His opening essay to that book, "Astonishment is our Natural State of Mind," reminds magicians of their own first experiences of magic and promotes the role of magician to stimulate others as "astonishment guides."[4] And like Henning on stage, Martin Gardner performed as a writer, exhibiting wonder over just about everything—including "nothing." The spirit of wonder revealed in his many columns and books has stimulated people in different disciplines over many years all over the world. It is an incredibly free spirit. More than any other single source, it has influenced both my creation of tricks and my thinking about magic. For a sample of his observations about wonder itself, read his essay "Surprise" in the collection *The Night Is Large* (New York: St. Martin's Press, 1996), pages 551-565. I have used his quotation from Dunsany as the epigraph to this book, just as I have used many other quotations as well as his own ideas. Martin Gardner's work is a wonder.

It is interesting that Henning and Harris say little about the actual experience of wonder. Sharpe and Gardner offer somewhat more, but not very much more. They all rely heavily on quotations. I understand why. When it comes to wonder, words fail; it is difficult to say anything. Nevertheless, the subject is about an experience that is fundamental to magic . . . but also to religion . . . and science . . . and the arts. So I will explore it anyway.

The opening chapter of this book considers five different approaches to wonder, some of which I believe to be quite limited. The following chapter, "Will Wonders Never Cease," is my basic attempt to articulate the nature and dynamics of the phenomenon; thus it is the best place to go to see my core view of wonder. Chapter 3 tackles the important topic of "mystery" and concludes that wonder occurs perfectly well outside of the language and notions of "enchantment" and "mysterious, hidden, transcendent reality." The last chapter, "Wonder Work," is about performance magic and contains comments on the function of this entertainment as related to wonder. As the table of contents reveals, each chapter also includes a number of my wonder tricks and wonder things, each of which relates in some way to the ideas of the chapter. My hope is that these performance offerings prompt the experience of wonder in you and the people with whom you share them.

It is quite wonderful to be re-considering these ideas and tricks in 2013, over thirteen years after they were originally created. This is not a sentimental affirmation but an evaluation of the content as both "awesome" and "awful".

To understand my complex reaction, please recall the first sentence of this preface, "Wonder is a subject that must be explored, but about which almost nothing can be said. So a great many thinkers mention it and then leave it alone." Should I have followed their lead? Should I have heeded their implicit advice? No. I would rather try and fail than not try at all. Besides, I do like my basic understanding of wonder as respect (about which I mean nothing sentimental either). And I also like my failures. I will like them even more if there are readers who are stimulated by them to discover their own understandings, especially if they differ from my own. Such differences are wondrous when we have the nerve to acknowledge and play with them. Perhaps differences between individual understandings are the most fruitful of all for illustrating the dynamics of wonder.

I am still wondering about magic. How could it be otherwise? And maybe it even *should be*. In any event, I am going about it the long, long way. My current project is writing another book. I have taken the theme from Shakespeare's Prospero, that old magician who breaks his magic wand while still alive. What if I, and the other magicians I know, did the same: break our wands while still alive? What might that look like? What would it mean? And since all of us are magicians in our everyday lives, what if we all did that, too? Is the old breakaway wand an apt symbol for a trick we need to play on ourselves? I don't know, but that is what I am playing with. What are the different ways of breaking a magic wand? Can it even be done? Would it be too destructive? Or might it be more liberating than we could tolerate? I don't know, but I continue to wonder.

In other words, my latest project continues to reflect and express this earlier one that is now in your hands: *The Sense of Wonder*.

Notes

1. S. H. Sharpe, *Words on Wonder*, second edition, in *Art and Magic*, edited by Todd Karr and Vito Lupo (No city: The Miracle Factory, 2003), pages 179-226. The first edition was edited by Todd Karr and published in 1984 by Wonder Publications.

2. Doug Henning, "Introduction" to *Words on Wonder*, in *Art and Magic*, pages 181 and 182, respectively.

3. Paul Harris, *The Art of Astonishment, Book 1* (Rancho Cordova, CA: A-1 Multimedia, 1996), page 311.

4. Paul Harris, *The Art of Astonishment, Book 1*, page 5.

5. Martin Gardner, "Surprise" in *The Night Is Large: Collected Essays 1938-1995* (New York: St. Martin's Press, 1996), pages 551-565.

Chapter 1
The Many Worlds of Wonder

Come, let us wonder about wonder. As Shakespeare allows it to be exclaimed, "O wonderful, wonderful, and most wonderful wonderful! and yet again wonderful, and after that, out of all whooping!"[1] Such babbling abounds from those who wonder about the wonderful. However, when Dr. Watson ejaculates, "Wonderful!" Sherlock Holmes replies, "Commonplace."[2] We should wonder about those who wonder.

Yet we are magicians and if so thaumaturgists, that is, workers of wonders. Perhaps our art or craft entitles and prompts us to become guardians of wonder and gurus of wondering. If so, magicians should be those entertainers who know about, exhibit, and inculcate wonder. That they don't do so hardly needs explication. The claim that they could and should do so needs much exploration.

This opening chapter is about how we wonder. It involves cursory reference to five worlds of wonder—the all too common worlds of the credulous, ironic, occult, and sentimental, and the more rarely employed world of language. These ways of experiencing and responding to wonder are wondrous in their own right but hardly to be welcomed without equivocation. We should wonder about those who wonder, especially when they are ourselves.

A. Credulous World

Imagine walking up to a large cabinet, peering inside, and taking note of the following: petrified eggs in which the yolk rattles, a hedgehog, pieces of amber with insects in them, amber cut in the shape of a heart with a salamander inside, a cock with four legs, a hen with two large spurs growing out of her sides, a hydraulic organ, and mechanical birds moving and chirping by the force of water.[3] It takes little further imagination to suspect that such a collection of curiosities is not contemporary. Other collections from the same general period contained a round horn that had appeared and grown on the forehead of an Englishwoman, the tail of a unicorn, and the hand of a mermaid.[4] The cabinet might contain yet another type of curiosity: porcelain from China, chain of monkey teeth, canoe with paddles from "India," a Turkish ruler's golden seal. An empty cabinet of the period might prompt a letter such as one seeking:

> All maner of Beasts and fowells . . .
> All sorts of Serpents and Snakes Skines and Espetially of that sort that hathe a combe on his lead Lyke a Cock

Chapter 1: The Many Worlds of Wonder

> All sorts of Shining Stones or of Any Strange Shapes

And indeed, the letter concludes:

> Any thing that Is strang.[5]

Some animals, early peoples, contemporary children, and just about everyone else, collect things that have managed to call attention to themselves. The cathedrals and churches of Europe were our early museums, holding beautiful and curious objects as well as holy ones. After the establishment of museums, collections spread enormously through magazines that revealed marvels with ease. Most recently, Marcel Duchamp and Joseph Cornell offered collections as artistic displays. But back between the cathedrals and the modern museums there occurred those displays of "any thing that is strange." They began in Italy during the sixteenth century and spread throughout Europe. Upper class gentlemen did not labor, had little else to do, and favored this sort of intellectual conspicuous consumption. They explored and exhibited antiquities, the arts, exotic cultures, and all the rarities and oddities of nature. The overly present taste for the curious and strange is denoted by the nomenclature "*Wunderkammern*" (Wonder-Cabinet). These collections predate, and led into, museums, and were formed and exhibited with some scientific interest. Wonder was regarded as an aspect of learning—a condition of the mind falling somewhere between ignorance and knowledge. As such it was an essential part of science. Francis Bacon supported the fashion and offered a prescription for them as well, suggesting that the "learned gentleman," in attempting to create within "a small compass a model of the universal made private," would want to have ". . . a goodly, huge cabinet, wherein whatsoever the hand of man by exquisite art or engine has made rare in stuff, form or motion; whatsoever singularity, chance and the shuffle of things hath produced; whatsoever Nature has wrought in things that want life and may be kept; shall be sorted and included."[6]

To modern minds, the breadth of such "science" is impressive. The mythological is included with the mundane, the supernatural with the natural. Anatomy was of interest, as were deviations from the normal. In addition to pickling jars of forked carrots and two-headed cats was a stuffed pelican mounted as if stabbing itself with its own beak.[7] Nor was there any hesitancy among some to moralize and preach. What was one to think about a tableau of the skull of a prostitute being kicked by the leg bones of an infant? Or how was one to contemplate a box of eggs from a fly taken from the anus of "a distinguished gentleman who sat too long in the privy."[8] It is no wonder that some scientists of the time grew distant from the collections. Descartes proclaimed, "What we commonly call being astonished is an excess of wonder which can never be otherwise than bad."[9] By the

Chapter 1: The Many Worlds of Wonder

end of the seventeenth century, the collections began to wither and the contents became prosaic.

Of course, wonders never cease. Wonders were nothing new. The cabinets were distinctive in featuring the connection of wonder and somewhat "natural" science. Although the eighteenth century lacked cabinets, it presented the current wonders in different ways. Perhaps we do, too. Suppose that we consider *Wunderkammern* as a metaphor. This is to assume that wonder-cabinets could be fashioned by anyone in any time, place, and culture. Further, it raises the question of content—what curiosities would be included? Something is always strange. The television set is such a cabinet when tuned to any one of a number of talk shows that collect contemporary social oddities.

Let it clearly be said that collections of curiosities have a strong tendency to be goofy. It is not only wonders that never cease; credulity is equally persistent. Yet we must be careful with our retrospection. Open-mindedness that seems unwarranted long after the fact is no spiritual crime. Oddities require investigation. Newton studied and wrote in both physics and alchemy. The lines between what was defined as "science" and what was not, as well as what could be easily investigated or what offered only frustration and disappointment, were drawn differently from the way they are now and not so clearly either.[10] Even so, many colleagues of the early collectors of wonders were highly critical of them.

Credulity can be detected in the present as well as in the past. Offering examples from the present can be difficult. Some seem relatively acceptable across a broad spectrum of society. For example, when a group of people wondered about a comet and then committed suicide in order to board a flying saucer accompanying it, the nation easily concluded that credulity ruled destructively. The belief in heaven is not so easily categorized by our society. The reality and nature of the wonder we label "hypnosis" is debated, not to mention a variety of paranormal phenomena. And what are we to conclude about theories of those perpetually wonderful experiences that occur to us during sleep: dreams?

There is a tension between credulity and skepticism that, I suspect, cannot be eliminated. The latter requires openness and the former supports it. The strange persists and so goofiness abides. It is reasonable to conclude that we participate in it, not contrary to our neighbors but only differently from them. So rather than merely berate or apologize for the goofiness of much focus on wonder, let us also be beware of it in ourselves.

B. Ironic World

One response to this tension is quite as curious and wonderful as the original cabinets. It is the Museum of Jurassic Technology, created by David Wilson, located in

West Los Angeles, and delightfully presented by Lawrence Weschler in *Mr. Wilson's Cabinet of Wonder.*

The storefront contains many gloomy alcoves filled with dusty exhibits, all carefully described in the pedantic and obscure language of scholars. One display features a stink ant of the Cameroonian rain forest. It is grasping a plastic fern with a thin spike sticking out of its head. The telephone beside this display reveals the natural history. This large ant, one of the few offering a cry that can be heard by human beings, usually forages for food on the ground. But it can inhale the spore of a fungus fallen from the trees above. The spore locates itself in the brain of the ant and causes it to climb up stalks and vines, finally grasping the plant with its mandibles and dying. The fungus lives on, eventually causing a protrusion to erupt from the head of the ant. The tip of the spike contains spores which fall down onto the forest floor for other ants to inhale and begin the cycle yet again.[11]

Here is the caption for a display of a vial of amber liquid accompanied by a small brush:

> Urine
> Like spittle, urine has beneficial or protective qualities, and clearly one of the most efficacious and widely practiced counter-charms involves the combination created by the practice of spitting into one's urine.

> On New Year's Day it is a common practice for the oldest woman in the family, employing a small brush, to sprinkle with urine the household animals and then, individually, the members of the family as they are getting out of bed.[12]

And here is another display of folklore with a moral message, the caption accompanying a large pair of scissors:

> Scissors at the Wedding Party
> One wishing ill to the bridegroom stands behind the happy man and, holding an open pair of scissors, calls his name. If the groom turns to answer the scissors are snapped shut whereupon the groom is rendered incapable of consummating the marriage.[13]

It is probably all too clear from the above selection of exhibits that this museum is some kind of a joke. But did you catch on immediately during your reading about the first exhibit? And is it really a joke? The museum presents, as one reviewer put it so very nicely, "phenomena known to science, if known at all, because of their appearance in the museum itself."[14] I doubt that it is so quickly and easily clear for one who actually visits and studies the curiosities. There are, in fact, weird alliances in nature between various forms of life. In general, human body products are deemed potent for good or bad. And the atmosphere of the place fully resembles that of the physically dingy and intellectually stodgy museums we know so well. So, is the Museum of Jurassic Technology a joke? Another reviewer says that it is not, suggesting it is the serious play of a childlike innocent. He notes, "Child's play, after all, when the adults are being imitated, is solemn, very grown-up in tone, and entirely without irony.[15]

Perhaps the creator of the Museum is without communicable irony. But it is hard to imagine that he lacks it entirely. And surely it is difficult for the viewer to not react with a postmodern mood. The museum makes fun of what? Of boring collections of stuff. Of human artifacts viewed totally without cultural context. Of dry descriptions. Of superstition. Of gullibility. Of astonishment. And maybe even of wonder itself. Author Weschler's reaction to curator David Wilson focuses on irony. Apparently, Wilson, informally or during his lectures, never betrays the joke, maintaining a serious composure in offering scholarly elucidation. The result is a delightful education, maybe even one that serves the cause of wonder. Wilson wonders about our wonder and prompts us to wonder about our wonder too.

Irony is a vital tool for illuminating human behavior. Wilson's displays are a most thoughtful art that can awaken the mind to the wonder of our own nonsense. We are humbled with good humor by his coyly impossible objects. But Weschler is reminded of Rainer Maria Rilke's advice to a young poet:

> Irony: do not let yourself be governed by it, especially not in uncreative moments. In creative moments try to make use of it as one more means of grasping life. Cleanly used, it too is clean, and one need not be ashamed of it; and if you feel you are getting too familiar with it, if you fear this growing intimacy with it, then turn to great and serious objects, before which it becomes small and helpless. Seek the depth of things: thither irony never descends—and when you come thus close to the edge of greatness, test out at the same time whether this ironic attitude springs from a necessity of your nature. For under the influence of serious things either it will fall from you (if it is something fortuitous), or else it will (if it really innately belongs to you) strengthen into a stern instrument and take its place in the series of tools with which you will have to shape your art.[16]

Indeed, a cabinet that only mocks the *Wunderkammern* is exceedingly limited, especially in inhibiting our awareness of previous and present versions that are not so clearly housed. There is more to our past and present wonder than can be revealed by such contemporary art. For both the ancient world and the

Renaissance, wonders were real, not make-believe in the service of irony. We still collect odd and beautiful objects, and we do so precisely because they are wondrous for us, not postmodern lessons. Even so, I do have a high regard for deliberate silliness. It is a delightful tonic for goofiness. No disrespect should be inferred from my acknowledging its limitations.

C. Occult World

One of the admired thinkers on the art of magic was S. H. Sharpe. His *Neo Magic: The Art of the Conjurer* and *A Thousand Thoughts on Art & Magic* are fundamental resources for understanding magic.[17] Equally valuable is his *Words on Wonder*.[18] It contains the fine insight of Sharpe's own thoughts about wonder and its relationship to magic, as well as an interesting collection of quotations from a variety of sources. It also raises the issue of the occult. Some of the quotations might give the secular humanist pause. For example, Sharpe quotes himself, "When wonder is genuinely evoked the wonderer is 'lifted out of himself,' or transported, so that all sense of the physical is momentarily lost in a surge of spiritual experience."[19]

Really? Is all sense of the physical left behind? A late quotation from Sharpe's collection of quotes goes further:

> That which we call our world is merely *our incorrect perception of the world*: the world seen by us through a narrow slit. *That world* (i.e., The spiritual world) begins to be sensed by us as *the wondrous*, i.e., as something opposite to the reality of this world; and at the same time *this*, our earthly world, begins to seem unreal. The *sense of the wondrous* is the key to that world.
>
> —P. D. Ouspensky, *A New Model of the Universe*[20]

The content and source of this last quotation are sufficient to encourage us to wonder about the occult. We are reminded that focusing on another world is a traditional motif in religion and the occult.

Sharpe's opening chapter, "The Evocation of Wonder," consists of mostly four very lengthy quotations, one from Ouspensky and three from Rudolf Steiner. From what they say, it is also clear that Ouspensky is concerned about discovering other worlds and Steiner is quite negative about science. Sharpe himself, in introducing these theorists, states his own goal precisely, "The underlying purpose of magic in its many aspects is not to deceive people but to encourage them to approach Life and Cosmos in a state of Wonder."[21] This is an admirable statement. I agree entirely. But he goes on to claim:

Chapter 1: The Many Worlds of Wonder

> The magician of ceremonial magic attempts to represent in external form a picture of the ideal perfected man when bathed in spiritual light. But the secular magician's lamp remains unlit until the occult doctrine begins to shine through his magic. Then he can start to show the Royal Road to others by its light. Mankind is on a quest of eternal life; but since individual men are at various stages of the journey their states of consciousness and susceptibility to wonder differ.[22]

Sharpe continues by stating that our emotions, of which wonder is one, are "secret doors between the natural and supernatural worlds."[23] I have no quarrel with this occult perception of wonder as one out of several, if not many, options. I believe that there are many ways to define and redefine "eternal life" and "supernatural." Some of these might even make sense to contemporary humanists. But surely this will not be an option for many people today. And the very presence of Sharpe's spiritual approach is a reminder of how constantly the occult arises both in connection with the experience of wonder and in opposition to the supposed barrenness of science.

The connection between wonder and the occult, and even the downright bizarre, seems to be ever-present. As an alternative to the goofy world of the credulous and the silly world of the ironic, it presents us with a crazy world. Several times Sharpe refers most affirmatively to the teachings of the "mystery schools" of the past. Such schools have remained and multiplied. Add your own examples to this minuscule list: UFOs, reincarnation, astral projection, out-of-body experiences, extraterrestrials, poltergeists, ESP, telepathy, channeling, clairvoyance, psychic healing, mind over matter, Atlantis, Stonehenge, the Bermuda triangle, the great pyramid, ancient astronauts, and the shroud of Turin. True, some of these phenomena can be positioned in the world of credulity. But it is also true that they are not just items to be created for the benefits of readers of *The National Inquirer*. They reflect actual organizations that function for many people as mystery schools.

Nor are these the only such schools in present society. There are others that appear less crazy to many of us. We will explore this theme later on in the chapter on mystery and enchantment wherein certain schools of psychology and of anthropology are usefully defined as contemporary mystery schools. And there is no doubt at all, I trust, about the whole host of healing groups that exist within, without, and on the fringes of both medicine and religion. Craziness abounds. This is not all bad. Occult behavior occurs because it works.[24] Mystery schools occur because they foster the effectiveness of occult behavior. And mystery is what we human animals covertly create and thrive upon. It may be crazy, but it may also be unavoidable. We will explore this more fully.

For now, perhaps it is useful to assume that the occult creation of mystery is fundamental and so variable that we may not be able to perceive our own participation in it. However, for reasons also to be suggested in chapter 3, we will find that the relationship of wonder can keep the occult in check.

D. Sentimental World

Wonder may have gone out of fashion before contemporary magicians rediscovered it. Max Maven, in the course of extolling the role of the magician in helping audiences experience mystery, adds this resounding cry, "And while we're at it, what about declaring a moratorium on the word 'wonder' as a wimpoid expression of what magic is supposedly all about."[25]

Wondering about the adjective for a moment, we can tentatively conclude that Max considers "wimpoid" applicable to anything that is weak, inept, and square. But is it wonder that is so spineless, whimpering, and behind the times? Is it the people in magic most prone to talk about it? Or is it the manner and meat of the talk itself? Whichever, surely one of the worlds of wonder we encounter in our art is wimpoid. It is corny.

A more traditional term to convey this meaning is "sentimentality." What is it? A sentiment is a mental attitude, thought, or judgment permeated or prompted by feeling. It is an emotional disposition. One who is sentimental has an excess of sentiment that appears artificial and superficial.

What I have heard about wonder reminds me of the middle-aged woman who remarked on seeing the Grand Canyon for the first time, "Oh wouldn't it look nice in Technicolor!" How could she have known? The Grand Canyon is very hard to see, actually. It is so immense that the eyes and mind cannot take it in. It requires hours, maybe days, and at least some descent into its depths, to begin some little appreciation of the space. A picture postcard of this natural monument is actually much easier to look at than the real thing. Perhaps the woman was indirectly expressing a desire for such an instant view. Or maybe she was reducing it all to something she could tell her friends about at home. Whatever the case, she gushed about the wonderful. But a participant is one who sees. And respect means "to see" something. So the true participant is one who respects. The woman's sentimentality was disrespectful. Because of such responses, wonder (as well as a certain comedian), "Don't get no respect."

We are all too often sentimental about wonder. Why? Perhaps this is only because, although we recognize the significance of wonder, we do not know how to talk about it meaningfully. There are other possible reasons. Among these is one suggested by Archibald MacNiece's definition of a sentimentalist, "one who insists on clinging to what he insists is gone."[26] Could our "wimpoid" reaction arise out of, and conceal, despair? Do we doubt that we will ever experience wonder again?

Wonder is no different in this regard than other common words for experiences of importance—love, trust, and caring, for example. Sentimentality trivializes whatever it touches and yet reminds us of our needs. However corny it may be, it does not eliminate our search for experiences of caring, trust, love, and, indeed, for wonder.

Or are we afraid of wonder and so behave sentimentally to protect ourselves from terror? If this seems unlikely, consider wonder as reflected upon in the following world.

E. Word World

An easy and fruitful way to begin thinking about wonder is to play around with definitions. An unabridged dictionary is informative, stimulating, and even challenging.[27] Agreement with its definitions is not necessary or even useful. The purpose is to begin thinking, not to end it. We will look briefly at a few of the words involved: *wonder* itself; the related terms of *surprise, astonish, amaze,* and *admire; awe* and *awful; thaumaturgy.* So if this discussion sounds awful to you, that is as it should be. If this is not your cup of tea, skim over this section lightly.

At the very least, these initial forays into the implications of the terms might remind us of the possible breadth and depth of wonder. At best, they may engender a little more awe over it.

Wonder

Something to wonder about is the fact that a "wonder" is a kind of sweet fried cake. I just thought you ought to know. Is that what some magicians fond of wonder are talking about? Beyond this definition, we end up in circular discussions that bring certain other terms into play repeatedly.

Here are two sentences that attempt to say all that needs to be said in summary form:

> To wonder is to be affected with surprise or admiration; to be struck with astonishment; to marvel. It can also mean to feel doubt and curiosity or to be in a state of uncertain expectation concerning something; to query in the mind; to be anxious to know or find out.

In these two sentences, far more has been suggested than we can quite comprehend. The definitions ask us to wonder about the nature of surprise, admiration, astonishment, marvel, doubt, curiosity, uncertain expectation, and anxiousness to discover. So it immediately is obvious that wondering can be a richly significant experience. Might it even be too rich for many magicians and their audiences?

A wonder is defined as something that causes surprise or astonishment. It is that which excites wonder as an incident, circumstance, achievement, or the like, of perplexing unexpectedness or unaccountability. The focus of this definition is on something perplexing, surprising, and mysterious. Wonder is also defined as the emotion we experience when excited by novelty, or as the presentation to the sight or mind of something new, strange, extraordinary, or not well understood. The feeling is that of being in a perplexed or bewildered condition of mind in the contemplation of something inexplicable or unaccountable.

Suggestions about the opposite of wonder are useful. The dictionary selects three words—*indifference, boredom,* and *ennui.* This is a rather restricted list. Also included would be *ordinary, customary, expected,* and *understood.* However, the suggestions do make it clear that wonder, however much a passive awareness, is a highly aroused state of being. A wonder is a powerful stimulation, and wondering is a state of great stimulation. Need it be observed that we do not always appreciate this condition?

A reference to an obsolete definition of wonder is especially interesting. It can mean *wrong, evil, destruction, harm,* and *grief.* This is probably surprising to us, especially if we have been captured by the sentimental world of wonder. But why is wonder so easily accepted as a totally pleasurable experience? We actually devote ourselves to avoiding the experience, and it is a good thing that we do or we would lose our sanity. Wonder can be awful in the worst sense, filled with the awe over destruction of the understandings that support us.

The related adjective is "wonderful." As we have been reminded by now, it means adapted to excite wonder; *marvelous; surprising; strange; astonishing,* and (obsolete) *miraculous.* It can also mean *admirable; surprisingly interesting, amusing,* and *lovely.* To avoid the sentimental view, note that not just the interesting or amusing or lovely is sufficient, for these must be surprising as well. Synonyms are *wondrous, marvelous, amazing, extraordinary,* and *astonishing.* Antonyms are *ordinary, commonplace,* and *usual.*

Finally, here is a reminder of the combinations offered by wonder: Wonder-bearing, wonder-charmed, wonder-dumb, wonder-loving, wonder-mocking, wonder-promising, wonder-raising, wonder-smitten, wonder-stirring, wonder-stricken, wonder-striking, wonder-teeming, wonder-waiting, wonder-worthy, wonder-wounded, wonder-writing, wonder-work, wonder-worker, and wonder-working.

This reminds us that wonder can charm (in the original sense of casting a spell), smite or strike, and wound us. Indeed, to the extent that we are wonder-workers, it probably has. Or are our efforts in magic devoted to warding off wonder rather than raising it in ourselves and others? Wonder is powerfully aggressive. If we tolerate it under only limited conditions, it would not be surprising. If we actually do welcome it under some circumstances, we should be surprised at ourselves.

Surprise, Astonish, Amaze, and Admire

Differing from the sentimental world of wonder, there is another approach from magicians that too simply equates wonder with surprise, the latter becoming the goal of performance magic. Clearly, the discussion thus far indicates that surprise is involved. But casual use of them as synonyms is not enlightening. For that matter, neither wonder nor surprise *per se* is sufficient for magic. Being hit from behind on the head with a hammer is a surprise and something to wonder about. But it is not magical in the slightest, unless the hammer is invisible, acting on its own, working at a distance, or the head remains uninjured.

To surprise means to seize by attacking unexpectedly, to take suddenly by storm. It is to strike with wonder or amazement because unexpected or different from what has been anticipated; variously, to astonish, awe, shock, unexpectedly please or disgust. Synonyms are *startle, perplex, bewilder, overwhelm, confound,* and *dumbfound.* Note that the reference to seizing, attacking, and taking by storm shows how aggressive surprise is.

Astonish and *amaze* are somewhat different. Astonish comes from a Latin term for thunder, meaning to stun, stupefy, and surprise greatly. Amaze, like maze, comes from a term meaning bewilder, confuse, and daze. The former stresses the shock of surprise, while the latter focuses on the inexplicable.

The dictionary concludes that surprise is the most general word, meaning to strike with wonder, especially at something unexpected. Astonish is stronger and implies the shock of surprise, especially at something inexplicable or unaccountable. To amaze is to overwhelm with bewildered wonder, whereas to astound is to stun or stupefy with amazement.

Another term brings judgment into the experience. To admire can mean to esteem, approve, delight in, revere, and idolize. So admiration can mean esteem or high regard. Originally, it meant wonder and astonishment. Perhaps the reasonable definition lies somewhere in between. Admiration is a wondering or marveling esteem accompanied by pleasure or delight. Synonyms are *appreciation, liking, esteem, adoration, reverence,* and *wonder*. Note the levels of feeling involved in this list, from the lowest degree, appreciation, to the highest degree, wonder. Antonyms are *condemnation, contempt, abhorrence,* and *hatred*.

The dictionary sums it up this way. Wonder expresses an awakened interest, but to a lesser degree than astonishment and with not so great an element of surprise. In amazement, the element of surprise is uppermost, but with no indication of like or dislike for the object exciting the emotion. In admiration, such valuation is given.

Awful Awe

These two terms come from the Greek language, meaning *pain* and *distress.* The original and obsolete meaning is great fear, dread, and terror. The modern meaning retains the original but is more complicated.

Awe is an emotion in which dread, veneration, and wonder are variously mingled. It can be profound and reverent dread inspired by deity. Or it can be abashed reverence and fear inspired by authority or power. Or it can be religious or superstitious veneration with latent dread, inspired by something sacred, mysterious, or morally impressive. Or it can be wondering reverence with a touch of dread inspired by the grand or sublime, especially in nature or art.

Note that valuation of liking and disliking is not ignored as it is with surprise. Nor is it only affirmative, as it is with admiration. The feelings are both positive and negative, being quite ambivalent, although very strong. There is nothing "wimpoid" about the wonder that is found in awe.

The synonym for awe is *reverence* and the antonym is contempt, both highly value-laden terms.

Lest one have any doubt, we consider the related term, *awful*. How is it to be filled with awe? By definition, awful. *Awful*, meaning filling with awe; inspiring dread or deep reverence; profoundly impressive; terrible; appalling. As we know, in a more weakened meaning, the term refers to what is ugly, very bad, ludicrous, or shocking. And the adverb, *awfully*, can just be a vague intensive, meaning exceedingly or very. But it can also mean in a manner inspiring awe; terribly; majestically; sublimely.

Awe is a combination of dread, veneration, and wonder. Surely the latter is provided with a powerful and meaningful context! What if the goal of performance magic was the inculcation of awe?

Thaumaturgy

From the Greek language also comes a group of words that have significance because they are applied directly to our art or craft of magic. For the record, and certainly not for memorization or even study, here is a list of the terms encountered.

Thaumaturgy is the performance of miracles or wonders, specifically magic. A thaumaturgist is the same as a thaumaturge or thaumaturgus, that is, a worker of miracles or wonders. The terms formerly were applied to saints, and now, more often, to magicians. Thaumaturgics refers to miraculous or magical performances but also to the art of the magician. Thaumatology is the science or lore concerning the working of miracle or wonders. And not just to complete the list but to add a warning: *thaumatolatry* means the worship or undue admiration of wonderful things. This is the most rare of all these rare terms, but what it points toward is common—idolatry about wonder.

What is important is the root meaning of the Greek combining form, *thaumato-, thaumat-*. It is from *thauma, thaumatos,* meaning a thing exciting wonder and used for miracle, miraculous, and magic. The Greek word for wonder is inseparable from magic and miracle. Performance magic done in the context of wonder is doing miracles.

So what can one do but slip in another definition? As we have come to expect in this circular discussion, *miracle* comes from the Latin verb meaning to wonder (as does *marvel* and also *mirror*—something to be wondered about there). A miracle is an event or effect in the physical world beyond or out of the ordinary course of things, deviating from the known laws of nature or transcending our knowledge of these laws. It can also be defined as an extraordinary, anomalous, or abnormal event brought about by superhuman agency as a manifestation of its power or for the purpose of revealing or manifesting spiritual force. In brief, a miracle is a wonder.

The Wonder Word

There are no simple conclusions to be drawn. Wonder and the bunch of words gathered about it—*surprise, astonish, amaze, admire, awe, awful, thaumaturgy, miracle*—can no more be captured with a simple understanding than can the wind be caught by a paper bag. Our experience can be so rich in breadth and depth it is no wonder at all that our responses trivialize it. Furthermore, such crucial words for us, whatever they may be—*love, trust, caring,* and/or these wonder words—are useful precisely because they are exceedingly vague. The vagueness allows them to be concretized by us in an appropriate variety of ways. Since no one of us can fully express the richness of wonder, the variation is to be appreciated.

Conclusion: More Worlds of Wonder

In the chapters that follow I will offer some other approaches to wonder. My purpose is to counteract the goofiness of the credulous world, the silliness of the ironic world, the craziness of the occult world, the corniness of the sentimental world, and the abstractions of the word world by presenting alternatives—which have their own limitations. Although we are right to wonder about those of us who wonder, we are also right to wonder about wonder.

The sixth world, developed in the next chapter, is a psychological perspective on the phenomenon of wonder. Chapter 3 presents the seventh world, which consists of the cultural atmosphere of enchantment and disenchantment and how wonder is related to them. And chapter 4 celebrates the eighth world: the world of performance magic and its relationship to wonder. These three additional worlds of wonder may not include your world, but they might remind you of your own approach to wonder and stimulate its development and application to our craft of magic. Let us hope in keeping with Stewart James, as he expressed it at the end of his "Interlude—On Creation": "Perhaps some of you will find your own world of wonder."[28] If so, we may become more able to help our audiences become true participants.

Notes

1. *As You Like It*, Act III, Scene II.

2. Sir Arthur Conan Doyle, "A Study in Scarlet," in *Sherlock Holmes: The Complete Novels and Stories, Volume 1*, New York: Bantam Books, 1986, page 19.

3. From a listing by Walter E. Houghton, "The English Virtuoso in the Seventeenth Century" in *Journal of the History of Ideas*, quoted by Mark A Schneider, *Culture and Enchantment* (Chicago: University of Chicago Press), 1993, page 129.

4. Items from collections mentioned by Lawrence Weschler, *Mr. Wilson's Cabinet of Wonder* (New York, Pantheon Books, 1995), pages 96-97, 81.

5. From a letter on behalf of the Duke of Buckingham to the Secretary of the Navy, quoted by Lawrence Weschler, *Mister Wilson's Cabinet*, page 95.

6. *Gesta Grayorum* of 1594, quoted by Weschler, *Mister Wilson's Cabinet*, page 76.

7. *Gesta Grayorum*, quoted by Weschler, *Mister Wilson's Cabinet*, pages 83-84.

8. *Gesta Grayorum*, quoted by Weschler, *Mister Wilson's Cabinet*, pages 85-86.

9. *Gesta Grayorum*, quoted by Weschler, *Mister Wilson's Cabinet*, page 89.

10. Mark A. Schneider, *Culture and Enchantment*, pages 1-2.

11. Lawrence Weschler, *Mister Wilson's Cabinet*, pages 3-4.

12. Quoted by Weschler, *Mister Wilson's Cabinet*, page 104.

13 Quoted by Weschler, *Mister Wilson's Cabinet*, page 105.

14. Lawrence Weschler, *Mister Wilson's Cabinet*, page 53.

15. Richard Jenkyns, "Child's Play," a review of *Mr. Wilson's Cabinet of Wonder*, *The New York Review*, July 17, 1997, pages 42-44. The quote is from page 42.

16. Rainer Maria Rilke, *Letters to a Young Poet*, quoted by Weschler in *Mister Wilson's Cabinet*, pages 113-114.

17. S. H. Sharpe, *Neo Magic*, published as Part 1 of Neo-Magic Artistry, edited by Todd Karr (no city: The Miracle Factory, 2000), pages 5-166. *A Thousand Thoughts on Art & Magic* is published in *Art and Magic*, edited by Todd Karr and Vito Lupo (no city: The Miracle Factory, 2003), pages 29-178.

18. *Words on Wonder* is included in *Art and Magic*, edited by Todd Karr and Vito Lupo (no city: The Miracle Factory, 2003), pages 179-226.

19. *Words on Wonder*, page 212.

20. *Words on Wonder*, page 221

21. *Words on Wonder*, page 183.

22. *Words on Wonder*, page 184.

23. *Words on Wonder*, page 184.

24. This issue is discussed in my manuscripts on illusion and on the mirror of magic. {*Editor's note: Bob is referring to the other two books in this Trilogy*—The Magic of Celebrating Illusion, *Theory and Art of Magic Press, 2013*—and An Essay on Magic, *forthcoming from Theory and Art of Magic Press in 2015.*}

25. Max Maven, "Ennui Are The World," in his "Parallax" column in *MAGIC Magazine*, Volume 1, Number 3, November 1991, page 15.

26. I am indebted for this quotation to Phil Alexander, a long-term friend, poet, and businessman.

27. The following expansion is drawn from definitions in *Webster's New International Dictionary, Second Edition, Unabridged.* Springfield, MA: G. & G. Merriam Company, 1955.

28. *Stewart James In Print: The First Fifty Years* (Toronto: Jogestja Ltd., 1989), page xxxi.

Performances for Chapter 1

One of Bob Neale's most revolutionary essays is "Many Magics," included in his book with Eugene Burger, *Magic and Meaning* (Hermetic Press, 1996). I refer to it as "revolutionary" because I honestly can't count the number of serious, even famous magicians who have told me that this essay changed the way they think about magic. What makes the essay so mind-expanding, I think, is Bob's carefully developed argument that there is no such thing as "Magic." On the contrary, there are many "magics," that is, *many varieties of magic* in human life and further, many varieties of performance magic itself. The implication is clear: for magicians (and scholars of magic, too) to talk and think about "Magic" is for them to remain stuck is an abstract generality that both ignores and obscures the actual facts—the complex multiplicity of magic.

In this first chapter of *The Sense of Wonder*, Bob extends this same approach to another of our most venerated words. Indeed, he argues here that there is no one, single "Wonder." Instead, he argues here that there are many *worlds of wonder*—many domains, arenas, areas of life within which wonder works in different ways and means different things. After explicating five common worlds of wonder in this chapter, Bob tells us that as the book unfolds he will develop and explore three additional ones.

However, before we turn to Bob's own innovative wonder worlds, we thought readers might enjoy spending time with some performance explorations of the five worlds discussed in this one.

"Rexile" (1.1) is a delightful, picture-perfect celebration of *Credulous World.* I have seen Bob perform it to great laughter and applause, and I think you might enjoy doing so, too. For certain performers in the right venues, it will add texture, humor, and a certain wise commentary on our credulity.

As for *Ironic World* . . . while Bob emphasizes above the limits of irony and ironic wonder, he also has a knack for creating delightful pieces that reside there, including these two rather biting samples, "The Line Between" (1.2) and "The Magic of Patriotism" (1.3).

"On the Romantic Card Trick" (1.4) and "The Affair" (1.5) come to us from *Sentimental World.* This is obviously true with the first routine, and perhaps a bit less obvious with the second one. However, if you spend a little time with "The Affair" you might come to see it as one of the more romantic presentations Bob has ever created.

As Bob argues above, *Occult World* has many different dimensions—to borrow Eugene Burger's analogy, there are many "rooms" in this particular "house." Over the course of his long career, Bob has created pieces for most of the rooms. Below, we present three routines from two different rooms: "Go to the Devil" (1.6), "Ultimately Sheep and Goats" (1.7), and "You Can't Beat the Devil" (1.8). The word "Devil" should tip you off which two belong to the same room!

To represent the *Word World* of wonder, it felt important to include "Two Stories I Carry with Me" (1.9). I suggested this to Bob because, over many years, these stories kept re-appearing in his books and unpublished manuscripts. Obviously, they were words that were keeping him in wonder.

May all these wonders work their ways upon you!

—Lawrence Hass

Performance 1.1
Rexile
(Credulous World)

Proceed to your nearest drug store. Purchase any over-the-counter liquid concoction that comes in a brown bottle holding about four ounces. Remove the label and drain the contents. Wash out the bottle thoroughly, fill it with tap water, and cap it. Substituting your own last name, type the following on a gummed label: Doc Neale's Rexile. Affix the label and you have completed construction of a classic object that is ever reappearing in new guises—snake oil. But this is one medicine you will use and pitch. Quite contrary to some of the over-the-counter remedies in the drug store, it is everything it claims to be. Rexile is both a remedy and a comment on "remedies." So it is worth as much as anyone will pay for it.

Script
Good afternoon, ladies and gentlemen. I am Doc Neale and I have been sent here by the Honest Indian Medicine Co., of 257 Park Avenue South, New York City [*the address of the Better Business Bureau*] **for the express purpose of informing you about their product. And friends, we have just one product—Doc Neale's Rexile.**

Rexile is spelled: "R," "E," "X," "I," "L," "E." Pronounce the "R," "E," "X" as rex, meaning king, kingly, or royal. Pronounce the "I," "L," "E" as in aisle, meaning path, passage, or way. Rexile means: *Royal Way*. Rexile is the royal way to health of body, mind, and spirit. It is curative, preventative, restorative, and oh, so refreshing.

Now you're going to say, "Well, what does it do?" Some of you will question, "Does it do anything?" Maybe a few of you will wonder, "Will it cure everything?" Ladies and gentlemen, I'm not going to lie to you. If I replied that Rexile does nothing, I'd be lying to you. And if I replied that Rexile does everything, that we had a cure-all, I'd be lying too. I do not have to lie. Our product Rexile, the Royal Way, is highly recommended by doctors as good for five things and five things only.

Here is how to use it. *One*, for buffering the stomach. Use one drop of Rexile in a glass of water for each pair of aspirin taken. *Two*, for relief of cold symptoms of dehydration, sore throat, and cough. Use one drop of Rexile in a glass of warm water. Repeat frequently each day. *Three*, for relief of the bowel dysfunction of constipation, diarrhea, nausea, and vomiting. Use one drop of Rexile in a glass of water about six times a day. *Four*, for relief of excess consumption leading to overindulgence and overweight. Use one drop of Rexile in a glass of water, preferably with ice and a twist of lemon peel. Repeat at will whenever craving food or alcohol. *Five*, for relaxation treatment of muscular pain, hemorrhoids, and insomnia. Use one teaspoon in a bathtub of hot water. Repeat at will until desired consequences occur.

That is all you need to know, folks! Rexile is simple to use and sure in action. The treatment is not for nothing and not for everything. It does not kill germs, heal broken bones, or cure cancer. If you are moribund don't buy a bottle, because it wouldn't do you any more good than that much rain water. But for these five common problems that plague even healthy people, Rexile is a cure-a-plenty.

You have heard claims about some of the thousands of medicines that you can buy. Hear now about Rexile. *One*, it is pure. Rexile has but a single ingredient and is not a collection of junk or a misguided and dangerous shotgun approach. *Two*, it is natural. Rexile is not artificial, but an unchanged substance directly from nature. It is so natural that human beings cannot live without it. *Three*, it is ancient. Rexile is so old that it has been used by animals before we humans arrived on the scene. And it has been used by early humans the world over. It is the most time-tested of all medicines. *Four*, as the newest version of the oldest remedy in the world, Rexile is highly recommended by the most modern physicians and medical researchers. It will do just what I have said it will do. I have not lied or offered any misleading suggestions about its function in curing our common problems. Modern science confirms what Rexile will do and highly recommends its use. *Five*, it does not harm. Rexile is probably more harmless than any other medicine on the market! Just think about the following advantages: you cannot overdose with it; it has no side effects; it is safe for children and need not be kept out of their reach; and it does not interfere with other medicines. Rexile fulfills that ancient hope of the physician—do no harm. *Six*, and finally, it is inexpensive. To put it simply and directly: refills for Rexile are free and easily obtainable. (Directions for refilling come with the bottle.) What more can be said about any drug? Rexile is pure, natural, ancient, highly recommended, and almost free.

There is one more claim to be made about Rexile. The company will not put it in writing and doctors will not recommend it, but I will mention it to you only because *I believe it to be true*. And this could be the most important thing I say here this afternoon. Unfortunately, I can't speak explicitly before a mixed audience of ladies and gentlemen, and people of all ages. But I will say this. If you are involved in an intimate relationship and either you or your partner has the problem of untimely headache or insufficient muscle tonus, Rexile will help you. I recommend one drop of Rexile in a shot glass of whisky for the one who is ailing, and also for the one who is not ailing. The couple taking this medicine together will be helped. This I can say most honestly, sincerely, and humbly: IF YOU BELIEVE IN WHAT I AM CLAIMING, YOU PROBABLY WILL BE HELPED IN THIS MOST INTIMATE MATTER. **Do yourselves a favor and share a bottle of Rexile with your loved one.**

Now, my friends, the price. Remember, Rexile is not yet available in stores or catalogs. I'm not really here to sell it, but to introduce and advertise it. A few bottles will be made available to you at one-third the regular price, simply to facilitate our word of mouth advertising. We have discovered that for every person who buys a bottle ten other households hear about it. The company charges you only to cover costs of our campaign. The price? Just a dollar a bottle. And with each bottle sold you receive this little brochure *[reprint of the pitch]* that describes the benefits of Rexile and how to use it for treatment of our common health problems.

This is a trial offer. If you use it and find that it does not work for you as I have claimed, return the bottle to the Honest Indian Medicine Company and they will refund your money. What can you lose? One dollar at most. What can you gain? Maybe as much as you are able and willing to believe in.

Performances for Chapter 1

Ladies and gentlemen, on behalf of Rexile, the curative, preventative, restorative, and oh-so-refreshing elixir of the Royal Way to health, I thank you. Simply raise your hand with a dollar bill in it and I'll be sure that you get one of my limited supply of bottles. Thank you for your kind attention.

Note: My conclusions for the use of water are drawn from publications of the U. S. Food and Drug Administration (FDA), The Public Citizen Health Research Group, a consumer organization founded by Ralph Nader in 1971, and Consumers Union, the nonprofit organization that publishes Consumer Reports. These three organizations agree in the vast majority of their evaluations.

Performance 1.2
The Line Between
(Ironic World)

Script

Good and Evil. Where and how are we to draw the line between them? We will do an experiment right here and now. Would you help? Here are our samples of good and evil. Which color is good and which color is bad? You decide. Okay. Remember then that the blacks are good and the reds are evil.

First, cut the cards anywhere and complete the cut. Now please cut them into two about-equal packets. Turn one packet face up. Finally, riffle shuffle the two packets together. Thank you.

Good and evil have been thoroughly mixed together; they are sometimes visible and sometimes invisible, just as they are in life. I will distribute them to you as random pairs. Some of the pairs may be all good, some all evil, and some a mixture of good and evil. We can see the nature of the face-up cards, but please do not peek at the ones that are face down. Allow those to remain unseen for now, just as with many hidden matters of the heart. Do not look at them until I look at mine.

Yes, I have the last pair in my hands. It consists of both good and evil. Look at your pair now. Right now, everyone who has a pair of both good and evil please raise your hands. All of us!

Where and how are we to draw the line between good and evil? As Alexander Solzhenitsyn, the Russian poet, novelist, and long-time inhabitant of a gulag stated, "If only there were evil people somewhere committing evil deeds, and it were necessary only to separate them from the rest of us and destroy them. But the line dividing good and evil cuts through the heart of every human being. And who is willing to destroy a piece of his own heart?"

Are we able to draw the line through our own heart? Please take your pair home with you as a memento. Perhaps you will stick the pair into a corner of a mirror, but keep both cards visible.

First Handling

Set up the entire deck in advance, alternating colors. Spread the cards casually to reveal the mixture of colors. Have the participant cut and complete the cut, cut the packet in half, turn one part face up, and riffle shuffle the two portions together. Deal off pairs from the top to members of the audience, and keep the last pair for yourself. If there are fewer than twenty-five people, set the remainder of the deck aside, casually cutting a card to the bottom so that the pairing is destroyed. (The pairs need not be given away.)

Second Handling
With this handling, the pairs need not be given away. Go through the deck openly and pull out twenty red and black spot cards, casually alternating the colors as you do so. Spread the cards casually to reveal a mixture of colors. Have the participant cut the packet and complete the cut several times. Have him then deal down half the packet into a pile and set the pile of remaining cards next to it. Instruct him to take a card from either pile and set it near him, and then to take another card from either pile and pair it with the first card. Have him repeat this pairing of face-down cards until the piles are gone. Turn over the piles to reveal the outcome. Either pass out the cards or not, as you choose.

Note
If you are interested in making a more formal gift, consider having the cards printed with a special back, one that consists of the properly credited quotation from Solzhenitsyn.

Sources
The effect relies entirely on what magicians commonly refer to as "The Gilbreath Principle." The principle is succinctly expressed by Charles M. Hudson in an article

titled "Norman Gilbreath's Second Principle" in the August 1966 issue of *The Linking Ring* (Volume 46, Number 8), pages 63-69. On page 63, Hudson says:

> When a repeating series of cards is riffle-shuffled into itself, with one of the packets to be shuffled in reverse order to the order of the other, the contents of each group in the series do not change—they are only disordered.

Norman Gilbreath first published his "principle" in "Magnetic Colors," a routine that appeared in the July 1958 issue of *The Linking Ring* (Volume 38, Number 7), page 60. For another one of my routines inspired by Gilbreath's wonderful principle, see "The Probability Pack" in *Life, Death & Other Card Tricks* (Seattle: Hermetic Press, 2000), pages 213-220.

For a review of the theme of this presentation in terms of historical events, psychosocial research, and excellent analysis with application to current events and to ourselves, see Philip Zimbardo, *The Lucifer Effect: Understanding How Good People Turn Evil* (New York: Random House, 2007).

The following statement by Alexander Solzhenitsyn is from his *The Gulag Archipelago* (New York: Harper & Row, 1973), page 168:

> If only it were all so simple! If only there were evil people somewhere committing evil deeds, and

it were necessary only to separate them from the rest of us and destroy them. But the line dividing good and evil cuts through the heart of every human being. And who is willing to destroy a piece of his own heart?

Performance 1.3
The Magic of Patriotism
(Ironic World)

Script

The magic of patriotism. *[A small packet of cards shaped like tombstones is shown.]* **In Arlington Cemetery, section 60, here are the gravestones of three Americans. Three young dead men, killed in Iraq while fighting for our country. One stone is unmarked as to religion. One is Christian. One is Jewish.** *[Three cards are shown, each with a different face—blank, cross, and star.]*

There is the magic of patriotism here in this Christian, this Jew, and maybe in this one who might have been a Humanist. *[The blank card is shown again.]* **But there is more.** *[The packet is turned over.]* **Looking closely, we see writing on the gravestones.** *[Three faces with apparent writing on them are shown.]*

And here is another gravestone we have overlooked in section 60—site 8441! *[Four cards are shown.]* **Looking more closely at it, we see awards—Purple Heart, Bronze Star, and the dates of his birth in New Jersey and his death twenty years later in Iraq. And there is the magic of his name—Kareem Rashad Sultan Khan.** *[The packet is spread widely to reveal the name card that is taken into the free hand.]*

No Christian cross, no Star of David, no Humanist absence of symbol. *[The fan of three is reversed to show the previous symbols again.]* **But the magic of the Crescent and Star for our American Muslim patriot.** *[The name card is reversed to reveal a Star and Crescent.]* **The magic of patriotism.**

Construction

Use four double blank poker size playing cards. Round off the one short edge on each card. The face of one card will remain blank. Use Sharpie markers to draw a yellow Christian Cross on one card (figure 2), a blue Star of David on another card (figure 3), and a green Crescent and Star on another card (figure 4). Outline these images with a black marker. On the other side of the Crescent and Star card, write "Kareem Rashad Sultan Khan" (figure 5). On the blank side of the remaining cards, make four wavy lines on each to simulate writing.

Routine

Stack the cards face up as follows from the top: blank, cross, star, crescent.

Show the blank face of the packet. Show three cards on the face by showing the blank followed by cross and star: push over one card, push another on top of it, and drop the final two cards as one on top of the other cards. Reshow the blank card by removing it from the bottom and replacing it there.

Performances for Chapter 1

Figure 2

Figure 3

Figure 4

Figure 5

Turn over the packet. Show three cards on the face, showing the wavy lines that represent writing: push over one card, push over two cards as one on top of it, and drop the final card on top of the other cards. Show four cards with apparent writing, doing an Elmsley Count, to be described below. Spread the cards widely to reveal the name card.

Remove the name card with the other hand. Twist the wrist of the hand holding the fan of three to show the three symbol cards fully. Twist the wrist of the hand holding the name card to reveal the symbol. This final display contrasts it with those in the other hand.

Note that with minor adjustments the various displays can be performed with the cards at chest level facing the audience.

The Elmsley Count

The Elmsley Count is a well-known and versatile false display of four cards that hides one surface of them. While it is commonly used in modern card magic, for the sake of completeness I will provide a brief description of it here. For a detailed description along with many fine points of handling, please consult Robert Giobbi's *Card College, Volume 2*, translated by Richard Hatch (Seattle: Hermetic Press, 1996), pages 311-314.

To perform: holding four cards in one hand, draw off the top card with your other hand. Then as you apparently draw off the second card onto the top card, in fact secretly place the first card on the bottom of the packet while pushing off the two top cards. Draw off the third card normally. Then take the bottom card (the original top card) onto the top of the packet.

Sources

While being interviewed on *Meet the Press*, October 19, 2008, Colin Powell referred to a photo essay in *The Washington Post* about Kareem R. Khan. To find details about his life and death, Google his name on the Internet.

I have rounded playing card stock to represent gravestones and coffins for many effects, beginning with "The Last Dream" in *The Magic Mirror* (Seattle: Hermetic Press, 2002), pages 119-126.

Performance 1.4
On the Romantic Card Trick
(Sentimental World)

Does he love me? Do I love him? Are we compatible? What will become of our relationship? Here are two tricks with different methodologies that underlie the same presentation on the theme of romantic love.

1. Very Romantic Card Trick

Script
These playing cards can reveal possibilities in relationship. Are the two of you compatible? Are you both, or will you become, truly in love with each other? The cards will reveal the answers.

First, are the two of you compatible? To find out, each of you must deal with the age in your teens when you first fell in love.

The woman declares first. What was the year in your teens? Fifteen. I'll deal that number of cards off the deck. You must also deal with the earlier age at which you very clearly recognized the difference between girls and boys. Adding the digits of your number—one and five—suggests the age to be six. I'll deal that number of cards back onto the deck. The next card represents your compatibility in the present relationship.

The man declares next. Your teen year of love discovery? Thirteen. I'll deal that number of cards. Adding the digits suggests the age of knowing the difference to be four, so I'll deal that number. And the next card represents your compatibility in the present relationship.

A woman is revealed to be compatible if she has found the romantic card representing her male partner. Check it out. The King of Hearts! The man is compatible if he has found the companion card. Turn it over. The Queen of Hearts! Very romantic!

So you are quite compatible. But are you, or will you become, truly in love with one another? As a result of dealing your own numbers we are left with this small packet consisting of a number of cards determined by chance. Or is it by fate? Remember when you determined love by plucking petals from a blossom, saying "He loves me, he loves me not"? I'll do the same with these cards on behalf of both of you.

"They love each other, they love each other not. They love, they love not. They love, they love not...." This last card occurred on "They love each other." So you both may be reassured. And not only that. A diamond ring will be *[or "has been"]* given and

received, as suggested by this Ace of Diamonds! Very romantic! Congratulations.

Routine

Set up the deck with the Ace of Diamonds on top, the King of Hearts in the ninth position, and the Queen of Hearts in the tenth position.

Deal the number called by the woman (between ten and twenty) into a face-down pile. Set the pack aside, pick up the pile, and deal onto the deck the number of cards equal to the sum of the digits of her number. Take the next card (the King of Hearts) and set it in front of the woman. Place the remaining cards on top of the deck.

Deal the number called by the man (between ten and twenty) into a face-down pile. Set the pack aside, pick up the pile, and deal down onto the deck the number of cards equal to the sum of the digits of his number. Take the *next* card (the Queen of Hearts) and set it in front of the man.

The Ace of Diamonds is on top of the remaining cards. At this point perform an Under and Down Deal with those cards. That is, place the top card on the bottom of the packet, deal the new top card to the table, place the new top card on the bottom, and so on. Reveal the final card to be the Ace of Diamonds.

To reset the deck, place the Queen on top, followed by the King, the tabled packet of seven cards, and lastly the Ace.

Performances for Chapter 1

Sources

Bob Ostin's "Romantic Card Trick" appeared in Aldo Colombini's column in *The Linking Ring* for July 1999 (Volume 79, Number 7), pages 74-76. Ostin created a plausible and interesting rationale for selecting the number and adding the digits. Such innovation for a standard method is to be greatly praised. He had a woman select one card with the pack face down and another card selected with the pack face up. Either Bob or Aldo, it is not clear which, suggested that the Ace of Diamonds could be positioned so that it would end up on the face of the deck for the diamond ring climax.

I prefer to use two participants, have the cards always face down, and have the climax reached by the Under and Down Deal using my favorite presentational reason—"she loves me, she loves me not." Of course, my routine can be done with one person. This makes sense when a single person wants a revelation about her or his future. When using an older married couple, present the routine as revealing the solidity of the relationship that is already firmly established.

Stimulation

What follows is a quick version of the above "Very Romantic Card Trick." It was prompted by Barrie Richardson's dislike of the dealing I used in the original. I did not find it as bad as he did, but agreed that he had a point. This stimulated me to develop an outline for a presentation to justify the different procedures.

2. Even More Romantic Card Trick

The effect and presentation idea: A couple tests the quality of their love for one another. The woman cuts to a card while she holds the deck behind her back. The man does the same. She has selected the King of Hearts and he has selected the Queen of Hearts, each signifying that, however blind their love, they have found the right person. How they will come to be together requires not only the blind love of passion but also a mature and wise love of vision. The couple together selects a third card while holding the pack in sight. They select the Ace of Diamonds, signifying their visionary love by representing a wedding ring.

Love is blind and love is vision. Both are required, the passion of the first and the comfort of the second. The first two cuts reflect the blindness of their individual loves. The first cut is simple blindness of strong passion. The second cut is a more complicated blindness of complicated passion. The final cut by both as a couple involves their mature and wise vision.

Performances for Chapter 1

Routine
The three cards are set up at the top of the deck with the Ace on the top: Ace of Diamonds, Queen of Hearts (face up), King of Hearts (face up).

Hand the deck to the woman behind her back. During this cover, flip the Ace of Diamonds face up. Instruct her to cut off half the deck, reverse it and replace it on top. Have her bring the deck back into sight, spread the cards, remove the top face-up half, turn it face down, and place it at the bottom of the deck. Ask her to remove the top card and place it face down beside herself.

Have the woman hand the deck to the man behind his back. Instruct him to do something a little more difficult. Tell him to cut off just a few cards from the top, a dozen or so, and replace them back face up. Ask him to cut far more deeply into the deck, turn the portion face up and replace it on top. Have him bring the deck back into sight, spread the cards, remove the top face-up portion, turn it face down, and place it at the bottom of the deck. Ask him to remove the top card and place it face down beside himself.

Direct the woman to reveal her card and then have the man reveal his card.

The final cutting is done in full view because it is even more difficult. Tell the woman to hold the deck face down, allowing it to rest on her open palm. Ask the man to cut off a few cards, about a dozen, and replace them face up on the deck. Tell him to make a deeper cut, about half the deck, and place them face up on the deck. Instruct him to make a far deeper cut, about three-fourths of the deck, and replace them face up on the deck. (The deck could be tabled instead with the woman cutting, the man cutting, and then the woman again.) Take the pack and spread it on the table, turning it over covertly during the broad movement of taking the deck to the table. As you spread the cards, casually cover the face card with your palm. Invite the woman to slide out the top face-down card toward the audience. As the card leaves the pack, gather the cards and restore them to a face-down condition.

Invite the man to reveal the card.

Sources
The first and second forces offer an interesting combination of ideas from Paul Curry and Henry Christ presented by J. K. Hartman in "Deep Voodoo," *Genii: The Conjurors' Magazine* (Volume 62, Number 6, June 15, 1999), pages 48-49. They are related to the more familiar Cut Deeper Force by Ed Balducci. The third force is a minor variation (for presentational purposes only) of the So Simple Force by Lin Searles.

Performance 1.5
The Affair
(Sentimental World)

Script
[1] He had been married many years when he began an affair with a mysterious *[2]* other woman. *[3]* For months, she had sent love letters saying that she saw him nearly every day, thought he was attractive, and very considerate of other people. She sent poetry. She sent a book—SENSUAL LOVE FOR SENSUAL COUPLES.

[4] One day a bouquet of roses arrived at his office. *[5]* The enclosed note asked him to meet her in the lobby of a nearby hotel that afternoon. She would be wearing a rose.

[6] He arrived early, used a side entrance, and looked out into the lobby. *[7]* Soon a beautiful woman entered wearing a rose. *[8]* He walked over to greet her. *[9]* His wife.

Corresponding Action
To begin: run through a shuffled, face-up deck and cut the Queen of Hearts to the top (back). Upjog the King of Hearts and either the Queen of Spades or Queen of Clubs. Turn the deck face down and remove the King and

Queen, placing them face down on top with the King uppermost.

1. Push over the King of Hearts and flip it face up with the right fingers. Pick it up with the right hand.
2. Push over the Queen of Spades and use the King to flip it face up.
3. Take the Queen on top of the King, spreading the two cards.
4. Bring the spread over to the deck, at the same time pushing over the top card, the Queen of Hearts. Close up the spread, lifting off the top three cards.
5. Peel the Queen off onto the deck, leaving it protruding from the side. Flip it face down with the two cards held as one. Lay the two cards as one on top of the deck and flip only the top card face down.
6. Deal the top card to the table or participant's palm face down.
7. Deal the new top card face down onto the table or the participant's palm.
8. Turn the King face up and move it close to the other card.
9. Use the King to flip the Queen of Hearts face up.

Performances for Chapter 1

Sources

This true account, slightly modified to fit the handling, is contained in *True Love: Stories told to and by Robert Fulghum.* (New York: HarperCollins Publishers, 1997), pages 90-92.

Performance 1.6
Go to the Devil
(Occult World)

Script

Go to the Devil? That is a curse. But it is also advice: we can defeat the Devil . . . by first invoking Him. This might seem dangerous but it is not, and we will find out why.

[The performer shows a sign with four names in a column.] **We invoke him by using names . . . these names: Lord of Lies, Tempter, Lucifer, Satan. Please call out any one of the names so we can spell it.** *[The performer deals out a row of five cards and continues laying down a card for each letter until all four names have been spelled.]* **Satan: "S," "A," "T," "A," "N." Another name please. Lucifer: "L," "U," "C," "I," "F," "E," "R." Lord of Lies: "L," "O," "R," "D," "O," "F," "L," "I," "E," "S." That leaves Tempter: "T," "E," "M," "P," "T," "E," "R."**

[The five piles are gathered into one packet.] **What we have invoked by spelling out, we now gather . . .** *[the performer gestures toward the list of names on the sign]* **. . . but only so that we can make a final invocation in which we use this preordained order of the names.** *[The letters of each name are used to form a pile, the last card*

being dealt in front of the pile. The end result is four piles, each with a card in front of it.] **Lord of Lies. Tempter. Lucifer. Satan. The full invocation of the Devil is done. Did we succeed?**

Of course we did. For better or worse, invoking the Devil always works. *[The cards in front of the piles are turned face up.]* **A six, six, and six. The Mark of the Beast. And in the realm of Hell, how many demons reside? We have it on good Renaissance authority that the infernal regions consist of 6,666 legions, each composed of 6,666 demons. So this last card is ... a six. How could it be otherwise?**

This is not the end of the matter. By invoking the Devil and succeeding we have also engendered the counteraction to defeat him. It is built into his mark, since a six can be turned upside down to form a nine. And 999 is the number of the Greek god of the heavens, of light and the sun—Apollo. *[The top cards of the piles are turned face up to reveal nines.]* **Here are the nine, nine, and nine.**

A question remains. After the initial battle between the good and evil when Lucifer and his cohort were cast out, which force had the overwhelming superiority? Well, we are told that in the heavenly regions there are 9,999 legions, each composed of 9,999 angels. So this last card is ... a nine. How could it be otherwise?

Go to the Devil? Yes, because the bearers of light will defeat the bearers of darkness. Be assured that it could not be otherwise.

Routine
Stack the deck from the top as follows: four sixes, indifferent card, four nines.

On a tent card or sheet of paper, write down the four names in big, capital letters in this order from the top: *Lord of Lies, Lucifer, Tempter, Satan.* Locate these names so that the audience can see the order and the spelling.

Shuffle the pack, keeping the nine cards on top. Have any name called out. You will be dealing five packets. Spell the first name by dealing the cards in a row from left to right. Deal five cards to form the row, and if necessary return to the leftmost card to continue the spelling. Call for another name and deal cards from the deck in the same fashion on top of the cards in the row already there, beginning at the pile at the left end of the row. Continue until all four names have been spelled.

Pick up the five packets in alternation, as follows. Pick up the leftmost with the left hand and then the rightmost with the right hand. Drop the left packet on top of the new leftmost packet and pick them up as one large packet. Immediately drop the right packet on the new rightmost packet and pick them up as one large packet. Drop the left-hand large packet on the remaining packet and then drop the right-hand large packet on top. You are simply gathering the cards with an easy rhythm.

You now deal the cards again into piles, but differently from the first time since you will create a pile for each name. Deal by spelling in the order of the names on your list. So begin by dealing and spelling *Lord of Lies*. Deal nine cards into a face-down pile and set the tenth card, the card falling on the last letter, face down in front of the pile toward the audience. Make a pile to the right by dealing and spelling *Lucifer*, setting aside the seventh card in front. Continue by forming the remaining two piles in the same manner.

Turn over the first three cards that have been set aside to reveal the three sixes. Turn over the fourth card to reveal the remaining six.

Turn over the first three top cards of the four packets to reveal three nines. Turn over the fourth card to reveal the remaining nine.

However, you are able to proceed as described in the preceding paragraph only half of the time. This is when the order selected by the participant begins with a word that has either ten or five letters, that is, "Lord of Lies" or "Satan." When either "Lucifer" or "Tempter" has been selected first, the nines will end up in pairs at the top of the center piles. When this happens, you will know it immediately with the participant's first selection. Remember this so that you can make this final adjustment at the end to display the nines: pick up the top card of each center pile, one in each hand. Lay them face down near you behind the left and right piles. Pick up the new top cards and lay them near you face down behind the center piles. Now proceed as usual, turning the first three cards face up, and then the fourth card.

Gesture to the display as you conclude the ritual.

Sources

This is a presentation for Harry Lorayne's "Any-Deck Tally-Ho Extended" published in *Genii: The Conjurors' Magazine* (Volume 66, Number 2, February 2003), pages 58-59. It is a development of "Tally-Ho" by Henry Christ. Lorayne suggests, "Use any words you like . . . . You are, as the platitude says, limited only by your own imagination." I agreed.

Demons have been catalogued and ranked for nearly two millennia. I was pleased to discover that, according to one authority, the German physician Dr. Johann Weyer (Wierus) in the sixteenth century, "Altogether there are in the infernal regions 6666 [sic] legions, each composed of the same number of devils." (Quoted by Lewis Spence in the entry on demonology in *An Encyclopaedia of Occultism*, Mineola, NY: Dover Publications, Inc., 2003, page 120.) Rosemary Ellen Guiley, in her entry on Dr. Weyer in *The Encyclopedia of Witches & Witchcraft, Second Edition* (New York: Facts On File, Inc. 1989), page 363, says he "claimed that there were 7,405,926 devils and demons organized in 1,111 divisions of 6,666 each."

Naturally, I prefer the neater numbers I have employed. That the Mark of the Beast is 666 (according to Revelation) is common knowledge. I had discovered in some forgotten treatise on numerology that the number of the Greek god, Apollo, is 999. The fact that sixes can be turned upside down has always been appealing, and I have employed it elsewhere in a magic square routine. Linking the three sixes to a fourth one is a happy consequence of the routine that demands it. Apollo is identified with light and the sun, although I had to make up the legions and numbers of angels. The result is synchronistic, to be sure. But historically, the question of how many beings were located in each place after the initial battle between Good and Evil was of serious concern.

Performance 1.7
Ultimately Sheep and Goats
(Occult World)

Script
[The performer shows four black cards and four red cards.] These are The Lord's Pasteboards, when they remind us that the Son of Man will come in his glory and sit on his glorious throne.

"Before him will be gathered all the nations . . . and he will separate them one from another as a shepherd separates the sheep from the goats . . . ." *[The cards are alternated by color into a face-down pile.]* They are mingled now, like this—sheep, goat, sheep, goat, sheep, goat, sheep, goat—just as they will be until the Day of Judgment. But then "he will separate them one from another . . . *[the black cards are shown to be together, being separated from the red]* . . . and the goats will go away into eternal punishment, but the righteous into eternal life."

[The cards are alternated face up.] The Day of Judgment is not here, so the sheep and goats are mixed —sheep, goat, sheep, goat, sheep, goat, sheep, goat. This is dangerous because the sheep could be led into sinful ways by the wicked. So the sheep pray for a miracle, knowing that the Good Shepherd said,

"Whatever you ask in prayer, you will receive, if you have faith." *[The blacks are shown to be together again.]* **And it is so.**

[The black pile is placed on top of the red pile.] **Yet this is not the whole story, for the sheep of the Good Shepherd are to serve him by serving the least of those among us—giving food to the hungry and drink to the thirsty, welcome to the strangers, clothing to the naked, and companionship to the sick and imprisoned.**

[The cards to spread to reveal the alternation of red and black.] **And so these sheep and goats are to be magically mingled by compassion until He whom we serve through the least of those among us, the Son of Man, comes in his glory.**

Sources

This is a gospel presentation for the classic card trick "Oil and Water." Four red and four black cards are openly alternated and then magically separate. The effect is repeated. When the colors are left separate, they magically alternate.

The history of this effect appears to start with Walter B. Gibson's "Like Seeks Like" in *The Jinx*, Number 91, 1940, page 569. Even so, definitional work on the effect—including the oil and water presentation idea, the now-standard use of four cards of each color, and a slew of first-rate techniques—was carried out by Edward Marlo. His earliest published routine was "Oil and Water"

The Sense of Wonder

in *The Cardician* (Chicago: The Ireland Magic Company, 1953), pages 111-117. But Marlo continued to refine the effect in many contributions to Howard Lyon's *Ibidem* magazine and elsewhere. For the early history of Marlo's work on the effect, see Jon Racherbaumer's discussion in *Kabbala, Volume 3*, Number 4 (New York: Louis Tannen, Inc., 1976), pages 45-46. Of course, since then countless variations and handlings have been devised. {*Editor's Note: Thanks to Stephen Minch for assistance with this paragraph.*}

Excellent routines for a three-phase version are: Dai Vernon's "Oil and Water" in *More Inner Secrets of Card Magic* (written by Lewis Ganson) in Dai Vernon's *Inner Card Trilogy* (Tahoma, CA: L & L Publishing, 1996), pages 20-25; Jon Racherbaumer's "Oil Slick and Water Wonderful" in *Kabbala, Volume 3*, Number 4, pages 46-48; J. K. Hartmann's "Fixit Mixer" in *Card Craft* (Kaufman and Greenberg, 1991), pages 376-378; and David Solomon's "Refined Oil and Water" in the Simon Aronson and David Solomon book, *Sessions* (no city, no publisher, 1982), pages 125-131. There are Marlo routines, several other Vernon versions, and many ideas for the effect in Verne Chesbro's *Ultimate Color Separation, No. 1* and *Ultimate Color Separation, No. 2* (no city: self-published, 1963 and 1965 respectively), along with a host of other sources as well. If interested in special cards portraying sheep and goats, note the routines in Bruce Cervon's *The*

Black and White Trick and Other Assorted Mysteries (Tahoma, CA: L & L Publishing, 1989).

I have listed all the sources above because I do not provide a specific handling for the above routine. Personally, I use the Solomon handling; to me, his handling is simple, easy, and elegant, worthy of careful study, and makes for an accomplished performance. However, such judgment is a matter reflecting many criteria, so no one routine will please everyone or even many people. I realize that it is not customary to describe a magic effect while leaving out the exact means to achieve it. But I have not left out the means of achieving a *presentation*. Indeed, the fit between the text and trick here is exemplary.

Note

Since most of us know the phrase "separates the sheep from the goats" but not everyone remembers the source and context, please see Matthew 25:31 to glimpse the spirit of the text. In appropriate situations, the performer might add more of the text. The focus of the text on compassion is sometimes missing in those who quote the phrase out of context.

Performance 1.8
You Can't Beat the Devil
(Occult World)

Script

When you spend enough time in a neighborhood bar, you eventually hear someone ask, "What ever happened to Bill Brown?" The answer is that nobody knows. He had been there daily for years and then just vanished. Most strangely, this disappearance happens in bars across the country. How come?

Who knows for sure? But there is a story making the rounds that might have the answer. The yarn ends with the advice, "Don't be like Harry Jones."

Apparently, Harry entered a bar and had a drink while waiting for a client. Next to him was a rather distinguished appearing gentleman toying with what appeared to be antique playing cards. Harry glanced over and showed interest. And because of what happened then, we are advised to never do the same. To tell the tale, I will play the comfortable role of that distinguished appearing stranger. Will you be Harry Jones? Thank you.

Yes, these are twenty-two cards that comprise the Major Arcana of a tarot deck. The images fascinate me because they are used for three things: gambling games, personality readings, and predicting your future. Here is the one to beat in all three—the Devil. You know everything that he represents. Not a good card. To be avoided if at all possible. Here's the Fool. He reminds us to trust our instincts even if they seem foolish. The Wheel of Fortune with its monkeys and kings. The spin of our fate—reminding us that our fortunes can turn either way, that what goes up must come down, and what goes down must come up. An easy way to understand a tarot reading is to think of it as about you on your journey through life. You start on the road and encounter all manner of people and events along the way, and through these experiences you learn life's lessons and become more enlightened and fulfilled by the time you reach the twenty-second card, which is called the World.

The gambling games are interesting. Would you like to play a simple one? Not for money. Just for fun. It is an earlier version of a game you might have played as a child. I place the top card face down anywhere. You place the new top card face up anywhere beside the first one. I place the next card face down beside them. Now you must place your face up card so that I do not complete a diagonal or row of three. Yes, we are playing Tic-Tac-Toe . . . . The game is a draw. Maybe we are both winners.

This fun game can also be about your personality. Would you like to have it revealed by a short reading? Good. We played together freely to build this matrix of nine cells. Now you alone will use your freedom again to make a selection of three cards. Do so now by selecting any row out of the three horizontal, three vertical, and two diagonal ones. Pick up those three cards, turn all of them face down, and mix them up. Now lay them out from your left to right.

The cards will tell you something about your action as a person in the past, present, and future. Your immediate past is represented by . . . the Magician. Recently you have exerted new power in some aspect of your daily life. Your present is represented by . . . the Pope. At this time you are concerned about conforming as well, being obedient to what you think is right. And your future is represented by . . . the Hermit. In your immediate future, you will be called to withdraw from the world and attend to your inner life. A serious transition is coming soon. Take care to remember this hint about your immediate future.

So we have used the tarot to both play a game and read your personality. But there is more. The tarot cards also deal out your fate. This is determined by these three cards you selected. Remember that the

Devil is the card among the twenty-two that you are to avoid at all costs? Let's see if you have.

Add the numbers of these three cards you have so freely chosen. What is the total? Fifteen. This is very good news. Deal down to the fifteenth card to discover your immediate fate. Death! Yes, "a serious transition is coming soon" and it is good news for me! *[Turn over the next card.]* My number is fifteen. And here I am, ready for Death to deliver you to me. Harry, you come along now.

So that is why it is said, "Do not be like Harry Jones." Thanks for helping us hear the tale. Please do not forget the advice.

Strategy

To learn the procedure, stack nine values in this order: five, ace, eight, two, seven, three, four, six, nine. You will follow a strategy created by Geoffrey Mott-Smith.

Table the packet. Pick up the top card and place it face down in front of the participant. Consider it to reside in the center square of the nine imaginary squares of the game. Have the participant pick up the new top card, turn it face up, and place it *"beside"* the first card. Casually point to the four sides as you speak. Consider this second card to reside in a side square. Please note: this verbal direction casually locates the card at one of the four sides and not at the corners. The spectator does not know yet the nature of the game being played. Place your next card in the imaginary corner on either side of the participant's card. This forces him to play in the opposite corner. You play the next card in the side square that contacts both of his previous cards. This forces him to play in the side square on the opposite side. You position the next card in the corner next to his last play. The remaining placements are forced.

The cards form a square of nine cells, the numbers showing on the one, two, three, and six. All the rows—vertical, horizontal, and the two diagonals—add to fifteen.

Routine

Use the twenty-two cards of the Major Arcana from a tarot deck. I prefer the images provided by the Tarot of Marseilles. Use the numbers on the faces to create the following stack: (from the top) thirteen, twelve, twenty-one, eighteen, ten, five, one, eight, two, seven, three, four, six, nine, twenty, nineteen, sixteen, seventeen, zero, eleven, fourteen, fifteen.

To begin the performance, spread the cards to show the backs and spread them again face up. Gesture toward the Devil card that is on the face. Spread the cards a little more to show the Fool card and then a great deal more to reveal the Wheel of Fortune and the World cards. Close up the spread.

With the packet face up, double undercut the Devil to the back of the packet. Turn the packet face down and overhand shuffle, running off three cards singly and tossing the remainder on top. Overhand shuffle again, running off three cards singly and tossing the remainder on top. The stack is in the required order.

Follow the instructions given above for playing the tic-tac-toe game. The one, two, three, and six will be face up. The game will be a draw.

Have the participant pick any row, column, or diagonal, arrange the three cards in a row, and turn them face up. Remove the other six cards, turn them all face down and place them on top of the remainder of the packet. (Note that the existence of a magic square is not exposed.) See the guide below for giving a brief personality reading. Always conclude the reading with the notice that, "A serious transition is coming soon."

Have the participant total the numbers of the three cards. It will be a total of fifteen. Death and the Devil have been positioned as required. Have the participant count down to the fifteenth card and expose it as Death. Turn over the card next to it to reveal that the Devil, which is numbered fifteen, had all possibilities covered.

As the Devil, reach for the hand of the participant and hold it as you ask him to accompany you. Change the grasp to a handshake as you return to the role of performer and thank the participant.

Personality Readings

The Fool: beginnings, transitions, courage, optimism.

The Wheel of Fortune: change in circumstances, especially those that are not understood but just experienced as happening.

The World: success, achievement, satisfaction; unification of an inner sense of being with outer activities.

The Magician: awareness of power in life, in self or other; beginnings already started; creative force; willpower, the will unified and directed toward goals.

The High Priestess: mystery in life; passive withdrawal; intuitive understanding of a problem; potential in our lives not yet acted on.

The Empress: passion, feelings, pleasure, either sexual or motherly; stubbornness, self-indulgent pleasure.

The Emperor: power of society, encounter with the law; stability, order; a person who holds power—father, husband, lover.

The Pope: orthodoxy, conformity; inner sense of obedience.

The Lover: choice about love, a specific lover or some relationship of value; help from such a person.

The Chariot: successful control of something; control of contradiction.

Justice: we are and have what we deserve; need to see the truth of this outcome; honesty, fairness, just decisions.

The Hermit: withdrawal from outer concerns, work in self-development; maturity.

Sources

This is a way of working and presenting "The Tic-Tat-Toe Trick." The idea for the trick was created by Martin Gardner and realized by Don Costello; see Martin Gardner, *Mathematics, Magic and Mystery* (Mineola, NY: Dover Publications, Inc., 1956), pages 28-31. The procedure required that an adjustment be made to the packet of cards after the spectator decided where to place his first card in relation to your first card. Dai Vernon provided a "subtle method by which this necessary adjustment can be made without the spectator being aware of it" (page 28). It required holding the packet in the hands and cutting it before placing it on the table for the rest of the trick. My simplification is to casually direct the participant to set the card *beside* my first card, which eliminates the corners from consideration and thus eliminates the need for adjustment. I recognize that this has pros and cons, too, and you may prefer the Vernon approach.

My script was inspired by a fine routine by an anonymous contributor (as were we all) to *The Devil of a Bar & Pub* (Leaping Lizards Publishing Company, 2007), a book compiling over sixty presentations that first appeared on the Internet bizarre magic site, "Shadow Digest." That routine, "That Devil of a Card," used three slips of paper numbered to force the number fifteen, which was then employed to count down to the Devil card in a tarot deck. I liked the premise very much, but I wanted to avoid using paper and to add a double duty approach for Death and the Devil.

The personality reading notes are from my notes from a book on the tarot by a Rachel Pollack, *78 Degrees of Wisdom, Revised Edition* (Newbury Port, MA: Weiser Books, 2007).

Performance 1.9
Two Stories I Carry with Me
(Word World)

I have about a half dozen stories that I carry with me. Actually, they carry me. They are companions that both comfort me and provoke me. To me, they are worlds of word wonders.

The first story from 1939 is by Deniil Kharms, who was born in Russia in 1905. He became an artist but was silenced by the Soviet officials in 1930. He survived by writing childrens' stories until he was arrested in 1941. He died under mysterious circumstances somewhere in the Ukraine in 1942, and the government made him an "unperson" by obliterating all records and references relating to him. However, he had written down some of his little stories and given them to friends. Talk about Word Magic! I came across this story, which is actually a story within a story, and the above information about Kharms in *Fiction of the Absurd: Pratfalls in the Void*, edited by Dick Penner (New York: New American Library, 1980), pages 61-67.

The second story is adapted from one told by Elie Wiesel as an opening epigram in *The Gates of the Forest* (New York: Holt, Rinehart and Winston, 1966), no page numbers are provided.

A Magician Who Lives in Our Time

"*[This is]* a story about a magician who lives in our time and does not work miracles. He knows he is a miracle worker and can work any miracle he wants, but he doesn't do it. They move him out of his apartment. He knows he would need only to wave his finger and he could keep his apartment, but he doesn't do it; he moves humbly out of his apartment and lives outside of town in a barn. He is able to turn the barn into a beautiful brick house, but does not do that; he goes on living in the barn and in the end dies without having worked one miracle in his own life."

The Last Magician

When a great magician saw destitution threatening his people, it was his custom to go into a certain clearing in the forest. There he would perform a trick with four pieces of parchment . . . one of them magically presenting a prayer . . . a hidden treasure would be revealed, and destitution averted. Later, when his disciple had occasion to intercede for the same reason, he would say, "Magician of the Universe, listen! I do not know the place, but I am still able to perform the trick . . . ." And again, the hidden treasure would be revealed. Still later, it fell to the last magician to overcome misfortune. He tried to perform the trick . . . and failed . . . and failed. He cried out, "I do not know the place. I cannot perform the trick. All I can do is tell the story, and this must be sufficient." And it was sufficient.

Chapter 2
Will Wonders Never Cease

We wonder together about wonder because we are magicians—as the Greeks said, thaumaturgists, that is, workers of wonders. Perhaps our art entitles and prompts us to become guardians of wonder and gurus of wondering. If so, magicians should be those entertainers who know about wonder, exhibit wonder, and inculcate wonder.

"Will wonders never cease." This common phrase can be an exclamation or a question. If it is an exclamation, then it's an assertion of wonder with the assumption that wonders will never end. If it is a question, then one could answer variously. Either way, my response would be the same. My basic assumption is that wonders never cease, even though wonderment does. As G. K. Chesterton puts it, "The world will never starve for want of wonders, but for want of wonder."[1]

And this death of wonderment is a wonder itself. Jorge Luis Borges voices his wonder about it:

> They never wonder at anything, no? They don't think it's strange that they should be living. I remember the first time I felt that was when my father said to me, "What a queer thing," he said,

"that I should be living, as they say, behind my eyes, inside my head, I wonder if that makes sense?" And then, it was the first time I felt that, and then instantly I pounced upon that because I knew what he was saying. But many people can hardly understand that. And they say, "Well, but where else could you live?"[2]

At the same time, an experience of perpetual wonderment would also be death. Wonder is not everything and not sufficient unto itself. Even so, I assume that our general problem today is not being possessed by too much or too lengthy wonder, but by lack of it. Wonders are everywhere, but we are elsewhere, living in the limbo of boredom, routine, paralysis, or just chronic and low-level depression or anxiety. From the situation of such a limbo, we need to romance a little bit about wonder. Thus, you might consider this chapter a waltz with wonder.

One such romantic was D. H. Lawrence. He said:

> The sense of wonder,
> that is our sixth sense.
> And it is the natural religious sense.[3]

Another such romantic was Albert Einstein. He said, "The man who has lost his power of wonder is a dead man."[4] (I presume that women die this way too.)

Chapter 2: *Will Wonders Never Cease*

Einstein states it more fully as well, speaking for people in a variety of, perhaps in all, the human disciplines. He recorded this full statement, which is often quoted and deservedly so:

> The fairest thing we can experience is the mysterious. It is the fundamental emotion which stands at the cradle of true art and true science. He who knows it not and can no longer wonder, no longer feel amazement, is as good as dead, a snuffed-out candle. It was the experience of mystery—even if mixed with fear—that engendered religion. A knowledge of the existence of something we cannot penetrate, of the manifestations of the profoundest reason and the most radiant beauty, which are only accessible to our reason in their most elementary forms—it is this knowledge and this emotion that constitute the truly religious attitude; in this sense, and in this sense alone, I am a deeply religious man.[5]

And there is one more romantic about wonder from whom I want you to hear. I have used the following quotation repeatedly, and more than any other, in my speaking and writing. It is one of those statements that, for me, nearly encompasses all that needs to be said. G. K. Chesterton is the source. He said:

> This at least seems to me the main problem for philosophers .... How can we contrive to be at once astonished at the world and yet at home in it? How can this world give us at once the fascination of a strange town and the comfort and honor of being our own town? .... We need this life of practical romance; the combination of something that is strange with something that is secure. We need to view the world so as to combine an idea of wonder and an idea of welcome. We need to be happy in this wonderland without being merely comfortable.[6]

And so, for me, the romance with wonder is a practical one. To use Chesterton's terms, I am concerned about wonder as combined with welcome. Wonder without welcome is too anxiety-prone. Welcome without wonder is too boredom-prone. But the two go together, I believe. We can recall experiences of wonder that welcomed us to greet the cause of the wonder. And we can recall experiences of welcome that elicited wonder in us as well. The problem may be not that the two conditions are easily separable but that we work too hard to separate them and keep them separate.

In this chapter we will look at wonder as an experience—what we might think of as Psychological World. We will also look at where wonder is directed, and what the stages of wonder are—the definition, objects, and outcomes of wonder. I hope my comments are useful enough to kindle our wonder about wonder, but not so useful as to encourage the wonder about wonder to be more interesting than all the other wonders in our living. The goal is to suggest the possible richness of our own experience of wonder and to underscore our opportunity to promote that experience in others.

A. What Wonder Is

What is wonder? I would call it *respect*. What is it to respect someone, something, or some event? The term comes from a Latin verb meaning "to see." To respect is to *really see*. Respect occurs, quite contrary to social manners, when we stare, point our fingers, and shout out, "look at that!" Respect is exclaiming that something really *is*. It is paying attention. So this is my working definition of wonder as an experience: it is recognition of a specific existence. What is it like to really see something, to witness something, to experience something? It is to wonder. Wonder is respect for what is.

Here is an example from a novel, *Zorba the Greek*[7]:

> One day, I remember, when we were making our way to the village, we met a little old man astride a mule. Zorba opened his eyes wide as he looked at the beast. And his look was so intense that the peasant cried out in terror:

"For God's sake, brother, don't give him the evil eye!" And he crossed himself.

I turned to Zorba. "What did you do to the old chap to make him cry out like that?" I asked him.

"Me? What d' you think I did? I was looking at his mule, that's all! Didn't it strike you, boss?"

"What?"

"Well . . . that there are such things as mules in this world!"

Just so. Wonder, as experienced, is respect for what is. Of course, what is so easy to state is not necessarily easy to understand. Nor may wonder be easy to experience.

Squatting

I hope you think for yourselves about my definition. Not to get the ultimate answer, but to get some line on how you perceive wonder. For myself, several other words come to mind. One is "suchness." This Buddhist use of the word is beyond my comprehension, but I have some feeling for the "suchness" of any object or event. There is something in what is that's impressive *per se*. I even composed this "poem" about it:

There's
There
There.

Another term is from the Protestant theologian, Paul Tillich—"Being Itself." This "being itself" is an attribute or feature of any object, event, or experience. We look around and can apprehend being. I can make fun of such jargon by responding with "buzz, buzz, buzz." Even so, everything does "buzz."

Still, the term that is more useful for me is *respect*. While "suchness" and "being itself" also refer to the recognition of a specific existence, I am trying to stay away from metaphysical assumptions and remain within a psychological approach, and "respect" works very well for that. So with respect in mind, the question is: what is it like to really see something, to witness something, to experience something? What it is like is this experience of wonder.

There are ways of putting this theme philosophically. Wittgenstein wrote, "It is not *how* things are in the world that is mystical, but *that* it exists."[8] And philosophers do speak of "ontologic wonder." For example, Plato said, "Wonder is the Seed of Knowledge." Aristotle stated, "In all things of nature there is something wonderful." In China, Lao Tzu observed, "From wonder to wonder, existence opens." And William James instructs us that this wonder is primal and unending, "Existence then will be brute fact to which as a whole the emotion of ontological wonder shall rightfully cleave, but remain eternally unsatisfied. Then wonderfulness or mysteriousness will be an essential attribute of the nature of things, and the exhibition and emphasizing of it will continue to be an ingredient in the philosophical industry of the race."[9]

From my perspective, all these observations are fine, as long as we do not assume we have to be professional philosophers in order to wonder. The philosopher C. E. M. Joad repeats the thought many people have shared on this, "I think one of the secrets of life consists of keeping alive a sense of wonder and awe, so that you look upon the world at least in part with the eyes of a child. All too quickly the horizon of our life contracts to the commonplace four walls of office or kitchen."[10]

So what we are talking about as wonder is something philosophers have recognized, but it is not exclusively for the adult thought technician. Nor is it only available to the adult artist, scientist, or religionist. Our practical romance about wonder is founded very much in our witness of the child in the state of wonder and in our desire to recapture the child's fresh recognition of what is. Recognition of a specific existence is precisely what a child can do best.

My visual image of wonder is that of a two-year-old child. She is squatting in that marvelous fashion we adults can no long manage. Her body is quite close to something. And she is fully open to the something with her entire being. It shows on her face. Can we at least remember such an expression? It requires this kind of spiritual squat.

Maybe we can experience a spiritual squat. Stand up wherever you are (unless on a form of public transportation), leaving some space all around you. Look ahead of you and pay attention to what is there—furniture, people, whatever. Turn around and face in the opposite direction. Spread your legs widely and plant your feet firmly on the ground. Bend over forward and grasp your legs. Continue bending deeper, moving your hands downward to support yourself as you do so. Look behind you through your legs. What do you see? Nothing that you have not seen before. But it looks different. Please do try this. Artists do it to get a fresh look at things.

The spiritual squat is a perspective that increases the likelihood of our seeing what is there. Reflect also on how foolish we look in this position. Wonder-struck. Some of you might be amused to contemplate that the squat is also a form of "mooning." And the possibility of two people viewing each other in this way lightens the spirit. Such a fresh look at ourselves is wonderful.

Wordsworth reminds us:

> My heart leaps up when I behold
> A rainbow in the sky:
> So was it when my life began;
> So is it now I am a man;
> So be it when I shall grow old,
> Or let me die!
> The Child is father of the Man;
> And I could wish my days to be
> Bound each to each by natural piety.[11]

Squatting More Fully

Recognition of a specific existence. What does this mean and what does it not mean? My basic observation is that wonder is a very simple condition of the human animal. There is a tendency to screw up our understanding in our heads by doing all sorts of things that complicate matters falsely. I do think we have many complicated conditions, emotional and intellectual ones, that cannot be spoken of simply. By contrast, wonder is simple. The complications all lie in our incapacity to wonder, not in our capacity. I will outline different objects for experiences of wonder and different elements in wonder. But I insist that wonder is, essentially, simple.

First, here are three caveats. One concerns the meaning of "recognition." The term can mean the identification of something as having been previously seen, heard, or known. Wonder can involve this, but not necessarily. I understand recognition to mean simply a perception of something existing. However, there are some other meanings of recognition that do seem to fit into our experience of wonder. Recognition can mean entitlement or validity; to recognize someone as having a claim; or something as deserving of some kind of appreciation. So I gather that the word "recognition" may have three basic kinds of meaning: 1) that something is, 2) that something can be identified on the basis of previous experience, or 3) that something has a claim upon us. Wonder involves the first sense for sure. It may or may not involve the second and third meanings.

My second caveat is a reminder about what is implied about basic forms of wonder. Acknowledging that we can wonder about anything opens up fundamental possibilities. For example, to experience that something is prompts wonder about what is not and how things come in and out of existence. Recall the toddler squatting and recognizing something. Suppose that it is a solitary ant wandering about. Suppose further that it is the toddler's first experience of a tiny moving thing. It is fascinating. Suppose even further that an adult is present who does not care for the sight of an ant in her kitchen. She stamps on the ant with her shoe and squashes it. The toddler sees a tiny black spot that does not move. Finally, suppose that you have been watching the toddler's face throughout this episode of something existing and going out of existence. Imagine the look on the face of the child when the ant is destroyed. I have seen it. If you saw it, you would never forget it. Wonder about life and death.

We can even wonder about wonder, about our recognition of something or our not recognizing it. Suppose again that the child is outdoors and comes upon a daffodil. Suppose further that this is the toddler's first experience of any flower, indeed, of any plant whatsoever. Most likely, the wonder is the wonder of something existing. Just this, and nothing more. At the other extreme, imagine an adult who has seen many daffodils and seen them many times, and further suppose that the adult is named Wordsworth:

> For oft, when upon my couch I lie
> In vacant or in pensive mood,
> They flash upon that inward eye
> Which is the bliss of solitude;
> And then my heart with pleasure fills,
> And dances with the daffodils.[12]

When Wordsworth recognizes the existence of daffodils, what is involved? I suggest that it is dancing in full wonder—wonder about something that exists and that does not exist, about something that is coming into and going out of existence, and wonder about wonder and the lack of it.

Of course, most human beings who see daffodils are somewhere between the toddler and the poet. And we do not have to be much beyond the toddler to possess the capacity for the poet's fulsome wonder. Consider any five-year-old. By that time, the child has seen these flowers more than once, can recall them in solitude, and has seen them grow and die. This child of five can and will wonder about the daffodils existing and not existing, coming and going. Maybe even the child wonders about wonder—about things coming and going from the mind as well as from sight. What are we considering here but the game of peek-a-boo that we play with babies? Could peek-a-boo be the primal example of wonder about being and not being, appearance and disappearance, life and death? Whether it is so or not, it reminds me of the theoretical physicist, Stephen Hawking. What is the leading interest of this one of the small handful of brilliant thinkers about the universe? What does he think about? What is the subject that most of his fellow theoretical scientists assume is pointless to think about? It is a very simple question he explores. How come the universe is rather than is not? Hawking is astonished that the universe is. I grant that it is cute, but I insist it is also precise to claim that Stephen Hawking is playing peek-a-boo with the universe. Such wonder involves the most developed mind but also the most open heart of the child.

So let us squat together. This final comment stems from a suggestion of David P. O'Neill in his book on joy written for parents of preschool children, *What Do You Say to a Child When You Meet a Flower?*[13] Please take the time to read carefully and critically what this author affirms:

> To approach a child without wonder is not to meet the child at all. Unless I join the child in the world of wonder, we are not being persons together.
>
> To test out what I mean, take your child with you for a walk. If you have no child yet who is two or three or five years old, find a niece or a nephew or the child of a neighbor. How can I tell you to be fully with this little boy or girl as you set out on your walk? This way ... right from the beginning, as you set out, give away everything in you except being present with this child. Give away your grown-up-ness and your worries and your anxieties. Give away your guilty feeling about wasting time so unproductively. Give away your feeling of being too important to be taking a child so seriously, and what, after all, will people think? Give it all away. Just be your self, totally.
>
> Stop at the first flower you see and talk with the child about it. It may be a daisy on a lawn or a dandelion or a rose or a jonquil ... just talk about it. If you are like most grown-ups, you will be wondering what to say. So you may start talking

objectively *about* the flower and *down* to the child. You may even give the child a little lecture about flowers. You may say something about botany and ecology and microorganisms. If you are practical, you may mention the price of roses in New York or the annual cost of clearing dandelions from front lawns. More likely, you will not be very sure what to say at all. What do you say to a three-year-old when you meet a flower?

. . . . You are in this quite unique situation in history—it has never happened before and it will never happen again. It is you, a real-life person; it is the child, another real person eager for life with you; it is this flower at this moment in its short span of living.

. . . . If you want to be real, you will be a person and meet the flower. You may pause with courtesy and simply experience the joy of meeting the beauty of life in this flower. If you feel free to use your imagination, you will enter into wonder . . . you will wonder what the flower is being to you.

. . . . Think now of your child companion in this meeting. Here is you being fully present. You are being a person to this flower and you are being open in wonder at its presence to you. This whole experience you will want to share with this little boy or girl. Here is an opportunity to share life and wonder and presence. Here is a deep reaching into reality.

Here the whole of you is open for sharing—mind and heart, hand and voice, imagination and fantasy. In this experience of life-in-depth, joy will be there when you least expect it. You will be full of the joy of being alive, of being your full self. You will have the joy of sharing your self with the child. Together as persons, you will both be present to the life and the beauty of the flower.

All of this so far can be a wordless experience, just a sensing of presence and of joyful wondering....

You may now like to tell the child the name of this flower. You may be able to sing a little song about the loveliness of the flower. You may be able to tell a story about its life and about how glad it is to meet this wonderful child. You may share with the child the favorite thing of your mind that the flower suggests . . . you may wonder why love is like a red, red rose . . . you may wonder why flowers are a language of love . . . and why do we bring flowers to a funeral . . . and where have all the flowers gone?

O'Neill's attempt to capture the requirements and spirit of such sharing of wonder will not excite everyone. The suggestion seems to verge on the sentimental, and I, for one, have heard more mention of "sharing" in my recent life than I can tolerate. The real danger is naiveté, that the reader, if not the author, may conclude that this meritorious appeal is easily met. But it is not. Trying to do what he says is most likely to fail. The cause is great, but the means elusive, perhaps even nonexistent. *Trying* to be fully present with a child, to live in the moment and to wonder, is a paradoxical challenge. It reminds one of the traditional spiritual disciplines in which one has to try and try and try until the futility of trying is fully realized, at which time success is granted. Being present, living in the moment, and wondering are gifts and quite rare gifts at that. In my opinion, those who assume otherwise are likely to end in either discouragement or self-deception.

However, O'Neill does put forth the valuable notion that wonder need not be experienced only in isolation and can be stimulated by means of relationship with others. As I would put it, we can squat together. And why not seek out those who might help us squat? Clearly, children can help adults in this matter. This is not to deny or ignore the fact that adults can help children. There is much more to wonder about a flower than this simple recognition noted by the toddler, including what the scientists can tell us. So we might question ourselves to discover who and what we can squat with, what individuals and disciplines might function for us as the toddler can. Poets and theoretical physicists serve me, as do short story writers and science journalists. Who are those with whom you could squat? Do we squat best with our most intimate loved ones or with friends or with strangers? Who are the people who support and increase our wonder? Who are those who undercut and diminish our wonder? For whose wonder do we offer our squatting together?

I have defined wonder as a *simple* experience that something is, but it can be expansive, involving something which does not exist or which is coming into or out of existence. We can even wonder about the presence or absence of wonder itself. The experience in all its fullness may be possible for any one of us. Perhaps there are more opportunities for wonder than we realize.

B. Where Wonder Is Directed

Wonder is one and the same thing whatever we wonder about. And we do tend to focus on different things. I can wonder about a bud of a flower that is just beginning to open, a feeling of attraction I have for another person, an abstract sculpture by Calder, or the Empty Tomb of Jesus Christ. There is not anything that cannot be wondered about, and this fact itself is something to wonder about. Equally obvious, and wonderful in its own right, is the fact that we do circumscribe our wonder in certain standard ways. We each tend to develop patterns of wonder according to which we wonder about some things and not about others. There may be many such patterns to explore. I will outline only three of them. They are sets of alternatives: uncommon or common, inexplicable or explicable, and disorderly or orderly. We can put it to ourselves as a set of questions to use to explore our own wonder: do we tend to wonder more about what is uncommon to us or common, what is inexplicable to us or explicable, what is disorderly for us or orderly? Answer the questions for yourself, and you will get an initial fix on the focus of your wonder.

Uncommon or Common
Some of us are struck most with wonder by means of the uncommon. We see person after person with black or yellow hair, and then are moved to wonderment by a person with red hair. We wonder at a deviation from the norm we have experienced. We wonder at the Grand Canyon because it is bigger than usual in size. We wonder at a little person who is so small. What is the *Guinness Book of Records* but a collection of wonders? A wonder of nature or of humanity is something that is *rare*. It calls attention to itself.

On the other hand, the common may be a stimulus for our wonder. An apple blossom is sufficient, if you really look at it. D. H. Lawrence wrote, "The one universal element in consciousness which is fundamental to life is the element of wonder. You cannot help feeling it in a bean as it starts to grow and pulls itself out of its jacket. You cannot help feeling it in the glisten of the nucleus of the amoebae. You recognize it, willy-nilly, in an ant busily tugging at a straw; in a rook as it walks the frost grass."[14]

I recall some forty years ago—in my "Zen period"—that I spent an afternoon in my graduate school dormitory room with a radiator. The reality of that radiator began that afternoon for me and still lives as a companion with me. There is nothing so familiar that it cannot be an object of wonder. The very familiarity stirs up the wonder. Remember from above Zorba's recognition of a mule.

John Cage wondered about music when he played his piano piece without touching the keys and the audience heard only the sounds in the concert hall for four and a half minutes. Not everyone wondered in response, but some did. Marcel Duchamp wondered about visual art when he placed a snow shovel and a mens' urinal in museum exhibits. So did some of the museum visitors. The natural history museum is even more oriented for wondering. Look at such a place as short story writer Stephen Millhauser does:

> Among the festive rooms and halls of the Barnum Museum, with their flying carpets, their magic lamps, their mermaids and grellings, we come now and then to a different kind of room. In it we may find old paint cans and oilcans, a

green-stained gardening glove in a battered pail, a rusty bicycle against one wall; or perhaps old games of Monopoly, Sorry, and Risk, stacks of dusty 78 records with a dog and Victrola pictured on the center labels, a thick oak table-base dividing into four claw feet. These rooms appear to be errors or oversights, perhaps proper rooms awaiting renovation and slowly filling with the discarded possessions of museum personnel, but in time we come to see in them a deeper meaning. The Barnum Museum is a realm of wonders, but do we not need a rest from wonder? The plain rooms scattered through the museum release us from the oppression of astonishment. Such is the common explanation of these rooms, but it is possible to find in them a deeper meaning still. These everyday images, when we come upon them suddenly among the marvels of the Barnum Museum, startle us with their strangeness before settling to rest. In this sense the plain rooms do not interrupt the halls of wonder; they themselves are those halls . . . .[15]

Uncommon or common. Weird or familiar. Either can be most wonderful. Perhaps neither would be wonderful without the other. If so, both are equally wonderful.

Inexplicable or Explicable

The inexplicable and explicable categories are similar but not the same as those of uncommon and common. The issue is *understanding*, because we can understand what is uncommon and not understand was is common.

Certain events seem inexplicable to us. As we experience it, something just happens. There is a lack of meaningful causality. For a simple example, suppose I am walking down the street and just happen to look down and to the side, noting a tiny patch of green paper. I look more closely and see a ten-dollar bill. I call this find "wonderful." Or I am looking up into the sky at night in the country at the stars. The specks of light are still. Then I see a speck move across the sky. Whether or not I know enough to call it a "meteor" or even a "shooting star," it is a wonder for me. Perhaps one of the best examples is an experience of what we call "coincidence." Suppose that I have just received an alumni magazine from my college and read about a classmate. On the same day, I go to the airport to pick up a relative. Lo and behold, I see the classmate I have just read about. Wondrous chance! The psychology of such coincidence is most revealing about human nature, although too large a topic to pursue here. The point is that we wonder about something we cannot explain. This is an object or event that is important to us and yet cannot be fitted into our past understandings of things.

Events that are quite explicable to us can be equally wonderful. There are events that are common, extremely familiar to us, and totally explainable by our everyday understandings, yet we are filled with wonder by them. Here are the obvious ones: birth, love, and death. These are so wonder-filled that we surround them with all sorts of special behavior. Yet they are as common as anything in our lives and are as explicable as anything in our lives. Here is a statement from Yehudi Menuhin about the familiarity that does not breed contempt:

> Today I believe I can play the Beethoven concerto better than I have played it in the past, largely because the music has become much more a part of me; in some ways clearer and more explicit, and yet just as full of wonder and mystery. I have never taken the Beethoven for granted. The beginning of the larghetto or the entrance of the strings in the first movement, when the violins repeat D sharp—these are moments which fill me with awe and astonishment. As a child, my performance gained unity through my intuition. Now logic has been added to that intuitive approach; I have gone through the period when I asked so many questions of myself and of the score. The wonder, the newness, the haunting originality—they all continue alongside the growing familiarity. But this is not the familiarity

that breeds contempt. Quite the contrary. For me, familiarity with anything or anyone increases the wonder.[16]

What is most common and most familiar to us can be extremely awesome. Scientists know this when they learn more and more about the human body or about the starry sky. So do lovers. A relationship of love or friendship between two people is a wonder, so much so that we call it a gift. To speak of it this way is to posit our wonder about it.

Both the inexplicable and explicable are wondrous. What appears quite inexplicable is a wonder because of that. What appears quite explicable is a wonder because of that. Recall the verse, "Twinkle, twinkle, little star/ How I wonder what you are!" This wonder can be either the wonder over the inexplicable or the explicable. The theme is wonder in relation to understanding. And the fact that there can be understanding is a wonder to the thoughtful. Scientists can be dumbfounded over the fact that we can think of numbers and that the universe can be comprehended in terms of numbers. How amazing that both the universe and the human being can be connected in this way! Even though we know that human beings are a product of the universe and so it is likely that their thinking will conform to it, it still strikes some scientists as a marvel. When we fall in love, we know full well that we are mammals and so, biologically, we need to cuddle both for pleasure and survival. But the occasion of cuddling still strikes us as a marvel. Equally marvelous are all the occasions in which events in the universe or between two people are revelatory of absolutely no connection whatsoever, in which the shock of understanding is absent. Recall the experience of Othello. Iago has planted a handkerchief belonging to Desdemona. Othello has found it. He remarks, "Sure, there's some wonder in this handkerchief." So presence and absence of understanding are equally a wonder. As with the uncommon and common, probably neither would be perceived as a wonder without the other.

Disorder and Order

To be a little disorderly myself, I will reverse the order of our consideration of these two poles of disorder and order. What might surprise us into wonder is the fact that some of our scientists wonder over the presence of order.

Martin Gardner reminds us that science can be surprised by order through his use of some quotations in his truly wonderful essay, "Order and Surprise."[17] Einstein said, "The most incomprehensible thing about the world is that it is comprehensible." The world can be understood. How about that! Bertrand Russell ended one book by concluding, "The final conclusion is that we know very little, and yet it is astonishing that we know so much, and still more astonishing that so little knowledge can give us so much power."[18] This is comprehensive wonder! We laypeople about science should be chastened a bit by the best of the scientists. Russell considers us fortunate not to live on an atom or on the sun. If we did we would be in a "higglely-pigglely" universe in which we could not formulate natural laws. Gardner informs us that Chesterton expresses this scientific wonder over order in his story, "The Man Who Was Thursday." His character Syme says:

> I tell you . . . that every time a train comes in I feel that it has broken past batteries of besiegers, and that man has won a battle against chaos. You say contemptuously that when one has left Sloane Square one must come to Victoria. I say that one might do a thousand things instead, and that whenever I really come here I have the sense of hair-breath escape. And when I hear the guard shout out the word "Victoria," it is not an unmeaning word. It is to me the cry of a herald announcing conquest. It is to me indeed "Victoria"; it is the victory of Adam.[19]

Things hold true. This is amazing for some of those who actually have sufficient imagination to think about it. There are features of a natural order, and we can make inferences from events to other events. Pattern occurs. Recognition of pattern occurs. Both are wondrous events. Think about such order in our own lives.

Regularity is with us all the time in literally thousands of ways. All our behavior assumes regularity, some kind of order. Simply consider the physical act of walking (which the toddler and clown have so much difficulty with)—the regularity of the body, the ground, and the connections between body and ground. There must be hundreds, no thousands, of kinds of order that make walking possible. There is so much order that it is hard to even begin thinking about it. Walking, perhaps, suggests the whole of order.

On the other hand, we may experience the wonder of disorder. Our experience is of a mixture of order and disorder. People, objects, our own inner lives, and the cosmos itself—all that is appears to embody some amount of chaos. Look into your own relationship with a loved one. It is untidy. Walk down the city street. It is untidy. (The country road is no different since it reveals nature's trash.) Look over the course of your life thus far. It, too, is somewhat untidy. International affairs are untidy. Electrons are untidy. Evolution, especially when we understand the role of mutation in the process, is quite untidy. Metaphorically speaking, we trip, stumble, and fall throughout our lives. Of course, we expend considerable effort to create and maintain cleanliness, neatness, and uprightness. So we do not see disorder so often. Then it gets forced into our awareness. Comedians learn how to "take a fall" for our benefit and do so when we need a reminder. And then it is a wonder. Sometimes, we shut out disorder as quickly and firmly as possible because it is too much of a challenge to our sense of order. Other times, when we open ourselves to it, it frees us from constraint, and we are prompted to create new order. In either case, we are wondering about something that does not fit. Sometimes there is even an order that itself becomes disorderly with regard to the whole in which it functions. This could be a relationship in our lives that has become nearly totally disorderly, a personal psychological habit that becomes too destructive of other personal orders, or even a scientific theory, such as the theory that light is only particles or only waves.

So the discovery of both order and disorder equally can be occasions for wonder. William James has an interesting approach to this:

> [O]rder and disorder . . . are purely human inventions . . . . If I should throw down a thousand beans at random on a table, I could doubtless, by eliminating a sufficient number of them, leave the rest in almost any geometrical pattern you might propose to me, and you might then say that that pattern was the thing prefigured beforehand, and that the other beans were mere irrelevance and packing material. Our dealings with nature are just like this. She is a vast *plenum* in which our attention draws capricious lines in innumerable directions. We

count and name whatever lies upon the special lines we trace, whilst the other beans and untraced lines are neither named nor counted.[20]

This is a good reminder about the order we create and then posit as outside ourselves. But our experience is even more complex. James appears to presume that disorder is the default rather than both order and disorder. He is, I suspect, astonished by order. Others of us may be more astonished by disorder. But both are wondrous. And there seems to be both order and disorder within us and without us. Both are beyond belief. I suggest that the situation is more like that when the beans are of two colors, some white and some black. This causes patterns that are actually there. We see them and tend to focus on them, ignoring the equally present lack of pattern. In any event, Santayana concluded, "A really naked spirit cannot assume that the world is thoroughly intelligible. There may be surds, there may be hard facts, there may be dark abysses before which intelligence must be silent, for fear of going mad."[21] For my part, I find both orders and disorders to be surds, facts that cannot be fathomed.

Our question has been, "Where is our wonder directed?" I believe that we might increase our capacity for wonder by taking a preliminary step of wondering about where we wonder. What kind of objects, events, people, inner life, and so on, are stimuli for wonder in us?

Taken more broadly, does our wonder tend to be connected more with the uncommon or the common, the inexplicable or the explicable, the disorderly or the orderly? Whichever our basic habits, the others offer new possibilities for occasions of wonder.

As a stimulus, delight in the poet Wislawa Szymborska's witness of miracles, which are, as we observed in our word world of wonder, nothing other than wonder-events:

> *Miracle Fair*
> The commonplace miracle:
> that so many common miracles take place.
>
> The usual miracle:
> invisible dogs barking
> in the dead of night.
>
> One of many miracles:
> a small and airy cloud
> is able to upstage the massive moon.
>
> Several miracles in one:
> an alder is reflected in the water
> and is reversed from left to right
> and grows from crown to root
> and never hits bottom
> though the water isn't deep.
> A run-of-the-mill miracle:

winds mild to moderate
turning gusty in storms.

A miracle in the first place:
cows will be cows.

Next but not least:
just this cherry orchard
from just this cherry pit.

A miracle minus top hat and tails:
fluttering white doves.

A miracle (what else can you call it):
the sun rose today at three fourteen a.m.
and will set tonight at one past eight.

A miracle that's lost on us:
the hand actually has fewer than six fingers
but still it's got more than four.

A miracle, just take a look around:
the inescapable earth.

An extra miracle, extra and ordinary:
the unthinkable
can be thought.[22]

C. Stages of Wonder

What is there to say about wonder?[23] What more can be discussed than the definition—recognition of a specific existence, the experience of suchness, being itself, the "thereness" of it all? Respect? Maybe nothing more can be said. So I will say a great deal, far more than is to be believed. This is how an academic attempts to respect wonder. The basic experience is simple, but we human beings are complicated and have all kinds of dynamics in our wonder. Here is an outline of what I think they are:

Stages, Elements, and Outcomes of Respect for What Is
- A. Stage of Attention
    1. Intellectual: witness—thereness, something happened
    2. Emotional: shock—surprise
    3. Spiritual: presence—receiving a gift
    Respectful outcome: simple greeting

- B. Stage of Awe
    1. Intellectual: puzzlement—something strange
    2. Emotional: dumbfounderment—astonishment and amazement
    3. Spiritual: empowerment—potential for movement and change
    Respectful outcome: ambivalent greeting

C. Stage of Action
1. Intellectual: exploration—curiosity
2. Emotional: expression—aesthetic elaboration
3. Spiritual: celebration—admiration and gratitude

Respectful outcome: sustained greeting in contemplative play

As the chart indicates, I will discuss these three stages of wonder, the three elements within each stage, and the outcome for each stage. The stages are: attention, awe, and action. The elements in each stage are: intellectual, emotional, and spiritual. And the outcome of each stage is a specific kind of respect. At the very least, I hope that you will find that there may be more to the experience of wonder than many of us have realized. At the very most, you may be prompted to think about your own wonder. That would be far more important than simply accepting what I say.

Stage of Attention

The first stage is *attention*. Something has to happen for wonder to occur. There is an event and we attend to it.

The intellectual element is simply to *witness* the occurrence of the event. We see mostly without seeing, experience without experiencing. This is very useful. If we could not do this, we quickly would become dysfunctional. Gliding half-awake through daily life wisely inhibits and prohibits wonder. But sometimes we are actually caught. We become conscious that we are witnessing something—a bird flying by, a smile from a passing stranger, a feeling of inner fear. We know that something is happening.

The emotional element is *shock*. By definition, the event is unexpected. It is an interruption of the normal. We exclaim not just "Look at that!" but also "How about that!" We are startled. To be surprised means to be seized by an unexpected attack, to be taken suddenly by storm. Wonder is surprising and aggressive. We may try to create the experience of wonder. But to say to ourselves, "Let's go out walking the streets of the city and wonder about the variety of people we meet" seems somewhat unpromising. The actual occurrence of wonder is beyond our control.

The spiritual element is *presence*. Wonder is a response to an encounter. It is not only about something happening, an event, but also about something being there. In some relationships, we have a casual sense of the other that may function well for us. We can actively use it or willfully ignore it. But in another kind of relationship, the other becomes real in a new way, it becomes really other. This other reaches out, grasps us, and gets our attention. We are more passive while the other appears active. It seems to present itself to us. This is not to say that a striking flower or moving poem is a spirit of some kind, although that is precisely what many have concluded about an experience of presence. However, it does say that wonder involves meeting and that the meeting for us seems more like an encounter with a person than with an object. We know that an individual we encounter is not necessarily a real presence for us. When a person is, we know the difference. It is the same with all objects and events, both those without us and within us. They can be a presence. The occasion is not only unexpected, it is also experienced by us as unearned. Presence is a gift.

In sum, the first stage, the stage of attention, involves witness, shock, and presence. The outcome is respect. And this is a very simple kind of respect—a *greeting*. As we know, respect means "to see," to really see something. When an African of a certain tribe meets another person, he says, "I see you." The respectful outcome of attention is "Hello." Whatever the words involved, the conclusion to the first stage of wonder is simple greeting. When we have actually witnessed and been shocked by a presence, we greet it.

Stage of Awe

The second stage is *awe*. We attend to what has happened with awe. And this stage is complicated.

The intellectual element is *puzzlement*. We know that something is happening and are puzzled by it. We see so well that we are propelled beyond our normal understanding. We witness something strange. This is because nothing fits into our patterns of understanding when we are fully in its presence. Consider such things and events as "surds." This term is not well known. An easy way to get a glimpse of what it means, as either adjective or noun, is to note that it is a part of another term, ab-surd. The original meaning of "absurd" defines it as something not clear or distinctly heard, sensed, or understood. The more usual contemporary meaning defines it as something without sense, irrational. To put it absurdly, a surd is something so silent as to be noisy because it is so hard to understand. Surds are puzzling. This is especially so when something formerly common and familiar becomes a surd for us—uncommon and unfamiliar. An unexpected vision of a tree known for years, a feeling within that is contrary to one's self-identity, or words from a loved one that are out of character. Something strange. Greeting is always, however partially so, with a stranger.

The emotional element is—please excuse the ugly word the dictionary recommends—*dumbfounderment.* The event is not only an unexpected interruption of the normal. It is dumbfounding. We exclaim, not just "Look at that!" or "How about that!," but also "Oh-oh!" To put it mildly, the experience of awe is daunting. For some of us, any surprise is something to be avoided as much as possible. And for most of us, there are certain areas of our lives that we protect very strongly from novelty. As we discussed during our verbal play in the word world in chapter 1, astonishment and amazement are both powerful versions of dumbfounding and somewhat different from each other. "Astonish" comes from a Latin term for thunder, meaning to stun or stupefy. "Amaze," like maze, comes from a term meaning to bewilder or confuse. The former stresses the shock of surprise, while the latter focuses on the inexplicable. Intellectually, we are puzzled. Emotionally, the puzzlement is stunning in the real sense of the word: inexplicable shock, dumbfounding.

The spiritual element is *empowerment.* The presence perceived in wonder is experienced as a powerful force. The best analogy to the experience is that of electricity: a power that can be stored in a reservoir, transmitted through objects and people, can help or hurt human beings, and which is difficult to control and does not always do what is expected. Wonder is not for wimps. Perhaps it is possible to have the initial experience of wonder in the stage of attention during which the presence is simply noted and greeted. But continued gushing about the wonder experience is a closing off of wonder. The "How nice!" reaction is a trivialization, a distancing maneuver that isolates the individual from a potential threat. An event that puzzles and dumbfounds us is too powerful to be cute about. Power is potential for movement, which means empowerment. However dangerous, it is a gift to those of us who are caught in routine stability. Wonder is about the possibility of change. We realize, "the strange might render me strange."

In sum, the second stage, the stage of awe, involves puzzlement, dumbfounderment, and empowerment. Something strange happens that is so astonishing and amazing as to have a powerful impact on us. So what is the respectful outcome of this stage? Greeting, yes, but a most *ambivalent greeting*. What is awesome is also awful. Because wonder is ambiguously both fascinating and daunting, we are both attracted to it and repelled from it. We are moved closer by the quality of fascination. Wonder is the source of rapture, bliss, and love. Equally, the quality of daunting pushes us away. Wonder is the source of weirdness, dread, and horror. What allures us with its charm also cows us and makes us tremble. We have a sense of our own reality. The wonder experience can strengthen it. But it also can weaken it. It saves and destroys. So wonder is both the most fruitful experience possible and the most threatening. Awe is the ambivalent element in our wonder. The respectful outcome of the stage of awe is ambivalent greeting.

Stage of Action

The third stage of wonder is action. The first stage of witness, shock, and presence is a quite passive noticing. The second stage of puzzlement, dumbfounderment, and power is somewhat more active in that the noticing is of ambiguity and the response is the mixed one of ambivalence. But it is in the third stage that our wonder becomes fully active. Having attended to the fact that something awesome has happened, we are empowered to explore, express, and celebrate.

The intellectual element is *exploration*. Something happens that puzzles us, so we want to find out what it is all about. In the first stage there is silence in our wonder. In the second stage there is the outcry of astonishment and amazement. But now there is the action of addressing the event by means of curiosity. The mind does not simply notice or puzzle, but actively explores by means of questions. What happened? How did it happen? What does it mean? Can it happen again? What can be done in response to it?

Some of these innumerable questions are answerable and some are not. Curiosity is an exceedingly open-ended wonderment that is not short-circuited by the possibility of answers but sustained by delight in questions. In wonder, we do not move instantly from puzzlement to solution. The stance is that of taking nothing for granted. One occupies a special place in which puzzlement is organized playfully into myriad ways of exploring possibilities. Needless to say, great minds enjoy this interim play with their own lack of understanding. They promote it, challenging not only accepted axioms but also newly suggested ones by raising yet another question and another. Lack of curiosity kills understanding as well as puzzlement. Dwelling in curiosity allows full play for the active organization of puzzlement. Curiosity itself is the pay-off from wonder. Beyond it is another fruit—knowledge. And arrival at knowledge does not necessarily prohibit a new or renewed occasion of wonder. Arrival at knowledge itself can be an occasion of wonder. When knowledge is pictured as an expanding sphere and the surface as being surrounded by the unknown, it is clear that knowledge only increases the arena for exploration and the potential for wonder.

The emotional element is *expression*. After the surprise and dumbfounderment comes the expression of the wonder event. The initial passivity is countered by an active communication about the experience. The wonderer is speaking to himself and his community but also replying to the powerful presence. Here is where all the arts come into play with image, sound, movement, and story. We proclaim not only "Look at that!" and "How about that!" but also "Here is that!" We dance, sing, paint, and tell a tale about it. The urge is almost inevitable and almost impossible to satisfy. The challenge is to communicate wonder. A painter sees an old woman and is moved to paint her. A poet writes about her. A dancer moves like her. A composer creates her music. A dramatist makes up the dynamics of her personal relationships. If their artistry is great, wonder is stimulated in others by their creations. Art has been described as a relatively "safe experience of chaos" and the artist as one who has a "rage for chaos." I would add that wonder is a relatively safe experience of chaos—our ambivalent reaction to the ambiguity of the uncommon, inexplicable, and disorderly, as well as the common, explicable, and orderly. The great artists wonder and open us up to the possibility of experiencing it ourselves.

The spiritual element of the stage of action is *celebration*. Wonder prompts us to admire what gives rise to the wonder. To admire originally meant to regard with wonder or astonishment. Admiration is a wondering or marveling esteem accompanied by pleasure or delight. The event is remembered, shared, and praised. A presence has been made known and empowered us. This is what is celebrated. The thing-itself is celebrated. In response to receiving a gift, we give thanks. Grace is followed by gratitude. But this need not be worship of some hidden divinity or sacred reality. Celebration *per se* is not worship. It does not go beyond the wonder event itself. We give thanks for the revelation of what is, gratitude for the gift of its presence, admiration for the "inviolable strangeness" of its existence. "Celebration consists of rejoicing in the presence of things."[24]

In sum, the third stage, the stage of action, involves exploration, expression, and celebration. Moving beyond passivity, we are engaged with what puzzles us, involve our creative talents to communicate and elaborate on the event, and proclaim our admiration by giving thanks. The respectful outcome is more than simple greeting and ambivalent greeting. It is *sustained greeting*.

One lives for a while in a condition of wonder. The space and time is devoted to playful contemplation. This is an odd situation. One is not entirely passive before the event, nor is one entirely active. One is in-between. The object is not used to work our will upon, not abused, but is not simply observed either. There is a relationship not of work but of play. The distinction between the thing and oneself is diminished. In the play reality, the self and other conjure up changes in each other without abuse. Respect for the unique novelty of self and other rules.

Conclusion

In our experience of things, wonder is respect. Our comments on recognition of what is, the foci of uncommon and common, inexplicable and explicable, disorder and order, and the proposed stages and elements —these are offered to entice us to spiritually squat, to open ourselves to the possibilities of respect. Believing in my thoughts would be foolish, maybe even an offense against wonder. It is better to wonder about our own wonder. Failing that, we can wonder about our lack of wonder. We all experience wonder. But it can disappear prematurely. Putting safety first, we close ourselves off from it. Or quite the opposite, wonder can be allowed and encouraged to take over our lives. Such lack of safety is no better. Wonder isn't everything and becomes destructive when it is considered so. Un-experienced by most of us, I presume, is the violent rage to wonder that destroys both the occasion and the possibility of it. The evil of Auschwitz may be beyond wonder. I do not really know. I do know the peril of responding to humanity's inhumanity to humans with cheap sentimentality or distancing rationale, both of which substitute for connection and change. There may well be a limit to what events can be wondered about.

On a somewhat less challenging note, I conclude by sharing a tale about going past wonder. However much there is a limit to wonder, there remains the danger of too easily and quickly going beyond it:

> One day a demon was traveling through the villages with his attendants. They saw a man walking who stopped to stare at something he had discovered on the ground in front of him. The attendants asked their master what was happening. He replied, "He is wondering." "Doesn't this bother you when someone wonders, o' evil one?" his attendants asked. "No," the demon replied. "Right after this they usually make a truth out of it, and eventually, it may even become a belief."[25]

May our wondering never cease.

Notes

1. Gilbert Keith Chesterton, *Tremendous Trifles* (New York: Dodd, Mead and Company, 1920), page 7.

2. Jorge Luis Borges, *Conversations with Jorge Luis Borges*, edited by Richard Burgin (Jackson, MS: University Press of Mississippi, 1998), page 6.

3. D. H. Lawrence, *The Later D. H. Lawrence* (New York: Alfred A. Knopf, 1959), page 382.

4. Editor's note: I have not been able to locate the text for this exact quote. Einstein said this kind of thing several times in different ways. His most famous expression is the subsequent quote in the text.

5. Albert Einstein. Quoted by Sharpe, *Words on Wonder*, page 212.

6. G. K. Chesterton, *Orthodoxy* (London: Bodley Head, 1949), page 4.

7. Nikos Kazantzakis, *Zorba the Greek* (New York: Simon & Schuster, 1965), page 152.

8. Ludwig Wittgenstein, *Tractatus Logico-Philosphicus* (London: Routledge & Kegan Paul, 1961), page 44.

9. William James, "Sentimentality of Rationality," in *The Will to Believe and Other Essays* in Popular Philosophy (New York: Dover Publications, 1956), page 72.

10. C. E. M. Joad. Quoted by Sharpe, *Words on Wonder*, page 210.

Chapter 2: Will Wonders Never Cease

11. William Wordsworth, "My Heart Leaps Up When I Behold," in *Poems in Two Volumes* (London: Longman, Hurst, Rees and Orms, 1807), page 246.

12. William Wordsworth, "The Daffodils," in *Poems in Two Volumes* (London: Longman, Hurst, Rees and Orms, 1807), page 303. The poem is widely available online.

13. David P. O'Neill, *What Do You Say To A Child When You meet A Flower?: A Book for Parents of Preschool Children* (St. Meinrad, Indiana: Abbey Press, 1975), pages 20-23. I am grateful to Brother Paul West for calling this book to my attention.

14. D. H. Lawrence. Quoted by Sharpe, *Words on Wonder*, page 224.

15. Stephen Millhauser, "The Barnum Museum," in *The Barnum Museum* (Normal, IL: Dalkey Archive Press, 1997), pages 89-90.

16. Yehudi Menuhin, quoted by Robin Daniels in *Conversations with Menuhin*. Quoted by Sharpe, *Words on Wonder*, page 215.

17. Martin Gardner, "Order and Surprise," *Order and Surprise* (Buffalo NY: Prometheus Books, 1983), pages 57-67.

18. Quoted by Gardner in "Order and Surprise," page 57.

19. Quoted by Gardner in "Order and Surprise," page 59.

20. Quoted by Gardner in "Order and Surprise," page 64.

21. Quoted by Gardner in "Order and Surprise," page 65.

22. Wislawa Szymborska, *View with a Grain of Sand: Selected Poems* (New York: Harcourt Brace & Company, 1995), pages 165-166.

23. Much of the following is greatly indebted to the superb observations and reflections of Sam Keen in "The Anatomy of Wonder," the first chapter of his book, *Apology for Wonder* (New York: Harper & Row, Publishers, 1969). The organization of the ideas into defined stages is my own.

24. Sam Keen, *Apology for Wonder*, page 209.

25. I have retold this tale "Buddha and Mara" from *The Heart of Understanding* by Thich Nhat Hanh. Quoted in *Stories of the Spirit, Stories of the Heart*, Christina Feldman & Jack Kornfield, editors (New York: HarperCollins Publishers, 1991), page 250.

Performances for Chapter 2

In chapter 1, Bob Neale informs us that chapter 2 will work to articulate a sixth world of wonder, an experiential or psychological one. To begin, he shares his view, his assumption, that for the most part, "Wonders are everywhere, but we are elsewhere." Our awareness and attention to them get waylaid by a variety of states such as boredom, routine, anxiety, depression, busyness, and so on. From this inspiration, Bob works to reveal wonder as an experiential state of mind.

This is no small thing. What he proceeds to do is offer a very rich, unprecedented account of wonder as "really seeing and recognizing—thereby *respecting*—a person, entity, or event in its specific being." While at first this might sound difficult, rest assured that Bob's many examples will quickly help you see what he means and see it in your own lives.

But this is not all that happens in this chapter. For once Bob puts the basic phenomena of wonder in play, he continues to explore how it works in human life: the different kinds of things upon which it can be directed and the three different stages of it, each one of which has different aspects and outcomes. By the time you are finished with this chapter, I suspect you will see that the living experience of wonder is different and far more complex than you might have thought before.

Given the purpose of this chapter, to carry out what I would call "a phenomenology of wonder," we have decided to include performance pieces that are especially arresting, that might well cause you to really see and respect something in its specific existence.

The first four items—"Toy Ball" (2.1), "Framed" (2.2), "Eye of the Needle" (2.3), and "Tortured Bill" (2.4)—are highly unique, impossible objects of the sort that Bob Neale is famous for creating. If you take the time to make these up and spend time seeing and exploring them, you will feel wonder. And yes, in 2.3 Bob has actually solved the ages-old problem of how to fit a camel through the eye of a needle!

The fifth item, "A King's Mourning" (2.5) is a story that promises to stop you in your tracks, setting you free to wonder.

—Lawrence Hass

Performances for Chapter 2

Performance 2.1
Toy Ball

The performer shows a ball that has been ever so slightly modified. Upon reflection, the object appears odd and possibly impossible. It has an inside and an outside. But it has only one edge and one surface. So perhaps it has only one side, and inside and outside are one and the same.

Before getting into my unusual ball, let's think more generally. A ball may well have been our first toy as children. Our early experience with a ball is beyond recall. It probably began sometime during the first year of life and continued for several years after. Indeed, it accompanied us from the nursery to the playground, and from there to the playing fields. The ball is a primal toy.

For your entertainment, I offer the following summary of the passion and wisdom of Friedrich Froebel, father of the kindergarten movement, concerning the toy ball. His intuition is sound, but the feeling and thought are clothed in a style of communication not exactly suited to our contemporary taste.

Froebel believed that the ball is one of our great gifts to the child. In *Pedagogics of the Kindergarten* (edited by W. T. Harris, translated by Josephine Jarvis, New York: D. Appleton and Company, 1895), he wrote (page 31):

Let us give to the child for its spontaneous and voluntary action an object which expresses stability and yet movability, which in this stability and movability can be grasped and handled by the child; in which, as in its own mind, the unity of all manifoldness is contained; which it perceives in its new existence, in which, therefore, though as yet quite unconsciously, it can see its own self-dependent, stable, and yet movable life, as it were, in a mirror, as well as test and exercise such life by such an object.

Extrapolating on this idea, the ball is an image of the world and of the self. From play with it, the child discovers object, space, and time. It presents presence, departure, return, seeking, finding, getting, catching, grasping, holding, rolling, sliding, turning, and spinning. It shows contents, mass, matter, space, form, size, figure, elasticity, stability, spontaneity, color, and sound. It becomes a connection between the child and its environment, especially its mother and father.

As Froebel puts it, "We see the human being as a child, yes, even as an infant, placed in the midst of his life, as of all life, by means of the ball and the play with the ball; for his own life, his mother's life, his father's life, and the life of all his surroundings become to him thus inwardly vital and jointly objective, as the life and the love of the mother has become one and objective to him in the fullness of the mother's breast which affords him nourishment, which itself appears to him a ball, and is his all" (page 58).

As the child develops, the play becomes more varied, free, and personal. The ball is put in and out of a box, rolled from hand to hand, tossed and caught, rolled on an inclined surface and caught, bounced on the floor or wall, and caught. Other people become involved in games of tossing and catching. Development of perceptions has been accompanied by discovery and perfection of skills. Froebel concludes that such play sponsors a "similar procedure to a solution of the highest problem of life, and *to hold fast the one high purpose amid all the vicissitudes of time and place*" (page 159).

Take delight in the obscure and the sentimental in Froebel, but please do not ignore the understanding of toys and the ball. At the very least, recall your own play with this toy, or that of children, or your play together. Just maybe, what the wheel is to civilization, the ball is to the individual.

Existence is a ball. This phrase is a physical and metaphysical joke as well as a verbal one. My "Toy Ball" is a trickster toy, so it will take some patience to see it fully. And the best way to see it is to construct it. (Even if you do not want to do so, attend to the following directions so you can understand the oddity that is created.) I will tell you how to make it first, then I will

The Sense of Wonder

describe what it is, and I will conclude by praising it (obscurely and sentimentally, no doubt) as a toy for adults.

Construction

My "Toy Ball" is made simply and quickly out of a toy ball. Obtain one of any size and material, but it should be hollow and solid enough not to collapse when slit open. The usual vinyl ball is perfect. (A large model made from the smallest size soccer ball is of pleasing appearance.) The ball is modified by making three slits with a knife to create a flap on each pole; the two flaps are then connected with tape or glue inside the ball. This is all there is to it.

Figure 6

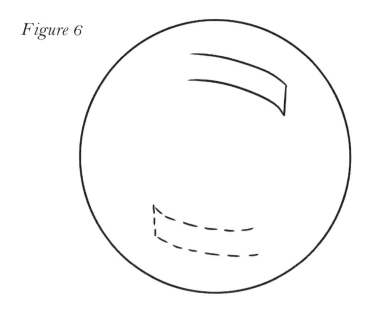

Performances for Chapter 2

Here are the details. Suppose your ball is about 3.5" in diameter. Figure 6 shows how to slit the ball. Please note: the slits should be exactly opposite each other, which is extremely difficult to represent on a flat page. To indicate this, one set of slits consists of dashes to indicate you are seeing them through the ball.

So to make the slits: imagine a rectangle at one pole that is about 1" by 3". Slit the two long sides and only one short side of this rectangle. On the opposite pole, imagine an identical rectangle, parallel to the first and running in the same direction. The way you slit this second rectangle is important. Again, you slit the two long sides and only one short side, but you must be sure to slit the correct short side. If you are holding the ball with the first rectangle facing you and the short slit is on the right, then as you look through the inside of the ball, the other short slit must be on the left. (Or if you are holding the ball as before and rotate it so that the first rectangle passes out of sight and the next one comes into sight, keeping both horizontal, the short slit is on the right of both.) The two flaps can be pushed inside the ball and will overlap. Tape or glue them together. The model is complete.

Demonstration

This simple modification of a ball may seem to have caused very little to happen. However, that little something is very tricky, so let's explore it.

The ball has only one edge and only one surface. Place your finger on the edge anywhere. Remember where it is or mark the place with a pencil dot. Now, run your finger along the edge, continuing until you arrive back at the starting point. There is only one edge. This is no different from a sheet of paper. It, too, has only one edge. But a sheet has two sides, one on each surface of its continuous edge.

Place your finger anywhere on the surface of the ball. Remember where it is or mark the place with another pencil dot. Now run your finger along the surface, covering the entire outside of the ball. Then run it inside the ball by letting it move onto the flap but do not cross an edge. Once your finger is on the inside of the ball, move it around so that it covers the entire inside. Finally, move the finger back to the outside of ball without crossing an edge, relying on the inner flaps. You have arrived back where you began. There is only one surface. This is quite different from a sheet of paper, which consists of one edge and two surfaces. The modification of a child's ball has rendered it a toy for adults.

We can think in the following odd way about this odd object. The ball has an inside and an outside. Yet, because there is only one surface, there can be only one side. So the inside and outside are one and the same. Therefore, when you put your finger in the ball it is also outside. When you put your finger outside the ball it is also inside. Furthermore, you can conclude that the little ball is truly empty, being nothing inside, and also truly full, containing the entire universe. And finally, since the latter can be the case, although you are holding the ball in your hand, it holds even you who are holding it.

This is a great toy! I had real pleasure when a friend took it to his fellow graduate students at Harvard's mathematics department for exploration. I recall my timorous presentation when revealing it to my own students as an example of one of my personal religious symbols. It remains my symbol of God, Life, Existence, Meaning, and much more. Yet I am quite clear that it is a toy. Never have I desired to redesign it as something other than a ball for play. The construction could be made from different materials and into different shapes, but the toy ball has the most appeal. A toy ball is for rolling, throwing, catching, and bouncing. This one is for bouncing the mind. We bounce most balls. This ball bounces us. And it is just this simple modification that transforms a child's toy into an adult's toy—a trickster's toy.

I confess that I rely on this ball to symbolize just about anything I have in mind at the time I am looking for a symbol. Until recently, my theme was perspective, and the ball plays very nicely. It is so strange that you have to look at it closely and carefully. And then you have to think about what you have seen. Once you have thought about the ball, then you have to think about how to see it because it presents options. Rather than ignore or disguise the observing process, this object tends to make you aware of it. Its strangeness calls attention to the strangeness of our thinking.

These shifts of thinking about inside and outside are shifts in perspective. Whether the ball has a finger on the inside or outside, is empty or full, is held by you or holds you—these are matters of the perspective that you have selected. Furthermore, you can change your perspective at will. And with practice, perhaps you can use two contradictory perspectives at once. The ball symbolizes multiplicity and opportunity of perspectives.

This ball is a nonsense creation. Both my creation and analysis of it are nonsense. Let this be most clear. The ball sponsors word play with our understandings of "surface," "side," "outside," and "inside." I do not claim to have played fair at all. But I do hope that the wordplay has prompted some new or renewed wonder about "outside" and "inside," as well as about perspectives. What does it mean to us to be "outside" or "inside?" We are objects that are contained or not contained in groups of various sizes. We can be in with God, out with a loved one, and so forth. It means a great deal to us. And we have perspectives that tell us whether we are in or out, and assumptions about whether we can change our presumed location. The ball is nonsense. So also is much of our perspective on sides. But it is necessary nonsense, for sure. The ball can remind us of such nonsense. At best, it can urge us to freedom with the nonsense of perspective, so that our perspectives can be put in their place, rather than our being placed by them.

The ball requires fully serious and fully silly effort of mind and will for us to see, interpret, and change perspectives. So my current vision of the ball is of an object. It presents itself fully to us, stimulating awareness of both objects and subjects. The ball is a serious but silly object that reveals serious but silly people. That is the glory of it and of us.

Have a ball!

Performance 2.2
Framed

The performer introduces a card with a very small frame in the center. The object looks quite impossible. It is shown how the entire card must have passed through the little frame, even though this could not have happened. But it has, and since this is the case, the little frame frames the whole card. Therefore, the part encompasses the whole. But, if the frame frames the whole card, it is also framing the frame. Could it be that a frame can frame itself?

Alternately, the performer recalls the common theory that magicians use trapdoors and introduces a small card that contains a trapdoor for the audience to examine. The door is discovered to be an impossible object. The opening is very small, yet it appears that the entire card has been passed through itself without damage.

Sources

It was Gustavus J. Simmons, an engineer in charge of research and development at Rolamite, Inc., in Albuquerque, New Mexico, who sent a curious topological problem to Martin Gardner at *Scientific American*. (This problem appeared in Gardner's column

Performances for Chapter 2

and then in his book, *Wheels, Life and Other Mathematical Amusements*, New York: W. H. Freeman and Company, 1983, pages 166-7, 173-4.) The challenge involved the need to put a loop in a flexible band having a slot in it and one end attached to an object too big to fit through the slot. Is that clear? No? Well, since this description is hardly sufficient, see figure 7.

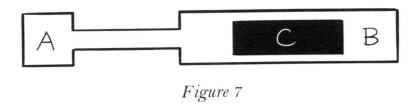

Figure 7

The ends are labeled A and B, and the slot is labeled C. The basic idea is to make the band intersect itself by ending with an end passing through the slot. You might make such a band out of file card to play with. For Simmons's Strip, cut a band that is 1" x 7". Consider it as divided into seven square units. End A is one unit, the slender portion of the band is two units, and the other end is four units in length with the slot itself being two units. (Color one side of the band for easy recognition of its varying conditions.)

We will consider the problem in stages. First, imagine that both ends are free. In this case the problem is easy to solve because end A can be inserted into and through the slot. Imagine what this end state looks like.

Second, imagine that end B is attached to a wall, large machine, elephant, or, indeed, yourself. Can the problem be solved? Of course. It is just as easy as before: end A can be inserted into and through the slot. Third, patient reader, imagine that end A is attached, maybe even being held by a friendly human being willing to be puzzled. With end A attached, can you imagine how to reach a solution? This is the problem. If we actually encountered it in circumstances of daily life, I assume that most of us would conclude that a solution was impossible, especially without putting permanent twists in the band. But Simmons and Gardner showed that it could be done simply. As I understand it, the solution amounts to turning the band through itself so that it becomes almost inside out. As we proceed, you may find a better way of describing the action. I did not solve the puzzle, but the solution prompted me to create some problems that others might wonder about, just as much as I had wondered about this one. This was not the first time my limitations in solving other people's puzzles generated such genteel revenge.

Here is how my mind played around and about. Thinking about impossibilities, I first saw end A as shaped into a camel. The narrow part of the band next to it became the camel's tail. Attached to the tail was the head of a needle with an eye in it. Then I saw end B as elongated to form a needle with a pointed end. You can guess what is coming. The relatively small needle was manipulated so that the finished object looked like a camel that had gone through the eye of a needle. (My "Eye of the Needle" object appears as the next performance piece.) Second, I saw end A as shaped into a very large rectangular card. A small rectangular section was cut out of the center. Hanging from the inner edge of the top rim was a stem from which hung a very small frame. That is, I saw a little frame hanging from the inside of a much bigger frame. After the appropriate manipulation, it looked as if the large frame had passed through the little one. After experimenting with large cards, I made this impossible object out of a playing card. Finally, I started exploring the possibility of doing the action in front of an audience, of creating an impossible event instead of an impossible object. This led to the simple use of a file card with a flap torn in it. Three of my early responses were published in a manuscript for magicians by Karl Fulves, *Robert Neale's Trapdoor Card* (Teaneck, NJ: Karl Fulves, 1983).

"Framed" was first titled "Trapdoor Card," and it was constructed from a playing card. When carefully examined, it does look impossible. Being unable to leave it alone, I added the idea of an impossible framing to accompany the visual nonsense. You might well decide to skip this presentation and simply allow the object to present itself visually. But I happen to enjoy the thought of a small frame that frames something bigger than itself and frames itself as well.

The Sense of Wonder

Construction

The frame can be made from a file card, business card, playing card, or dollar bill. It is best to practice making and folding the card with 3" x 5" or larger file cards. Fold the card in fourths each way. (The creases are used as guides for cutting the card while making samples. Models for display and performance are without them.) Make slits in a 3" x 5" card to form the outline given in figure 8. The shaded areas indicate parts of the card that have been cut out and discarded. The result is a flap with a hole in it that is attached to the rest of the card by a short stem.

Figure 8

The flap is 1¼" x 1½" with a rim ¼" wide. The stem, and the holes on either side of it, is a ½" wide and 5/8" long. These dimensions need not be exact. Eventually, you will probably want to make a smaller flap than this on an even larger card.

Manipulation

When you are thoroughly familiar with the following moves, you can do them with only a single crease being made. When you are thoroughly practiced as well, you can do the moves right in front of an audience. All extra creases give away the method of creating the card and should be avoided. However, to learn how to create the card creases are advised. Once you understand the process, you can roll the card through the steps without creasing.

For the frame to appear, only the flap itself is manipulated. In general terms, what happens is that the three free outer edges of the flap are passed through the hole in it and the fourth connected edge is creased. To do this, you will first pass the two side edges through the hole, then the bottom edge, and finally make the crease with the fourth edge. The end result is depicted in figure 9 (see next page).

Here are the details of this operation. The folding required is indicated by figures 10-16. (Please note: in these figures only the flap and its stem are referred to.) Getting started with figure 10: the dotted lines indicate the two creases that are to be made. Fold the left and right rims of the flap in toward the center. Figure 11 is the result.

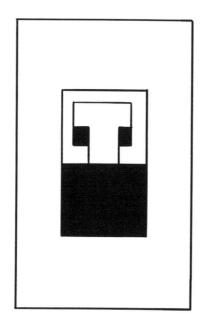

Figure 9

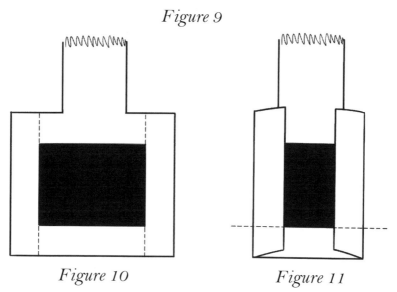

Figure 10 *Figure 11*

Performances for Chapter 2

The dotted line in figure 11 shows the next crease to be made. Fold the bottom rim of the flap up toward the center. Figure 12 is the result.

The dotted lines in figure 12 show the next creases to be made. Fold the flap up and over against the stem. Figure 13 is the result.

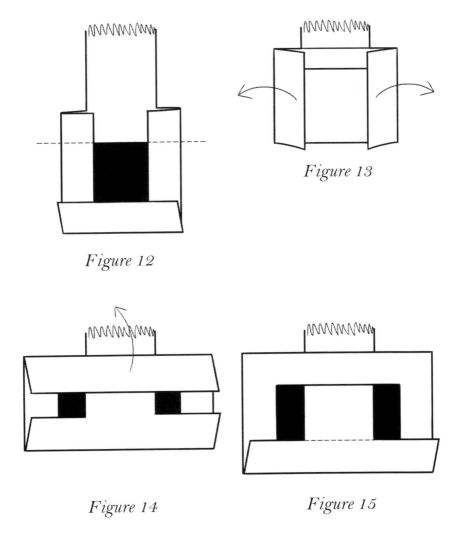

Figure 12

Figure 13

Figure 14

Figure 15

The Sense of Wonder

The arrows in figure 13 indicate the next move. Unfold the left and right parts out to the left and right. Figure 14 is the result.

The arrow in figure 14 indicates the next move. Unfold the upper part upward. Figure 15 is the result.

The dotted line in figure 15 gives the last fold. Crease along the connection of the rim and stem to move the entire rim upward along the stem. Figure 16 is the result.

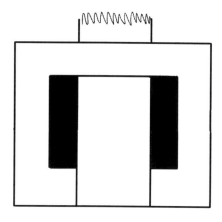

Figure 16

Demonstration

The object may be labeled a frame or a trapdoor. Whatever the label, some words can be used to assist the eyes of the audience. If the object is defined as impossible and handed out for examination, not everyone will see the issue quickly. So it is helpful to state that the object is made from one card with no hidden cutting and pasting.

Then point out the single crease in the object and state that it is the only crease that has ever been made. Finally, claim that, therefore, the large card has passed through the small frame in its center. Such an introduction is both necessary and sufficient. After it, pass the object out for inspection and exploration. Then offer whatever verbal nonsense appeals to you.

Performance 2.3
Eye of the Needle

The effect: the performer states that her goals for this life and the next one are money and heaven, respectively. With due respect for the admonition, "It is easier for a camel to go through the eye of a needle than for a rich man to enter the kingdom of God," the performer reveals her symbol of success in both worlds—a camel and needle. The large camel and the small needle, with a very small hole for an eye, are made from one piece of paper, yet the camel has gone through the eye.

As discussed in "Framed" directly above, "Eye of the Needle" is my response closest to the original statement of the problem concerning a slotted band attached to a large object. Look at the drawing that follows this explanation. The camel is the large object. The slotted band is the tail with the long needle attached containing a hole in it for an eye. This is simply a more graphically pleasing approach to the problem, redesigned as getting the camel through the eye of the needle. Impossible objects of any kind often appeal to the intellectually curious. This one has the advantage of also referring to a familiar saying about impossibility. The spirit is that of challenge. The game is that of rendering the impossible possible and the possible impossible—playing with our experience of possibility.

Construction

Constructing this object is a variation of "Framed," and the same manipulation is required. Refer to "Framed" for details of manipulation for construction. Of course, it is not the camel but the needle itself that goes through the eye, but this is not immediately apparent to the observer. Figure 17 is the completed model.

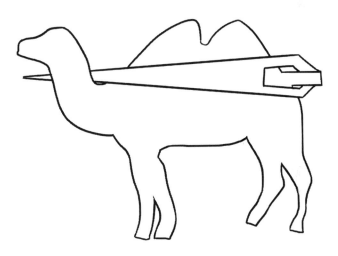

Figure 17

Use light cardboard or paper that has a different color on each side. Note that the head of the needle is connected to the end of the camel's tail. The needle is long enough to pass over, and rest on, the neck of the camel. The only restriction on the size of any part is that the eye of the needle must be big enough for the remainder of the needle to pass through it. Practice with a rough model of a needle attached to a tail cut out of a sheet of typing paper. First, bend the end of the needle through the eye, then the two sides go through together, and conclude by making the one necessary crease.

Performance 2.4
The Tortured Bill
(A Presentation and Method for Harry Eng's "Impossible Bill")

The effect: a dollar bill is borrowed. It is folded a few times, then unfolded and torn a little bit in the center, and finally refolded. The result is returned to the owner. It is a strange configuration, seemingly impossible. Half of the slenderized bill faces one way and half the other way.

Note: if the owner does not care to keep the bill in unusable condition, the performer quickly returns it to the original simple rectangle. A tiny slit remains, but it is hardly noticeable and not a problem being accepted by banks or stores.

Script
Do you have a thing about money? A negative thing? The "root of all evil" sort of thing? Loan me a dollar bill and I will help you express it.

I fold and crease it, hoping it experiences some distress . . . . I tear it a little . . . . Maybe it feels some pain . . . . Now I shove a part of it into and through itself . . . . Yes, make it give itself "the bird" . . . . Finally, one pull to complete this joyful torture.

Here it is, an impossible mess—half inside out and half outside in. May your tortured bill please you.

If you want me to restore it to its commercial value, I will instantly remove the folds, causing only a little pain. It will be nearly whole again and totally usable.

Construction

1. Place the bill face up in front of you with the narrow ends pointing toward and away from you. Fold the top edge to the bottom edge (figure 18). The bill may be either face up or face down. Please note: in all these figures we will indicate one side of the bill as white and the other side as shaded, but again it doesn't matter which side is which.

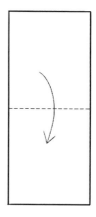

Figure 18

2. This step divides the bill into thirds. It is best to begin with an estimated fold on the left that splits the remaining area to the right in half as exactly as possible. Folding the edges on the right will show if the first crease is properly situated; if it is not, adjust it as appropriate. So fold the left edges over to the right, making the crease one-third the width of the bill. Unfold. Fold the right edges over to the left crease, making the

crease one-third the width of the bill. Unfold the bill entirely (figure 19).

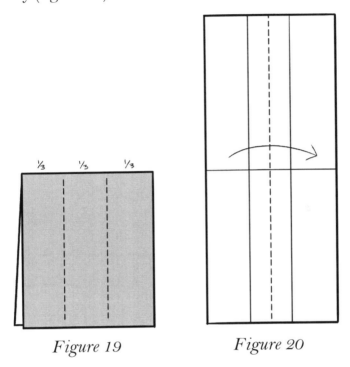

Figure 19   Figure 20

3. Fold the left edge to the right edge (figure 20).

4. Make a short tear, running from the left folded edge to the creases just made so that the slit occurs in only the center third of the bill (figure 21). Unfold and refold the bill in half the other way as done for step one.

5. Open up the upper layer of the left third and squash down at the top to flatten each of the two layers, one to

the left and the other to the right (figure 22). See figure 23 to understand the goal.

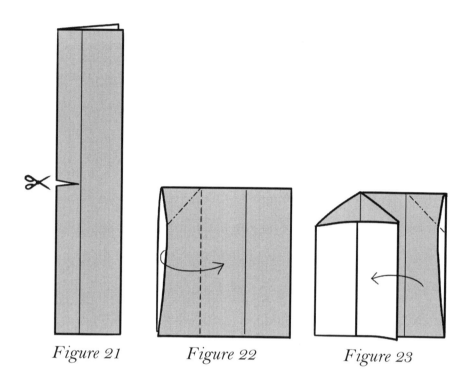

Figure 21 *Figure 22* *Figure 23*

6. Repeat the folding and squashing with the right third of the bill (figure 23).

7. The bottom end of the column in the center is going to be pushed underneath itself and up through the slit at the top (figure 24). To do so, it is best to make a horizontal mountain crease near the upper end as indicated in the figure. Lift up the column in order to do this. Then thread the end of the column through the slit behind. It will go

all the way out the top as far as the horizontal crease you just made.

8. Fold over the left flap on the crease that is already there (figure 25). Please note carefully the two different fold lines: the bottom part of the flap is valley folded to the right, but the top layer of the top part of the flap is mountain folded. This top part of the flap goes all the way to the right as well and is tucked underneath the upper end of the right flap.

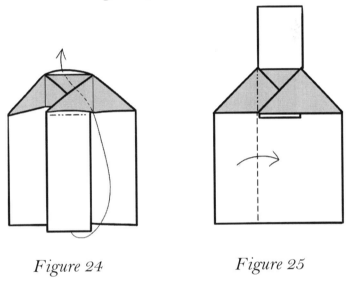

Figure 24 *Figure 25*

9. Push over the upper layer of the right flap inside the left flap and as far as it will go to the left (figure 26). Again, please note the two different fold lines: the bottom part of the right flap is valley folded to the left and the top part of the flap is mountain folded and is tucked underneath the folded-over left flap. It is difficult to make

the upper part go all the way to the left inside the left flap. You can assure this by pushing the upper part with the pencil. But it is sufficient to just shove it in the best you can. It does not need to be done perfectly at all.

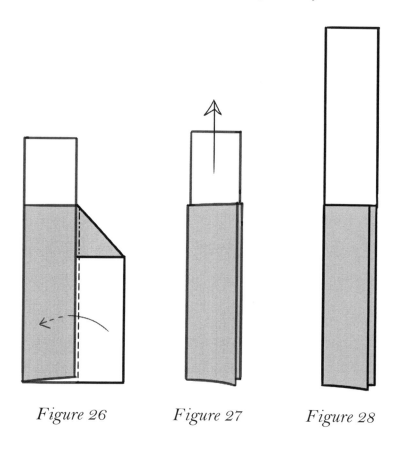

Figure 26   *Figure 27*   *Figure 28*

10. Hold the bottom end of the column firmly and pull up on the top half of the column (figure 27). It will go up the rest of the way (figure 28). The construction is complete.

Disassembling the bill is very simple. Bend the top end of the column back away from you. Insert this end into the slit from above and shove it down a ways. Open up the flaps at the bottom of the column and reach inside to pull the end all the way down to the bottom of the bill. Then it is easy to unfold the rest.

Routine

Do not just show the completed model. The construction is an interesting part of the presentation and helps sell the strangeness, so construct it openly. Few will be able to follow the process. Borrow the bill. This adds a little drama, especially when you tear it. Skip the lines about giving itself the finger if you must, but refer somehow to the interesting process of pushing part of it through itself. Point to one half of the model as you refer to "inside out" and to the other half when saying "outside in." Flip it over sideways to show both sides. Be sure to offer to disassemble the model. And even be prepared to exchange the bill for an un-torn one of your own. At best, the model can be a gift that one treasures.

Sources

Harry Eng was a high school teacher who challenged his students to do the impossible. One of his examples was putting something into a narrow-necked bottle that could not be fitted into it in any possible way, for example, a ping pong ball, a full and cased deck of playing cards, a master lock, or even a tennis sneaker. I met him only a few times and we exchanged only a few objects and emails, but once he did something for me during a convention. He asked for a dollar bill, received one of mine, turned his back for a while in silence, and then presented me with my bill in a quite odd configuration. This was the oddity that I have described above. Due to my own play with paper puzzles, it was not hard to discover a procedure. What took time was eliminating unnecessary steps and adding a presentation. Harry died at an early age. It is my great pleasure to preserve and present this small reminder of his talent.

Doubling the Procedure: An Action Model
I developed a variation of Harry Eng's model with three equal segments, the middle one showing the portrait and both ends showing the green sides of the bill (see figure 29 to see the result). To construct this, the folding procedure will differ in four ways: 1) folding begins with the bill face down, 2) it is folded in thirds rather than in half, 3) two slits are torn rather than one, and 4) and one end is treated a little differently than the other.

For step 1 with this model, place the bill face down. Rather than folding it in half, fold it in thirds, following the recommended

Figure 29

procedure for estimation.

Follow steps 2 and 3 as before.

For step 4, make a slit on each of the two creases made in step 1.

Follow steps 5, 6, and 7 as before, except you are carrying out the processes with an end third of the bill rather than with the bill folded in half.

For the next step, a new step 8, handing of the other end is just a little different. In the old step 5, the opening and squashing began on the left side and then was repeated at the right side. The required change for this step is to do the opposite, beginning on the right side and repeating the action on the left side.

For the next step, a new step 9, you do the old steps 8 and 9 for both ends simultaneously. The action is a little different. The top and bottom of each side are moved together. The first one to be moved is the one that was moved first in original instruction for this step, the one on the left. Tuck both sides in as neatly as possible, employing a pencil if necessary. The construction is completed. Only the middle segment is visible. The portrait is on one side.

Here is the action. Holding each end with the face of the president toward the audience, pinch the inside ends with the thumb and forefinger of each hand. Slowly pull them away from each other, releasing the hidden green parts surprisingly to reveal the whole bill. (To render grasping easier, make the outer thirds a very small bit longer at the very beginning of construction so they will stick out just a very small bit from the middle section at the end.)

The model can be constructed in advance and exhibited with only the middle section observable at the beginning of the presentation. Alternately, it can be folded and torn and then unfolded and pressed flat so it is ready for a very quick public construction.

The presentation might be about what happens to Washington in Washington as the following script illustrates.

Alternate Script: The Tortured President
Do you have a thing about money? A negative thing? The "root of all evil" sort of thing? And how about our government? And our president? Loan me a dollar bill and I will help us express our feelings.

I fold and crease it, hoping it experiences some distress . . . . I tear it a little . . . . Maybe it feels some pain . . . . Now I shove a part of it into and through itself . . . . Yes, make it give itself "the bird" . . . . Here it is, an impossible money mess—part inside out and part outside in.

But this is not all. The mess is about more than money, so the torture continues.

The government of Washington is meeting President Washington . . . . Washington is capturing Washington . . . . But which is which? The situation, like this bill now, is quite obscure. So much is concealed.

But here it is for our contemplation. We pull on the situation, like this, to see the fully impossible obscurity! May your tortured bill please you, disturb you, or simply confuse you.

If you want me to restore it to its commercial value, I will instantly remove the folds, causing only a little pain. It will be nearly whole again and totally usable. The political value I cannot restore.

Performance 2.5
A King's Mourning

Script

The incident of a king's mourning. It occurred over two thousand years ago. Yet this story, passed to us from ancient Egypt, still kindles astonishment and thoughtfulness. We will all wonder "why?" Why did the king mourn when he did? And we will have different answers from the magic of our own imaginations.

[The performer shows a small packet of playing cards.] Here are the characters involved in the incident: *[the face of the packet is shown to reveal the King of Hearts]* this is the king who will mourn . . . *[the packet is spread to reveal the Queen of Hearts, Jack of Hearts, and the Jack of Spades as well]* and here are his daughter, his son, and his servant. These four will act so as to tell the tale. *[The spread is closed.]*

[The King of Hearts on the face of the packet is shown again to the audience.] This Egyptian king has been beaten and captured by a Persian king who is bent on humbling his prisoner. He gives orders to place him on the road along which the Persian triumphal procession is to pass. *[The Queen of Hearts is removed from the packet and passed back to it, being placed face-to-face*

with the King.] **And he further arranges that the prisoner should see his daughter pass by as a maid going to the well with her pitcher.** *[The Queen is removed from the packet in the other direction, exposing the King again, and placed aside.]* **While all the Egyptians are lamenting and bewailing this spectacle, the captured king stands alone, mute and motionless, his eyes fixed on the ground.** *[The Jack of Hearts is removed, passed back to be placed facing the King, and then removed to expose the King again and placed aside.]* **Then when presently he sees his son, who is being taken along in the procession to be executed, he likewise remains unmoved.** *[The Jack of Spades is made to act identically to the Queen and Jack of Hearts, eventually being set aside, but revealing a transformation of the King of Hearts to a King of Spades.]* **But when afterwards he recognizes one of his servants, an old, impoverished man, now in the ranks of the prisoners, he beats his fists against his head and gives all the signs of deepest mourning.**

So how come? Why does the king mourn when he does? May we enjoy our imaginations.

The Method

Stack five court cards as follows from the face: King of Hearts, King of Spades, Jack of Spades, Jack of Hearts, and Queen of Hearts.

The cards will always be displayed chest-high. Hold the packet by the short edges from above with the right hand so that the face of the packet is shown to the audience. Call attention to the King of Hearts. Take the packet with the left hand and spread them one at a time to show the Queen of Hearts, Jack of Hearts, Jack of Spades, and the King of Hearts. Close the spread, returning to the original grip.

Slide off the Queen of Hearts into the left hand with a twisted wrist so that the thumb is on the face and the fingers on the back. Show it a foot away from the packet. Now you represent the procession passing by the King of Hearts. Reverse the twist to make the Queen face away from the audience. Move the Queen to the packet, and lay it face-to-face with the King of Hearts, creating a grip on the left edge of the packet with the thumb nearest you and the fingers on the side nearest the audience. Let go of the packet with the right hand while maintaining the grip on it with the left hand. Slide off the Queen of Hearts with the right hand, fingers on the back and thumb on the face, move it away to the right about a foot, and set it aside. Place it out of sight (in a shirt or jacket pocket, pants or skirt pocket, or on a flat surface). Repeat this action with the Jack of Hearts. Repeat the action with the Jack of Spades, but shove off two cards aligned as one, the left fingers pushing both Jack of Spades and King of Hearts to the right and the thumb simultaneously pushing one card to the left. Grasp and move the double card to the right. Discard the double card while concealing the extra card behind it, and placing them aside with the others. The appearance of the King of Spades focuses attention away from the double card. Handle the King of Spades casually enough to suggest that it is a single card, for example, tap the card with a free finger of the left hand holding it.

This handling is very easy and secure while perfectly illustrating the passage of the individuals past the King of Hearts.

For a large audience, consider using more visual variety. For example, depict the daughter as the Ace of Hearts, the son as the Ace of Diamonds (or Two of Hearts), and the servant as the Ace of Clubs (or Three of Hearts). Such a selection renders the change of the King from red to black clearer.

The Sources for the Story

Herodotus was a Greek historian who lived in the fifth century B.C.E. He has been called the "Father of History" and was the first historian known to collect his materials systematically, test their accuracy to a certain extent, and arrange them in a well-constructed and vivid narrative.

Walter Benjamin was a German Jewish literary critic, philosopher, social critic, translator, and essayist. Born on July 15, 1892, he died on September 27, 1940, committing suicide at the border between France and Spain while attempting to escape from the Nazis. The following excepts are from his essay, "The Storyteller: Reflections on the Works of Nikolai Leskov" (in

Illuminations: Essays and Reflections, New York: Schocken Books, 1969, pages 83-110). I invite you to read carefully because there is a lot to take in.

Walter Benjamin on the Story:
The first storyteller of the Greeks was Herodotus. In the fourteenth chapter of the third book of his Histories there is a story from which much can be learned. It deals with Psammenitus.... When the Egyptian king Psammenitus had been beaten and captured by the Persian king Cambyses, Cambyses was bent on humbling his prisoner. He gave orders to place Psammenitus on the road along which the Persian triumphal procession was to pass. And he further arranged that the prisoner should see his daughter pass by as a maid going to the well with her pitcher. While all the Egyptians were lamenting and bewailing this spectacle, Psammenitus stood alone, mute and motionless, his eyes fixed on the ground; and when presently he saw his son, who was being taken along in the procession to be executed, he likewise remained unmoved. But when afterwards he recognized one of his servants, an old, impoverished man, in the ranks of the prisoners, he beat his fists against his head and gave all the signs of deepest mourning.

Walter Benjamin's Theory:
From this story it may be seen what the nature of true storytelling is. The value of information does not survive the moment in which it was new. It lives only at that moment; it has to surrender to it completely and explain itself to it without losing any time. A story is different. It does not expend itself. It preserves and concentrates its strength and is capable of releasing it even after a long time.

There is nothing that commends a story to memory more effectively than that chaste compactness which precludes psychological analysis. And the more natural the process by which the storyteller forgoes psychological shading, the greater becomes the story's claim to a place in the memory of the listener, the more completely is it integrated into his own experience, the greater will be his inclination to repeat it to someone else someday, sooner or later. This process of assimilation, which takes place in depth, requires a state of relaxation, which is becoming rarer and rarer. If sleep is the apogee of physical relaxation, boredom is the apogee of mental relaxation. Boredom is the dream bird that hatches the egg of experience. A rustling in the leaves drives him away. His nesting places—the activities that are intimately associated with boredom—are already extinct in the cities and are declining in the country as well. With this the gift for listening is lost and the community of listeners disappears. For storytelling is always the art of repeating stories, and this art is lost when the stories are no longer retained. It is lost because there is no more weaving and spinning to go on while they are being listened to. The more self-forgetful the listener is, the more deeply is what he listens to impressed upon his memory. When the rhythm of work has seized him, he listens to the tales in such a way that the gift of retelling them comes to him all by itself. This, then, is the nature of the web in which the gift of storytelling is cradled. This is how today it is becoming unraveled at all its ends after being woven thousands of years ago in the ambience of the oldest forms of craftsmanship.

Some Whys

Herodotus gives no answers. Benjamin offers four—the first one is a quote by Montaigne, the other three are his own:

> 1. "Since he was already overfull of grief, it took only the smallest increase for it to burst through its dams."

Performances for Chapter 2

2. The king is not moved by the fate of those of royal blood, for it is his own fate.
3. We are moved by much on the stage that does not move us in real life; to the king, this servant is only an actor.
4. Great grief is pent up and breaks forth only with relaxation. Seeing this servant was the relaxation.

To these responses, I offer six more:

5. The servant, although neither a relative, nor royal colleague, and merely an employee, is his best friend.
6. The king witnesses kindness, the action of his servant who is occupied caring for a fellow prisoner.
7. While the daughter and son keep their composure, as did their father, the servant smiles at the king.
8. The servant carries the family pet, a small dog. Alive or dead?
9. The servant carries a small, broken toy, presumably lost since the childhood of the king.
10. The king has last seen the servant caring for his queen and realizes she is lost to him forever.
11. The servant is actually the unacknowledged biological father of the king.

The Sense of Wonder

Clearly, the possibilities are unending. One can focus on the king or the children or the servant or any combination of them. The approach can be visual, psychological, social, and nearly any other perspective. Please wonder.

Chapter 3
The Mystery of Enchantment

There is a condition we presume we have lost, one that both children and earlier peoples have possessed or been possessed by: enchantment. Along with this assumption is another one held by many people, that the loss is to be regretted. One solution is re-enchantment. But another alternative is wonder within disenchantment, wonder apart from mystery.

In this chapter, I will write about the mystery of enchantment by utilizing some issues of faith and religion that are not often discussed in performance magic circles. The omission is quite understandable because such matters are personal, controversial, and of little significance for magic when it is taken to be no more than an entertaining diversion. But if performance magic has any connection with contemporary offstage practices of magic and religion, the issues should be confronted. Needless to say, sharp differences of opinion, belief, and faith will have to be tolerated. Lots of luck to us. Better, lots of maturity.

A. Enchantment and Disenchantment

Our modern focus on enchantment and disenchantment is largely indebted to Max Weber, who used this language to discuss what he saw happening at the beginning of the twentieth century.[1] He believed that the natural world was in the process of being stripped of its capacity for meaning—"disenchanted," he says.

Enchanted meaning, for him, is related to perception of a general order of things. Throughout history, this order has been provided in several basic ways. Weber says that magic is perhaps the most universal of them. Popular belief in magic involves the experience of power. The power is thought to reside in certain objects and behaviors. It can cure disease, create love, discover what is lost, kill enemies, and so forth. Whether conceived in systematic ways or not, there is in this an assumption of two realms, a magic one of power and the mundane one that can be changed by the use of such power. When especially good or bad things happen, there is a reason for it—magic. And when the latter occurs, there is something that can be done about it—counter-magic. One who lives by means of such perceptions has an enchanted world that is meaningful.

Such a world can be destroyed.[2] To do so, divide the enchanted world into two categories, the mundane and magical, and then stigmatize the latter. It is the disenchanted ones who find it odd that a fossil and a horn of a unicorn are located in the same wonder cabinet. For them, such a thing merely puzzles. But there is more involved. Here are two quotations that express the mood of disenchantment. The novelist Salman Rushdie has a character say:

> *Star light, star bright* . . . we look up and we hope the stars look down, we pray that there may be stars for us to follow, stars moving across the heavens and leading up to our destiny, but it's only our vanity. We look at the galaxy and fall in love, but the universe cares less about us than we do about it, and the stars stay in their courses however much we may wish upon them to do otherwise. It's true that if you watch the sky-wheel turn for a while you'll see a meteor fall, flame and die. That's not a star worth following; it's just an unlucky rock. Our fates are here on earth. There are no guiding stars.[3]

Another novelist, Gore Vidal, has the mood presented differently, but just as clearly:

> Naturally, there are puzzles. I would like to know whether or not the universe is finite or infinite. I would like even better to be assured that the two words are meaningless. But excepting the sort of puzzle which makes our passage here interesting and gives incentive to our questioning games, I see no mystery at the heart of things and take comfort from Wittgenstein's profoundly unpop-

ular dictum, "Philosophy simply puts everything before us, and neither explains nor deduces anything. Since everything lies open to view there is nothing to explain. For what is hidden, for example, is of no interest to us."[4]

The mood of one quote is sad and the other disdainful. In either, there is no mystery, no revelation of another world of reality. In these specific examples, there seems to be no wonder either. Is this necessary? Can there be wonder without enchantment?

B. Traditional Enchantment

Magic is universal. What archeologists and anthropologists can inform us about the past magic of early cultures, sociologists and psychologists can update with analyses of current magic. But magic is not the only vehicle for enchantment; philosophy and religion serve as well.

In the philosophy of Plato, reason is an ultimate order by means of which we can order ourselves for virtue. We do not create this ultimate order. We discover it. It is what is most real, and one becomes real by getting in touch with it. Nor is anything else in existence real other than by participating in the cosmic order. Physical reality is of interest because it embodies ideal essences. Look at an apple and one can grasp "apple-ness." Plato argues that the latter is more real than the former; the former participates in mystery because of the latter.

On this thinking, disenchantment comes when the ideal essences, rather than being the bases of reality, are seen as the contents of an individual mind. We moderns understand ourselves as thinking about being good and doing good. The "good" is just a concept created by our brain. We use it to communicate with other people, not with the cosmos. It is real only insofar as we think about it. It is hard to grasp what the experience of the enchanted view of the Good would be. Perhaps objects and activities would possess what we would refer to as richness and depth in contrast to being either unnoticed or used as disposable commodities. Disenchantment is related to the instrumentalist society.

Enchantment is also provided by religion. It establishes the essential categories of the sacred and the profane. The sacred is the locus of power and order, and it provides the general meaning for the believer. Religion creates general conceptions of meaning that make sense of human experience, especially those that challenge our everyday view of things—issues of incomprehensible events (such as earthquakes) or of justice (such as the loss of little children through disease).[5] By means of symbol, myth, and ritual, people can rely upon and renew the effect of such meaning on their daily lives. As we know, this kind of enchanted world, too, can be destroyed. The gods leave the scene of their creation; they die or perhaps just fade away.

In his remarkable analysis of the creation of our modern identity, *Sources of the Self* (Cambridge, MA: Harvard University Press, 1989), Charles Taylor argues that more was involved in this shift from enchantment to disenchantment in the modern western world than the success of scientific rationality.[6] Consider the Victorian age. Surely the scientific advances in geology and biology helped create and determine the outcome of the battle between Theology and Science. Institutional changes—industrialization, technology, urbanization—eclipsed the influence of church institutions. But Taylor argues that what accompanied such changes was a new belief. It became a matter of pride in our secular knowledge, powers, and maturity of self to abandon traditional religious authority.

Taylor shows there were, and are, three components of this belief: an obligation to make up our minds without bowing down to any authority; a spirit of heroism that looks into the reality without blinders and accepts what is seen without flinching; and a concern for human betterment, which offers aid to others for the sake of progress. Taylor offers a compact example of this belief in a moving statement by Thomas Huxley. In a confession of his early immorality and subsequent reform, Huxley affirms that any religious hope of immortality or future reward played no part whatsoever:

> No, I can tell you exactly what has been at work. Carlyle's *Sartor Resartus* led me to know that a deep sense of religion was compatible with the entire absence of theology. Secondly, science and her methods gave me a resting place independent of authority and tradition. Thirdly, love opened me up to a view of the sanctity of human nature and impressed me with a deep sense of responsibility.[7]

This example illustrates what Taylor stresses, that the late Victorian change away from religion was a new belief. A more contemporary example of this shift can be seen in Albert Camus's novel, *The Plague*. The novel is about the heroism of non-heroic people who, entirely without religious belief, face a disaster that cannot be justified or removed, and who labor with sympathy and love on behalf of their fellow human beings.

Again, the modern shift away from religion, as exemplified by Huxley and Camus, is not a shift toward scientism in a narrow sense, but toward a new piety. The mystery of religion is removed, and what is left of religion is regarded as cowardly sentimentalism. Of course, whether or not *mystery* has been avoided is another question that I now want to consider.

C. Contemporary Re-Enchantment

So let us consider the new enchantments. There has been a tendency to assume that enchantment is in the past, destroyed by the dynamics of the modern western world. This is not so. As in other matters, it is easier to perceive the enchantment of others than that of oneself. Perhaps enchantment is only known when one becomes disenchanted. In any case, I am delighted to suggest some locations of enchantment. What enchants us?

Sociologist Mark A. Schneider offers us a fine definition of the experience and of the cause.[8] Enchantment happens to us when something happens that is so wonderful and mysterious that we raise the prospect of an unknown order which would change our understanding of reality. In fields of study, some subjects are relatively easy to think about because they are simple, regular in their occurrence, and easily observed. The human action of walking is an example. But other subjects are very complex, quite irregular in behavior, and observable with difficulty. Experiencing a ghost is an example, as is a dream. Such areas in which we have limited competence give openings for enchantment. In contrast, where we are fully competent, enchantment disappears.

The social organization of inquiry also plays a role. We are flooded with many and contradictory reports about the world, which thus require organization to become useful. Consider the "community" represented by

Chapter 3: The Mystery of Enchantment

buyers of the American tabloids, *The Star* and *The National Inquirer*. It has no systematic organization centered on alien abductions and other oddities. Indeed, one supposes that these buyers would prefer none since it might endanger the enchantment they seek. In peasant communities, the miracles always occur next door. Lest we be accused of classism, please note that our solidly middle class urban myths nearly always are presented as having happened not to oneself but to an acquaintance of some sort. By contrast, a scientific community offers brakes on credulity. It is the combination of incompetence and credulity that fosters enchantment.

Schneider finds this very combination at work in the modern study of culture, in the thinking of two influential anthropologists, Claude Levi-Strauss and Clifford Geertz. They were social scientists, captured by the need to observe, report, and think in scientific ways. They exhibit this need, but also present a further sort of significance that they each claim to have discovered. What they discover has been quite compelling to the students of their works: that there is some kind of deep meaning underneath human behavior. However, there is no way of knowing if this deep meaning is realized by or reflected upon by the participants who are observed, nor is there anyway of testing it out. In a scientific sense, one cannot do anything with it. For example, Geertz claims that the Balinese cockfight experience is a story they tell themselves about themselves, and proceeds to suggest what this story is. The story he recounts is fascinating. The question is whether it is there or not, and there is no way to find out. Aware of this, Geertz states that his understandings are fictional, but only "in the sense that they are 'something made,' 'something fashioned' . . . not that they are false, unfactual, or merely 'as if' thought experiments."[9] Yet Geertz does not offer any way for social consensus to put brakes on these understandings. Schneider concludes that the power of the contributions of Levi-Strauss and Geertz is considerable. Indeed, it is enchanting.

I find the "discoveries" of Sigmund Freud and C. G. Jung equally so. The id, ego, and superego of the former and the archetypes and objective psyche of the latter are enchanting. Both thinkers were highly involved in exploring the world of dreams and related hidden worlds omnipresent yet extremely difficult to objectively observe. Freud considered psychoanalysis to be a replacement for both religion and science. Although recent Freudians have a tendency to treat the concepts of unconscious, preconscious, and id as simply mental constructs that are useful for organizing and understanding experience, for many psychoanalysts they became and still function as a hidden world, one as mysterious as the religions Freud sought to supplant. In fact, certain psychoanalysts have openly affirmed that they held a new faith because they could no longer hold a traditional one.

Chapter 3: The Mystery of Enchantment

Jungians have been far less concerned to balance their concepts with modern scientific understanding. They frequently present and discuss "The Self" or "Objective Psychic" and its contents, "the Archetypes," as mysterious entities in a hidden world. Jung mentions that he is basically a collector of religious experiences and that theorizing is only a hobby, but in general he seems to grant far more reality to his initial concepts than this.

Both the Freudian and Jungian systems are remarkable examples of the discovery of hidden order where it can be found in modern society—*within*. Symbol and myth are as powerful as ever in the understanding of these two theorists. Unlike traditional peoples, their enchantments focus on the mystery of an "inner world," rather than an outer one. But the point is that this presumed inner world is as mysterious and far removed from common understanding and experience as the presumed supernatural world of the traditional thinker. That is, it is equally supernatural.

I have mentioned only the hidden realms discussed by Mark A. Schneider and those experienced by myself. It seems fair to suspect that there are other realms in which enchantment can and does occur. For example, I have found it in the attachment of some people to psychological theories of the human life cycle and of creativity (which are strikingly parallel to earlier theological theories of revelation). The question is: where do you find enchantment yourself?

D. Mystery

Mystery: for some of us this is an enchanted word. It is used so casually and superficially in advertising and more pompously by certain magicians. There are even such persons as Jeff McBride, Eugene Burger, and myself who speak of "Mysteries" and "Mystery School." But what is meant? Here is an occasion to clarify what we can mean by the term and what I now mean.

There are several different meanings, and it is all too easy to slip and slide from one to another and back again without knowing it. Here are some definitions of mystery gleaned from the dictionary:

> 1. A profound secret; something unknown that has not been explained.
> 2. Something that cannot be explained; hence, something beyond human comprehension.
> 3. A miraculous or divine power.
> 4. A secret religious rite to which none but duly initiated worshipers are admitted.
> 5. A cult, often called a mystery religion, characterized by such rites mentioned in 4.
> 6. Profound and inexplicable quality or character; incomprehensibility; inexplicable features or circumstances.[10]

The above list highlights the problems: mystery can refer to something that can, or cannot, be explained; a

Chapter 3: The Mystery of Enchantment

divine or mundane entity; an experience or an institution centered about an experience. In addition, I suspect that we have a tendency to be vague and deceptive about our own definition of the term when we use it. Note that three of the six definitions (3, 4, and 5) are about some hidden reality, one likely related to a sacred reality. It is my experience that some depth psychologists refer openly to dreams and other striking phenomena quite prosaically, but gently and most indirectly hint at the possibility, or even fact, of miraculous power behind them. Some magicians may do the same thing. And perhaps there is a tendency to shield oneself from accusations of having unacceptable assumptions about reality.

My own previous use of the word *mystery* illustrates the initial confusion and subsequent traps of understanding. First, I do assume that what is a mystery to me is different from a puzzle. A puzzle, in my view, has a solution, regardless of whether or not I know what it is, even if that solution is a "profound secret." A mystery, in my usage, is not a puzzle. That is, with a mystery there is no understanding possible.

But here is the question: for any so-called mystery, why is no solution deemed possible? Is it simply because, for whatever reason, none is available to me? However that answer means the "mystery" is really only a particular kind of puzzle. Or is no solution possible because some other reality is involved that is beyond understanding? This answer sustains the distinction between a puzzle and a mystery but is loaded with metaphysics: "some other reality."

To be clear, in my previous use I was not thinking that a mystery required a hidden *divinity* of any sort. Thus, my assumptions were closest to the second and sixth definitions given above. Unfortunately, at the same time I was also involved in exploring religion, especially the spiritual experience in traditional mysticism. Here is where the slipperiness came into play. Were my fleeting and partial mystical experiences a "mystery" that were, in principle, beyond all understanding? "Certainly," I assumed. But why? Why did I assume this? Because some other reality was involved? Intellectually, I disavowed that conclusion. But my feelings were different; they kept clinging to one. I see now that I was sliding back and forth from one perspective to another without paying attention to it. Was my willful deviousness necessary? Perhaps, but now I am well rid of it.

The preceding confession explains my current position. There is a profound, deeply affecting, even inexplicable quality of various experiences that happens without the need to posit some hidden reality with extraordinary power to inform daily reality. In short, to use two fundamental terms, I do not experience the sacred, but I do experience wonder. Indeed, my focus on wonder is, I suspect, my way of coming to terms with my lack of concern for and interest in the rites and religions termed mysteries. My personal conclusion then, which

Chapter 3: The Mystery of Enchantment

quite surprises me, is that I now reject mystery, the very thing I used to think was so important. It helps me now to only employ the term to signify rites and religions. For what I really care about—experiences in this world that are profound and inexplicable—I speak of wonder. As the previous chapter demonstrates, this approach focuses on the phenomenon itself and doesn't bother with metaphysical speculation or religious beliefs. And as the above argument conveys, it is vigilant about smuggling those things in through unquestioned assumptions or feelings.

I do remain delighted to wonder about our human propensity to assume a "hidden reality of mystery." You may well be equally delighted to wonder about my determined refusal to explore such a possibility. Maybe we all can wonder about our likely self-deceptions on the matter. We are interesting. Indeed, we are wondrous—profound and inexplicable.

Using the above observations and the previous ones of Mark Schneider, we can conclude that there may always be realms of human experience in which we are incompetent and which resist organized, systematic inquiry. These difficulties provide openings for "enchantment"—the creation of a "mystery," a hidden world that powerfully impinges on this one. The stereotype we have of the mysteries of the past—the symbols, myths, rituals, and divinities—should not prevent us from acknowledging the temptation to be enchanted by new mysteries. Remember the saying of Xenophanes:

> Ethiopians imagine their gods as black and snub-nosed; Thracians blue-eyed and red-haired. But if horses or lions had hands, or could draw and fashion works as men do, horses would draw the gods shaped like horses and lions like lions, making the gods resemble themselves.[11]

The thought should not be left to rest with divinities described only traditionally. The "divinities" may be the deep meanings uncovered by anthropological analysis and the deep structures of the psyche. Academics in the social sciences may create gods of meaning like themselves and psychologists may create gods of dynamics like themselves. How could it be otherwise? And these new mysteries have their own "mystery schools." A psychoanalytic training center has a process of complex and powerful training that has been compared to that for those in training for Roman Catholic priesthood and can be compared also with earlier shamanic training. Again, how could it be otherwise?

    Oh yes, lest we forget, such creativity might occur in the realm of hard science too. Consider scientism, the belief, as Charles Taylor defines it, "that the methods and procedures of natural science . . . suffice to establish all the truths we need to believe."[12] He points out that there is an "ought" here to not bow to outdated authority and to make up our own minds. It is based, in part, on a moral vision involving both freedom and heroism. Yet this pious new belief that science is not only a valid realm but also replaces all other ways of establishing the truths we need to believe suggests that science is a mystery for some people. That would seem inevitable, given our investment in it and our proclivity for creating mystery. Once more, how could it be otherwise? Disparagement of enchantment can be overdone, and when it is, it may reveal a battle between enchantments more than anything else.

 I conclude that there are two negative results of disenchantment. One is adherence to formal mysteries without enchantment. Clinging to a formal mystery without mysteriousness, through long habit or new adoption, is a convenient perniciousness for those who feel hopelessly diminished by the ruling spirit of disenchantment. It sustains congregations of traditional western religions and weekend spiritual shoppers of New Age occultism. Perhaps this is better than nothing. But it is hardly better than the other negative result: the new false belief occasioned by the modern temperament that allows concealment of one's mysteries from oneself. So let us begin to explore an alternative.

E. Wonder

Can we get beyond both enchantment and disenchantment? Maybe. Wonder is, I believe, more primal than enchantment. I believe the latter is a response to the former. We will begin the remainder of this chapter by considering the frequent battle between poet and scientist and end by exploring the epiphany of being.

Poet and Scientist

One of Martin Gardner's delightful columns[13] offered a collection of complaints and counter-claims about science that underscores an issue of concern for the past several hundred years. The battle is between, among others, some poets and some scientists. Here are a few of the poets Gardner selected who suggest that science destroys wonder:

> The goose that laid the golden egg
> Died looking up its crotch
> To find out how its sphincter worked.
> Would you lay well? Don't watch.
> —X. J. Kennedy, "Ars Poetica"

> I'd rather learn from one bird how to sing
> Than teach ten thousand stars how not to dance.
> —e. e. cummings

Chapter 3: *The Mystery of Enchantment*

> Sweet is the lore which Nature brings;
> Our meddling intellect
> Mis-shapes the beauteous forms of things: —
> We murder to dissect.
>
> Enough of Science and of Art;
> Close up those barren leaves;
> Come forth, and bring with you a heart
> That watches and receives.
> ——Wordsworth, "The Tables Turned"

It surely is possible for a scientist, just as anyone else, to lose sight of beauty and miss the experience of wonder. But many people assert that this is hardly necessary. The physicist Richard Feynman is a person whose scientific life overflowed with wonder. In response to an artist friend who suggested that science takes a flower apart and makes it dull, he said:

> I think he's kind of nutty. First of all, the beauty he sees is available to other people—and to me too. Although I might not be quite as refined aesthetically as he is, I can appreciate the beauty of a flower.
>
> At the same time, I see much more about the flower than he sees. I could imagine the cells in there, the complicated actions inside, which also have a beauty. I mean, it's not just beauty at this

dimension of one centimeter; there is also beauty at a smaller dimension—the inner structure. The fact that the colors in the flower are evolved in order to attract insects to pollinate it is interesting—it means that the insects can see the color. It adds a question: does this aesthetic sense also exist in the lower forms? Why is it aesthetic? All kinds of interesting questions, which a science knowledge only adds to the excitement and mystery and the awe of a flower. It only adds. I don't understand how it subtracts.[14]

Elsewhere, Feynman also wrote:

It does not do harm to the mystery to know a little about it. For far more marvelous is the truth than any artists of the past imagined! Why do the poets of the present not speak of it? What men are poets who can speak of Jupiter if he were like a man, but if he is an immense spinning sphere of methane and ammonia must be silent?[15]

I could not agree more. Even Charles Taylor, who has great reservations about contemporary science, still finds it easy to assert that believing ourselves to be part of a vast physical order awakens wonder and considerable awe over both the power of the natural world and that fact that out of this world evolves our thought, vision,

Chapter 3: The Mystery of Enchantment

and speech.[16] The contemporary theorist of science and other fields, Douglas Hofstadter, writes:

> Perhaps my lifelong training in physics and science in general has given me a deep awe at seeing how the most substantial and familiar of objects or experiences fades away, as one approaches the infinitesimal scale, into an eerily insubstantial ether, a myriad of ephemeral swirling vortices of nearly incomprehensible mathematical activity. This in me evokes a cosmic awe.[17]

I suspect that there are people within any of the human disciplines who are prone to wonder and those who are not. Feynman and Hofstadter, for example, are exceptionally playful individuals open to wonder. For that matter, so too is Martin Gardner. There seem also to be those people who are exceptionally closed to wonder, whether in science, religion, or anywhere else. Contemporary science is not the problem. And note that mystery, in the sense that I have been discussing it, is not present and need not be. What we know from science about the first three minutes of creation may prompt revitalization of the mystery of God for some, but need not do so. Our wonder *per se* about creation, a flower blossom, or a dream can be quite self-sufficient.

As philosopher Richard Rorty puts this point, "The secret in the poet's heart remains unknown to [scientists], despite their ability to predict his very thought, utterance, and movement by monitoring the cerebroscope.... We can know which thoughts pass through a man's mind without understanding them. Our inviolable uniqueness lies in our poetic ability to say unique and obscure things, not in our ability to say obvious things to ourselves alone."[18]

Agreement with Rorty's insight neither diminishes the scientific approach nor supports the mystery approach. Scientism is not upheld. Enchantment is not required. But there is much to wonder about—the richness of our experience.

F. Epiphany

Where are we when we are beyond enchantment, disenchantment, and re-enchantment? Surely we are in a Post-Romantic Age. And we are in a Non-Scientism Age. What does that leave us with? Much more than the enchanters, disenchanters, and re-enchanters suspect. We are left, in a word, with wonder. And to speak of this in the modern western world of literature, we can use James Joyce's term—*epiphany*.

Epiphany refers to a manifestation, but not the traditional one of a god.[19] And this is not the romantic conception of art portraying something in such a way as to reveal a greater reality. The focus is on the work itself. There need not be extra meaning suggested. To the contrary, there may be an "unveiling of things in their meaninglessness."[20] Here is Emile Zola's appreciation of a painting by Pissaro:

> This is the modern countryside. One feels the passage of man, who digs up the earth, cuts it up, saddens the horizon. This valley, this hillside, manifest a simplicity and an heroic frankness. Nothing could be more banal, were nothing greater. The painter's temperament has drawn a rare poem of life and force from ordinary reality.[21]

The epiphany is of "ordinary reality." And modern artists have gone further, or differently, than relying on such straightforward presentations of nature. The use of juxtaposition creates an epiphany that occurs in the collision of images. Charles Taylor provides this remarkable example from T. S. Elliot:

> Let us go then, you and I,
> When the evening is spread out against the sky
> Like a patient etherized upon a table.[22]

And this ordinary reality is presented with a clear denial of the depth—the heavy meanings—so beloved by the romantics of all ages. The freedom of escape from enchantment is illustrated by D. H. Lawrence:

> No home, no tea. Insouciant carelessness. Eternal indifference. Perhaps it is only the great pause between carings. But it is only in this pause that one finds the meaninglessness of meanings—like old husks which speak dust. Only in this pause that one finds the meaninglessness of meanings, and the other dimension. The reality of timelessness and nowhere . . . nothing is so meaningless as meanings.[23]

This is a strong refusal of depth. The focus is on the thing to be presented. Taylor reports that Ezra Pound once saw people getting out of the Metro, one beautiful face followed by another. He struggled for a year to express his experience, and created the following:

> *In a Station of the Metro*
> The apparition of these faces in the crowd;
> Petals on a wet, black bough.[24]

It is very difficult to explain what happens by means of the title plus the two lines of the poem. Taylor and his sources resort to much aesthetic jargon. But the result is not the kind of epiphany that reveals a deeper reality. It focuses on the mundane world, entirely and exclusively. Something does appear, but it happens between the images, according to Pound himself, as an energy or energies made available. He also says about a work of art, "An 'Image' is that which presents an intellectual and emotional complex in an instant of time."[25] What is rejected is expressed meaning. The object is offered opacity. The very power of the image comes from the refusal to be directly expressive. Finally, here is a more recent example of such presentation from a contemporary Polish poet, Herbert:

> The stone
> is a perfect creature
>
> equal to itself
> obedient to its limits
>
> filled exactly
> with a stony meaning[26]

Where do these examples lead us? Toward an alternative to both the mysteries revealed by enchantment and the boredom revealed by scientism. Into wonder and out of both enchantment and disenchantment. Wonder without enchantment. Wonder without mysteries.

What we must consider is an epiphany of what is. For me, no one has considered this more wisely than

Jorge Luis Borges. He is obscure, but no more so than the others I have mentioned. In the essay, "The Wall and the Books," Borges concludes with this evocation:

> Music, states of happiness, mythology, faces belabored by time, certain twilights and certain places try to tell us something, or have said something we should not have missed or are about to say something; this imminence of a revelation which does not occur is, perhaps, the aesthetic phenomenon.[27]

His story, "Pedro Salvadores," states the theme again:

> As with so many things, the fate of Pedro Salvadores strikes us as a symbol of something we are about to understand but never quite do.[28]

What is Borges is talking about? Does it help to label it, in summary, as the "permanence of revelation's imminence?" The idea is that there is something about to happen that does not happen. It is something to be desired beyond all else, but never received. It is an unending pregnancy of experiencing the ultimate. And despite never coming to the possible conclusion on revelation, knowing the continued absence of revelation, the experience is awesomely affirmative. How come?

Commenting on this theory, one literary critic, Carter Wheelock, has said, "The 'imminence of a revelation' is perhaps the ultimate knowable reality and men do not create it. They comprise it, behold it, and try to transmute it into language. This idea precludes any esthetic theory—that is, any rule or formula for producing an imminent revelation."[29]

His comment, as well as that of Borges above, needs expansion to include other realms than aesthetics. The experience precludes any philosophic or theologic theory as well. And human beings try to transmute it into symbols of all kinds, not merely language, and expand it into myth and ritual. The claim is that the imminence of a revelation is the "ultimate knowable reality." This experience is a breaking into our capsulated selves and closed mundane realities, indicating their insufficiencies, yet affirming them as well.

Some would find this claim quite insufficient when compared to those of the established religious traditions with their fulsome details of revelation pertaining to this world and others. Others would find it quite unnecessary, a vague, sentimental gushing, acceptable only for those incapable of scientific realism and rigor. But I find it exactly right in expressing the human condition. It is given, on a somewhat lower level, with Charles Dickens's character Macawber, who is, against all odds and all previous experience, persistently affirming, "Something will turn up." To know this is already to have received something. This experience, I believe, is not about getting something in the future, although it may be expressed that way and given such concrete details to render it into revelation. Rather, it is having received something. It is not the promise of a gift, but the reception of one. When truly received and accepted, it is all that is necessary and, therefore, not transformed into a promissory revelation.

Borges, no less than any human being perhaps, creates "revelations." Since they are defined by his readers as poems, stories, and essays, these responses to the permanency of revelation's imminence are not believed, but received as metaphorical reactions to the initial experiences. Borges, for example, is intrigued by Coleridge's fantasy, "If a man could pass through Paradise in a dream, and have a flower presented to him as a pledge that his soul had really been there, and if he found that flower in his hand when he awoke—Ay!—and what then?"[30]

But Borges also considers dreaming itself an experience of revelation's imminence. This is underscored when he ponders, in a variety of ways, who is dreaming whom? The flower is not necessary. Or to put it another way, the "flower" is dreaming, twilight times, or however one is led into the experience.

Let Borges speak once more, "There is an hour of the afternoon when the plain is on the verge of saying something. It never says it, or perhaps it says it infinitely, or perhaps we do not understand it, or we understand it and it is as untranslatable as music."[31]

How wonderful is this expression of options! Is something not said; said infinitely; said infinitely, but not understood; or said infinitely, understood, but not translatable to oneself and/or others? Any single option renders the phrase, "permanence of revelation's imminence" too limiting. This is as it should be.

Epiphany. Wonder without the mystery of enchantment. We can talk about this in a somewhat different way, and perhaps more clearly (or perhaps not). Depth of the traditional kind suggests that another reality is present. In the modern sensibility I am suggesting, a depth occasion may be wondrous, but not mysterious in the sense we have been dismissing. The depth, if it be such, is about what is and about what both might be and might not be. The vision of the object is sufficient unto itself. Expectation occurs and is sufficient in and of itself. Here are two examples, first a negative illustration of shallowness followed by a depth affirmation of wonder.

Popular culture abounds in trivial sentiment that fosters shallow mysteries of cheap enchantment. It is present in the tales told in supermarket magazines and shown on television fantasy programs. A recent example is being promoted at bookstores, *Small Miracles: Extraordinary Coincidences from Everyday Life*.[32] The two authors are Jewish women who inform us, "Both of our fathers were Holocaust Survivors whose lives were saved by inexplicable sets of uncanny coincidences."[33] They quote the writer Doris Lessing as having said, "Coincidences are God's way of remaining anonymous." And a well-known writer on healing, Dr. Bernie Siegel, wrote a preface to the book in which he affirms, "I believe that *nothing* is a 'coincidence.' It's all part of creation and God's plan and our response. We just have to be open to seeing it."[34] Siegel continues by giving an example of such vital revelation—his finding of pennies wherever he goes. And on a penny is written, "In God We Trust." So he concludes that he is getting a message from these remarkable events, "a reminder that God is directing my energies, God is here, and I am on my path."[35]

His example is a fair indication of the sort of tales that will be told in the main body of the text. Here is one of them. A man is walking along a dark street and hears the noise of an attack upon a woman. After some hesitation he interferes and battles with the assailant who runs away. The man discovers the woman to be his daughter.

Here is another. All twenty members of a church choir just happened to be late to a rehearsal for highly individual reasons. This was fortunate because the building blew up just before they all arrived.

And here is just one more. A woman locked herself out of her house just as a mail carrier arrived

Chapter 3: The Mystery of Enchantment

with a letter containing a duplicate house key a friend had borrowed previously.

Of course, my summaries have stripped the stories of the details that make them interesting. Each of the tales is followed by a maxim and all are considered to be "small miracles," revelations of divine providence, of a god who cares.

What is one to say? I find the book profoundly silly and equally revealing of us all. I also suspect that it may well be a spiritual insult to their fathers who probably had a more sophisticated theology. Fortune, good or bad, is impressive and surely something to wonder about. But creating a mystery about a happy coincidence is silly to me. Worse, there is the hidden assumption in such tales as these that the entire world is rearranged by some special power just for the sake of one individual. The implicit egoism is extraordinary. However, I probably create such trivia myself elsewhere —being an academic, more likely with words and meanings than with pennies and such. The book is a clear illustration of our delight in the mysteries of enchantment. The wonder of the authors sponsors perception of the reality of another world. Probably they would approve of this bumper sticker, "We are not human beings on a spiritual journey. We are spiritual beings on a human journey."

Quite contrary to this creation of mystery when wonder alone would do is a poem by a woman who died of leukemia at the age of forty-nine. I encourage you to read it aloud, to become the voice of this poet.

>*Otherwise*
>I got out of bed on two strong legs.
>It might have been
>otherwise. I ate
>cereal, sweet
>milk, ripe, flawless
>peach. It might
>have been otherwise.
>I took a dog uphill
>on the birchwood.
>All morning I did
>the work I love.
>
>At noon I lay down
>with my mate. It might
>have been otherwise.
>We ate dinner together
>at a table with silver
>candlesticks. It might
>have been otherwise.
>I slept in a bed
>in a room with paintings
>on the walls, and
>planned another day
>just like this day.

> But one day, I know,
> it will be otherwise.[36]

This is a very quiet poem. It neither moans nor laughs. There is an acceptance of what is and of what is to come. There is no mystery created. And perhaps there is even wonder about it all. In every phrase, as I read the poem, there is wonder about what is and what might not be. It is so very simple. And the absence of mystery is hardly a lack. The wonder is sufficient. For me, the apparent depth in those coincidence tales is shallow, and the apparent shallowness of the poem is deep indeed.

An epiphany of being is a revelation of what is. What is is evocative of wonder. Well, what could be more miraculous in the old-fashioned sense of the term, that is, more wonderful? The miracle of interest to me is that we do have the experience of wonder. What more could we want?

Notes

1. Max Weber observed, "As intellectualism suppresses belief in magic, the world's processes become disenchanted, lose their magical significance, and henceforth simply 'are' and 'happen' but no longer signify anything." This quote is from *Economics and Society, Volume 2*, edited by Guenther Roth and Claus Wittich (New York: Bedminster Press, 1968), page 506.

2. As sociologist Mark A. Schneider puts it in *Culture and Enchantment* (Chicago: University of Chicago Press, 1993), page ix: "Disenchanting the world, as a social process, involves sorting its behavior into mundane and magical categories—and stigmatizing the latter, making it a disreputable object of inquiry. We become disenchanted only when this invidious distinction is developed, and remain so only while it lasts: in its absence, by contrast, the magical and the mundane appear to us largely indistinguishable."

3. Salman Rushdie, *The Moor's Last Sigh* (London: Jonathan Cape, 1995). This and the following quotation are used as epigraphs in Christopher Hitchens's delightfully muck-raking book, *The Missionary Position: Mother Teresa in Theory and Practice*. New York: Verso, 1997, page 35. The book was given to me gleefully by Eugene Burger.

4. Gore Vidal, *Two Sisters*, quoted by Christopher Hitchens, *The Missionary Position*, page 75.

5. See Clifford Geertz, "Religion as a Cultural System," in *Anthropological Approaches to the Study of Religion*, editor Michael Banton (London: Tavistock Publications, 1965), pages 1-46.

6. Charles Taylor, *Sources of the Self: The Making of the Modern Identity* (Cambridge, Massachusetts: Harvard University Press, 1989), pages 402-410.

Chapter 3: The Mystery of Enchantment

7. Quoted by Taylor, *Sources of the Self*, page 405.

8. Schneider says enchantment happens when "phenomena are encountered that behave so wonderfully and mysteriously as to raise the prospect of an order as yet unfathomed, familiarity with which would fundamentally alter our understanding of the world" (*Culture and Enchantment*, Chicago: University of Chicago Press, 1993, page 10). He also says, "Limited competence causes us to behave clumsily, suffer misunderstandings, be surprised by events, and fail to predict outcomes beyond chance. Yet with these difficulties comes an opening for enchantment: our very awkwardness can suggest powers or principles at work that are not just beyond our ken but quite possibly of another order. In contrast, where we are fully competent not only does our awkwardness disappear, but the enchantment along with it. The ease with which we negotiate the world and our failure to be surprised by its behavior underscore the ultimate intelligibility of the circumstances in which we live. Whether or not the assumptions that allow us to operate deftly are 'true' in any ultimate sense, the facility they afford us indicates they work. Hence our competence is defined pragmatically and is symmetric with disenchantment" (pages 7-8).

9. Clifford Geertz, quoted by Schneider, *Culture and Enchantment*, page 77.

10. These definitions are teased out of those provided by *Webster's New International Dictionary, Second Edition, Unabridged* (Springfield, MA: G. & G. Merriam Company, Publishers, 1955). Several of the definitions lumped together what "cannot be explained" with "what has not been explained." I preferred to separate these alternatives for the sake of clarity.

11. Xenophanes, quoted by Christopher Hitchens, *The Missionary Position*, page 1.

12. Taylor, *Sources of the Self*, page 404.

13. Martin Gardner, "Science vs. Beauty," in *The Skeptical Inquirer*, Volume 19, Number 2, March-April 1995, pages 14-16, 55.

14. Richard P. Feynman, *"What Do You Care What Other People Think?": Further Adventures of a Curious Character* (New York: W. W. Norton and Company, Inc., 1988, page 11.

15. Feynman, *The Feynman Lectures on Physics, Volume 1* (Reading, MA: Addison-Wesley, 1963), page 3-6.

16. "The belief that thinking beings are part of a vast physical order can awaken a kind of awe, wonder, even natural piety. The reflection which moves us is that thought, feeling, moral aspirations, all the intellectual and spiritual heights of human achievement, emerge out of the depths of a vast physical universe which is itself, over most of its measureless extent, lifeless, utterly insensitive

to our purposes, pursuing its path by inexorable necessity. The awe is awakened partly by the tremendous power of this world which overshadows us—we sense our utter fragility as thinking reeds, in Pascal's phrase; but we also feel it before the extraordinary fact that out of this vast blind silence, thought, vision, speech can evolve." Taylor, *Sources of the Self*, page 347.

17. Quoted by Taylor, *Sources of the Self*, page 348.

18. Quoted by Schneider, *Culture and Enchantment*, page 158.

19. The following discussion is totally indebted to Taylor, *Sources of the Self*, pages 419-495.

20. *Sources of the Self*, page 431.

21. Quoted by Taylor, *Sources of the Self*, page 433.

22. Quoted by Taylor, *Sources of the Self*, page 466.

23. Quoted by Taylor, *Sources of the Self*, page 466.

24. Quoted by Taylor, *Sources of the Self*, page 474.

25. Quoted by Taylor, *Sources of the Self*, page 475.

26. Quoted by Taylor, *Sources of the Self*, page 485.

27. This quotation by Borges is taken from John Dominic Crossan's *Raid on the Articulate* (New York: Harper & Row, Publishers, 1976), page 169.

28. Borges, quoted by Crossan in *Raid on the Articulate*, page 169.

29. American critic Carter Wheelock, quoted by Crossan, *Raid on the Articulate*, page 169.

30. Borges, "The Flower of Coleridge," in *Borges: A Reader* (New York: E. P. Dutton, 1981), pages 163-165. See also in the same volume "The Other," pages 321-326.

31. Borges, "The End," *Ficciones* (New York: Alfred A. Knopf, 1993), pages 127-130.

32. Yitta Halberstam & Judith Leventhal, *Small Miracles: Extraordinary Coincidences from Everyday Life* (Holbrook, MA: Adams Media Corporation, 1997).

33. *Small Miracles*, page xii.

34. *Small Miracles*, page iv.

35. *Small Miracles*, pages iv-v.

36. Jane Kenyon, *Collected Poems* (Graywolf Press, Saint Paul, Minnesota, 1996), page 266,

Performances for Chapter 3

In this highly significant chapter, Bob Neale clarifies and defends his big claim about the experience of wonder as respect. He says in no uncertain terms, "For me, wonder is sufficient." That is, no more flirting with mystery, no hidden realities, no "deep" subterranean levels and meanings. For him, all these are loaded with implicit or explicit metaphysical assumptions. All these are sustained by and weave a spell of beguiling enchantment that thereby leaves us vulnerable to the threat of disenchantment. But also, and perhaps worse, the spell keeps us blind to the extraordinary wonders of *this* world.

"Epiphanies": following Joyce and Borges, this is what Bob Neale here calls the complex manifestation of things and other people in the world that call for our respect. No deep meanings, depth dimensions, or extra hidden realities required. For Bob Neale, re-attuning ourselves to the perpetual, pregnant "imminence" of their "revelation" is well enough for wonder.

It is in the spirit of this re-attunement that Bob and I have selected the routines for this chapter. We hope that each one will serve as an epiphany (not a "mystery"), and one you can share with others. As Bob says about the Jane Kenyon poem that closes his above reflections, they neither moan nor laugh (although some of them are rather humorous). They accept what is. They do not create or point toward some great, grand mystery. And if we learn to re-tune ourselves, there is wonder about what is in this world and what is not, what is possible and what is impossible, which is rather deep indeed.

I cannot think of a better way to start than with "Prometheus's Box (3.1). It is a picture-perfect, trickster exploration—and potential performance—of Bob's views in this chapter. I have a feeling that Borges would have loved it and could have written a whole essay about it.

"Arrow of Good Fortune" (3.2) is a wonderful visual oddity. Both the moral and the magic unravel binary thinking and happen on the surface without hidden or inner depths.

The playful exploration of rich surface effects continues with "Open Book" (3.3) and "Easy Reader" (3.4). With both of them, I heartily encourage you to construct the models, play with them in your hands, and wonder at these books without end. Simply reading about them will not convey the ideas and subtle sensations they provoke.

Finally, what has less depth and mystery than another Elmsley Count card trick for cardicians? Even so, because it is so, because of its juxtapositions, "Saint of the Cardicians" (3.5) is fun and funny—perfect for laughs at the magic club or a magic convention. Who other than Bob Neale would have written it?

—Lawrence Hass

Performances for Chapter 3

Performance 3.1
Prometheus's Box

Imagine a small box with a lid. Each edge is equal in length, as is each of the six surfaces. It looks like a cube. The box is made of wood. There are two metal hinges connecting the lid to the box and a metal latch to keep it closed. This is the object for our meditation.

The Experience

Remember Pandora's Box? Zeus created Pandora as the first woman on earth. After Prometheus had stolen fire as a gift for human beings, Zeus sought vengeance by giving her to Prometheus's brother along with a box containing all human ills. Curiosity caused Pandora to open it, letting them loose over the entire world. Hope, also in the box, was the only thing she prevented from escaping. The antidote to Pandora's Box is the box you see before you now. The hope she kept back can be released by this new box—Prometheus's Box. (He created it after he was freed from the mountain where vultures daily consumed his liver.)

This box contains a great secret. It is a secret you already know and have known for years and years. Yet you have forgotten it, over and over, every day and every year. That is as it should be. However, recollection of the secret should also occur, over and over, every day and every year. This box can be the reminder. After you have opened it the first time, just to see it again will re-expose the great secret that can freshen our humility, humor, and sense of wonder. So I also call it "Whatabox!" And you will too.

Don't you wonder what is inside? What the great secret is? What is it that can so simply renew your life? Here. Open the box and you will find out.

Surprise! There is nothing inside. Absolutely nothing. There is not even empty space. In fact, there is no inside to the box. What we thought was a box is not a box at all. It is a cube with the top portion sliced off and reattached to give the appearance of a box.

Prometheus's Box is a joke. But it is a serious one. It is a joke about our expectations, especially our "great expectations"—our hopes. And it can do what I have claimed, if we let it. We might well experience the fruits when we come to find the joke equally silly and serious.

It is interesting to ask ourselves what surprises us. Some theoretical scientists are surprised that there is order in the universe, while others are surprised by disorder. On a more mundane plane, some of us are pessimists and others optimists. It helps if we are not stuck entirely with either expectation. Remember the story about the elders who used to meet to discuss the serious events of the world? All the talk centered around the darker view of the situation. Then one day an elder announced that he was an optimist. In amazement, the others responded, "Then why do you have that worried look on your face all the time?" The optimist replied, "Do you think it is easy being this way?" This makes sense because an optimist should be somewhat worried. And a pessimist should wear a carefree look on his face. Surprises reveal that our expectations are necessary but limited.

We are governed by our expectations. These are based on specific needs seeking satisfaction and on generalizations from past experiences. Thus, we have goals and means. Moreover, they tend to serve each other. Expectations are what we live by and are to be respected. We could not leave home without them.

However, these governors of behavior are not to be elevated into gods. Possession of them neither provides absolute justification for them nor guarantees success with them. Expectations are overturned by events. This is all to the good, otherwise there would be neither novelty nor learning.

Unfortunately, though understandably, we are upset by the unexpected. This is putting it mildly. Consider our reaction to the "unexpected." This term can be a synonym for "horror." When someone leaves on a trip a spouse will say, "Be careful. I wouldn't want anything to happen to you." "Accident" tends to be a most negative term. For a positive meaning, we have to put "happy" in front of it. When the goal has become an accident-free world our expectations have become idols.

Such expectational idolatry is not functional on the material level or the psychological. It prevents perception of reality and appropriate responses, and it diminishes satisfaction. It may even risk extinction.

So it behooves us to seek surprise. Not very often. And not in crucial situations. Surprise should be sought safely. Then the experience of the unexpected can be enjoyed and absorbed. The expectations that govern us remain but do not rule exclusively. The expectation of the unexpected has been added.

"Prometheus's Box" is a gift of spiritual fire. It is a genuinely practical joke about our expectations. At its best, it fosters the really "great" expectation of a surprising world.

Construction

It is easy to construct such a box for yourself and others to experience. At a craft supply store, you can obtain a 1.5" cube of soft white pine, some miniature hinges, and a latch. Saw off a quarter slab of the cube and reattach it. Or more simply, construct the box out of index cards and tape, using colored plastic tape for the hinges and latch.

But why stop there? This is only the first Promethean Box. By definition, the number in a set of such boxes would be unlimited. A surprising world includes surprising meetings of our governing expectations too. Construct another box that looks the same, but is hollow inside—a normal box. Present this one after the previous one has been examined. A surprising world includes being surprised about the surprising. Construct a box that looks like the others, but cannot be opened at all (sawing around the cube only enough to make a deep groove). Or make a box that looks just like the others, but twists open. There are other Promethean Boxes to be created as gifts for the human race. Invent one for yourself.

Performance 3.2
Arrow of Good Fortune

Script and Performance

[The performer shows a three-dimensional arrow made of cardboard.] **This is a model of an ancient Asian artifact. The Chinese call it the Arrow of Good Fortune.** *[It is held with the point up.]*

When your good fortune reverses into bad fortune . . . *[the arrow is twirled to point down]* **. . . and you cannot change it . . .** *[the arrow is twisted up and down again, but fails to reverse itself both times]* **. . . turn to a new perspective to see the good fortune in the bad.** *[The arrow is turned sideways to change its direction.]*

Then all reversals will bring good fortune to you forever. *[The arrow is twirled three times and yet always points up.]* **And that would be a good trick!**

Note: this effect is based on my discovery that an arrow of three dimensions can behave oddly—maintain its orientation despite being twirled one hundred and eighty degrees—without any hidden means. (Having said that, the shape does lend itself to paddle moves.) The result is not so much a trick as it is a demonstration of an odd movement.

Construction

The arrow can be cut out of wood, but it is easier to construct and carry one fashioned from an index card. Use a white, unlined index card that is 4" by 6". Cut off a strip of 2" from the end to form a 4" x 4" square.

Fold the square into fourths and unfold. See figure 30.

Cut the top and bottom as indicated in figure 31.

Use two markers to color as indicated in figure 32. The design accentuates the direction of the arrow. For the best visibility, use fluorescent pink for the ends and fluorescent yellow for the middle.

Attach the two straight edges with transparent plastic tape to form a tube. The tape should be on the inside. See figure 33.

A portion of the remaining strip is used to provide stability to the tube during performance. Cut off a piece that is 4" by 15/16ths of an inch. Color it the same as the ends of the tube. Fold the short ends to meet at the center. See figure 34.

Insert the strip into the tube. Tape the short ends to each end of the tube. When this strip is flat, the tube can be flat, and the strip will stick out at one end. See figure 35. Carry it in this condition.

For performance, open the tube and push on the protruding strip. This moves it inside to hold the tube open. When the routine is concluded, the arrow is closed flat again, then put away from participants who might want to toy with it.

The Sense of Wonder

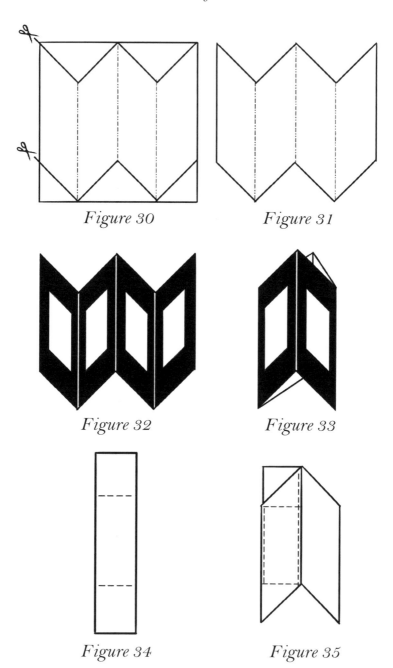

Figure 30

Figure 31

Figure 32

Figure 33

Figure 34

Figure 35

Performances for Chapter 3

Routine

Hold the arrow with your left hand in front of your body. Grasp the middle of the arrow, opposite edges of the sides held by the left thumb and forefinger, palm toward the body. The arrow points up. Keep your other fingers curled out of the way.

"This is a model of an ancient Asian artifact. The Chinese call it the Arrow of Good Fortune."

Your right forefinger twirls the arrow one hundred and eighty degrees, upside down. **"When your good fortune reverses into bad fortune."** The arrow points down.

At the end of the twirl, move the left thumb and forefinger counterclockwise around the arrow, re-grasping it by the opposite side panels. The right forefinger gives stability during this shift. Note that the arrow itself does not move. The arrow still points down. Now twist the left hand at the wrist away from you and down, turning the arrow upside down. Unexpectedly, the arrow remains pointing down. Reverse the twist to restore it to its former position. The arrow still points down. Be sure to keep the arrow facing the audience in the required orientation so it does not reverse itself. **"And you cannot change it."**

Grasp the bottom of the arrow with the right hand. Twist the arrow slowly counterclockwise so that it openly changes direction. Re-grasp the arrow with the left hand by the new set of opposite sides. The arrow points up. **"Turn to a new perspective to see the good fortune in the bad."**

The right forefinger twirls the arrow one hundred and eighty degrees, upside down. The arrow still points up. Again, be sure to keep the arrow facing the audience in the required orientation so that it does not reverse itself. **"Then all reversals will bring you good fortune . . ."** Repeat the twirl. **" . . . forever."** Repeat the twirl.

"And that would be a good trick!"

Sources

This arrow is inspired by "The Pirish Compass," an invention of the English ventriloquist and magician Terri Rogers. See *Secrets: The Original Magic of Terri Rogers* (London: Martin Breen Publishing, 1986), pages 15-25. She devised a flattened tube with a pointed head and indented tail that resembled an arrow and could reverse itself. (It could also be presented as a bomb, chevron, or a head of a cat.)

This marvelously clever idea has inspired several variations. Three of mine, including this one, were published in my booklet *Three Magic Arrows* (Leeds, MA: self published, 1991). "Arrow of Good Fortune" appears on pages 8-10.

Performance 3.3
Open Book

The performer shows a folded card with the title, "Open Book." It has a slit in the center of the front and a red seal that passes through it. Exploration reveals that the book cannot be opened and is one-sided. It is argued that the book is open in three different ways and concluded that an open book is an empty one.

I like the idea of a closed book that is open and vice versa. The title is the content, making this book not so different from some I have had the misfortune to read. Speaking metaphorically or not, most open books are short.

Construction
The card is made from a 5" x 8" file card. Cut two vertical slits, each one 1.5" long, and 2" from the short edges. See figure 36.

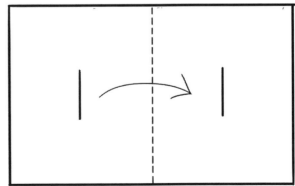

Figure 36

Fold it in half. The two slits should meet, one being on top of the other. Procure two 1.25" round, red removable labels. Slide one halfway into the slit and onto the inside of the card, sticky side down, and attach it. Repeat this process on the other side, sliding the label halfway into the slit. The card has been sealed shut and rendered one-sided.

Figure 37

Next, write the title with a red marker. With the open edges to the right, write "Open" horizontally across the top, and "Book" horizontally across the bottom. The model is complete. See figure 37.

Demonstration

Bring out the card and read the title aloud. Say that it is a prototype and that you will use it to define what an open book really is. Insert the tip of a finger to show the slits on both sides. While noting that the label seals the book shut, slide the finger between the covers, making it travel on three sides, showing that the book cannot be opened. Assert that the book has only one surface, and then trace with your finger all over the presumed front, around to the back and to the front again, through the slit, and then mime traveling inside the book while lifting up the cover a bit. State that the finger travels all about the outside and the inside without crossing over an edge, and conclude that the book has a single surface. Assert that the title is accurate and define the claim in your own style.

At least three points are possible. The book is open because it has only one surface and therefore no inside. It is open because there is no writing that is not fully visible on the cover. And it is open because it does not say anything at all. For a conclusion, it can be suggested that an open book is an empty one.

Performance 3.4
Easy Reader

This is a permutation of the previous concept—an endless book without a beginning. A storybook of apparently eight pages is shown. Each page contains a single word and a visual direction as to what page to turn to next. When the book is read aloud, it is discovered that the story is unending and written on a single page.

    This is one more of my attempts to solve the problem of writing appropriate nonsense on a one-sided surface. Making sense out of nonsense is a challenge that perhaps cannot be won, but the battle is engaging. I borrow the idea of an endless story and combine it with both a one-sided object and the idea of a book that is read without being opened. You can judge how successful I am at combining these three kinds of nonsense.

Construction

The materials required to make the book are: two unlined, 5" x 8" white file cards; black, red, and green markers; and four green, 1.5" diameter round, removable labels.

    Fold each file card in half along the width so the crease runs from the center of one long edge to the center of the other long edge. Slit this crease in both cards from one edge to the center of the crease (figure

38). Place the two cards in the same plane next to each other so that the beginnings of the slits touch (figure 39). Shove the cards so that they are woven together. The result is that the two cards are together, but one half of one card is on top of the other one, while the other half of this card in beneath the other one. Stick a green round label right on the exact center of the cards (figure 40), which holds both cards together and provides a hinge.

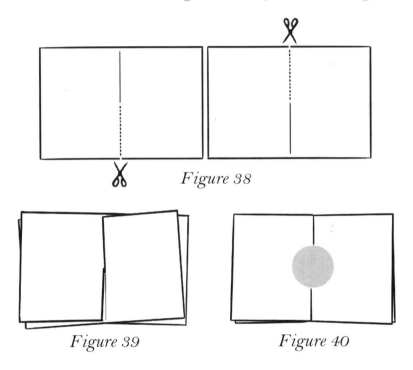

Figure 38

Figure 39   Figure 40

Turn the two cards over and stick another label on the exact center of the other side. Open the pages of the book to find another two sides and stick labels on them. Fold the cards in half along the creases already made to make a book of eight pages. {*Editor's note: Since the pages will be turned a lot, I recommend using glue to help affix and secure the labels.*}

To decorate the book correctly, it is important to have it oriented properly. Place it on a table with the spine and labels to the left. You are looking at the cover. It will have a cut, single edge of a card at the upper or lower part of the spine. If this cut runs along the top part of the spine, the book is oriented properly. But if the cut runs along the bottom part, simply turn the cover to the back of the book, making the next half of a card the new cover. This one will have the cut running along the top part of the spine. (You will understand why this is important as we proceed.) Now follow figures 41-45 by writing the title "Easy Reader" in red, the rest of the words in black, and the lines in green. Figure 41 indicates the book cover, figure 42 indicates pages 2 and 3, and so on.

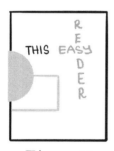

Figure 41

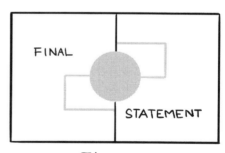

Figure 42

Performances for Chapter 3

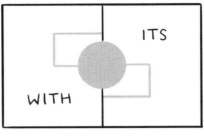

Figure 43

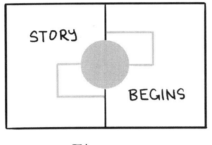

Figure 44   *Figure 45*

Script and Demonstration

[Depending on the performing circumstances, the book may be held horizontally or vertically. Either way, begin so the audience can see the front cover.]

This book is, as the title states, an easy reader. *[Use your fingers to casually turn and show the pages.]* **We might think that the reader is "easy" because it has only one word on a page, so few pages, and even this green line to show how to find the next page. This does make it easy, but we'll read it together to find out how easy it really is.**

[Point to the black word on the front cover.] **The first word is "This." Now we follow the green line.** *[Trace the green line with your right forefinger. When you get to the spine, clearly slide your forefinger through the slit and use your fingers to open up the book to what are, in fact, pages 6 and 7. Your forefinger traces the green line to the word on page 6, which is "story."]* **Ah, the line goes through here to another page. And it comes to the next word, "story."** *[Follow the line onto page 7.]* **And now it continues to the next word, "begins."** *[Continue tracing the line through the slit, open the book to page 4, and follow the line to the word "with." Then trace the line to the word "its" on page 5, go through the slit and turn to page 2 to read "final," and trace the line to "statement" on page 3. After reading that word, openly go through the slit, turn the book one hundred eighty degrees, and follow the line to the word "that" on the back cover. As the script conveys, say the word at each step.]* **On to "with," "its," "final," "statement," and "that." We are back to where we started.**

Did that seem difficult, even though the green line guided us? Well, it was not really as difficult as it seemed. The story is: *"This story begins with its final statement that . . . This story begins with its final statement that . . . This story begins . . . ."* **The story is endless. So it is the longest story that can be read. Yet we have read it all. How easy can a reader be?**

But it is even easier. Remember how we followed the green line? We never crossed over an

Performances for Chapter 3

edge, but always had our finger on the surface. So this reader has only one surface and therefore only one page. It was not difficult to turn pages because there are not any to turn. The book does not even have to be opened because there is only the one surface. How easy can a reader be? This is it: a book that tells the longest tale ever told without being opened.

Performance 3.5
Saint of Cardicians

Script
There have been saints of all kinds, but no saint for those magicians who specialize in card tricks—*cardicians*. However, things change. Sainthood is all the rage these days. Pope John Paul declared four hundred and sixty three saints during his reign, more than all the popes of the past four centuries combined. (That is, he discerned those God had made saints.) Some parishioners have complained, but one cardinal affirmed, "There cannot be too many saints."

I agree with such discernment. The necessary stages may be more easily traveled than we might imagine. After all, a married couple that did not have sexual relations for twenty-four years was beatified by stage four. And a sixteenth century Mexican man who did not exist was sanctified by stage five. So there must be room for many more of us. For example, me.

[The performer holds a small packet.] These three playing cards represent the early stages. *[An ace is shown on the face of the packet.]* **Stage one is "Recognition"**: the name is reported to the Vatican. I have already sent in my name.

[A two is shown.] **Stage two is "Servant of God":** **many believers find their prayers answered through the candidate's intercession. Ask around of cardicians you know. They credit me with contributions.**

[A three is shown.] **Stage three is "Venerable": at least one verified miracle is attributed to his or her intercession. Okay, here it is.** *[The packet is turned face down and counted, showing four blue-backed cards.]* **There were three cards, but now there is the creation of a fourth card!**

And stage four is "Blessed": after the miracle has been officially attributed, he or she is beatified. I have just worked the miracle, so I should be beautified.

And not only that, because stage five is the final one of "Sainthood." When a second miracle has been attributed, he or she is recognized as a saint. *[The cards are counted to show one face up.]* **The new card is now face up. My second miracle is accomplished.**

Please inform the new Pope that this humble cardician awaits his response. And if more is required, here is another miracle. *[The back of the face-up card is shown to be red.]* **This red back of the new card signifies my passion for sanctification.**

Routine

Use the ace through four of any of the suits, the first three of these with blue backs and the fourth with a red back. Have the cards in sequence from the ace down to the four, with the latter reversed at the bottom of the face-up packet. Show the cards in the fashion of an Elmsley Count to reveal three cards only: peel off the top card, the next card, and lay the last two cards as one on top. You have shown three cards representing the first three stages. Turn the packet over and perform an Elmsley Count in the normal way to show four face-down cards. This is the first miracle. Reverse Count the packet to show that the card has turned face up. This is the second miracle. Reveal the different color back. This is the third miracle.

Note

If an Elmsley Count is used instead of a Reverse Count with the last card placed at the bottom, the packet can be reset by simply replacing the face-up four on top.

One may perform this impromptu by skipping the different color back.

Sources

Information about the saints was taken from the cover story on October 3, 2002, in *USAToday* by Cathy Lynn Grossman.

The story notes that about eighty percent of the saints discerned by past popes have been martyrs. The performer of card tricks in bizarre magic circles certainly qualifies on this basis.

Chapter 4
Wonderwork

What is magic? What is it that we magicians do? What is it that we pretend to do? Can we define it? Do we need to be able to define it? Maybe not, but it would be odd to simply leave it at that, content with not knowing what we are doing. Of course, if magic is trivial then our not knowing is both normal and sensible. But perhaps magic needs to be enchanted and we must labor to re-enchant it. Or is it possible our magic can avoid both trivia and re-enchantment by focusing on wonder? I believe that it is. Here follow some introductory pontifications, perhaps even spells.

A. Magic as Trivial

In my view, no magic trick is trivial. But most presentations of tricks are. This is as it should be. What else could our presentations be in a nightclub or bar act? What else could they be in any group that prefers flash and surprises to the experience of wonder and mystery? Most people most of the time seek distraction during their leisure time. It would be foolish to totally ignore this need.

But people also read thoughtful books, serve on community organizations, worry about the state of the nation and world, and attend church and synagogue during their free time. So there are occasions, perhaps even while performing for magicians, when a performance can be non-trivial. Further, many acts could be improved magically by the addition of a trick that engages the heart and stimulates the mind rather than merely satisfies or distracts. Good comedians are as troubling as they are amusing. Good music is not entirely easy listening. Good magic? Is magic, as it is typically performed, the least provocative of the lively arts?

Three dangers of serious magic are immediately apparent. One is *sentimentality*. There are laudable attempts to relate tricks to life that are, for me, warm-fuzzy-yuk presentations that have become trite because the seriousness is so shallow. A second danger of a non-trivial presentation is *pretentiousness*. To pull together two common observations, "If you want to send a message, use Western Union; if I want to receive one, I go to church." Serious magic can be both boring and stuffy. A third danger of non-trivial magic is *destructiveness*. Magicians who function as psychics and healers can help, but also do damage. Those who do not go so far can still raise the discomfort level beyond utility.

Unserious magic can be either cute or confusing. Magic for magicians tends to be both cute and confusing. Children's magic and gospel magic tend to be both cute

Chapter 4: Wonderwork

and immature. They need not be either. Most good magic can entertain children. Good gospel magic need not be so entertaining, but the performer then risks suffering the fate of the founder of the faith.

But no trick is trivial in essence. This is because the occurrence of one impossibility in the world means that anything is possible. In principle, if a magician can make a coin vanish at his or her fingertips, then the participant can be healed, saved, or win a lottery. In fact, however, most magicians present the coin vanish in a trivial way and so the underlying principle is scarcely brought into play. But make no mistake: most people's fascination with magic is due to the principle. The trivial trick is only distraction.

B. Magic as Re-enchantment

The presentation of tricks as trivial is largely due to the fact that modern performance magic in the western world essentially is disenchanted. This dominant style of presentation developed, in part, out of a revolt from enchantment. Performers of enchanted magic were subject to persecution and, eventually, exposure and ridicule. Recall that the early books on the subject were a protest against belief in witchcraft. The result was not just secularized entertainment, but a version of it that is devotedly, perhaps even defensively, no more than diversion. Most magicians seem to communicate, "Look everybody, we are totally harmless, being quite irrelevant to life and in league with nothing but our psychosocial regressions." Perhaps they have over-reacted. Secularization has not so drastically curtailed the heart of the other lively arts.

Amid such a constrained performance tradition, a few exceptions arise. One was the gifted German performer, Punx. He labeled his life "Eternal Longing" and wrote:

> I was seeking miracles, the wonders that lift the heart and make it tremble. I found them everywhere, but still I could not capture them.
>
> So I invented miracles, clothed them in the magical cloak of my fantasy and gave them the wings of my longing for the incomprehensible. I took the magic away from its life on the "other side" for a few moments and let it illuminate our reality.
>
> Is everything illusion? Is the incomprehensible also unreal?
>
> Nothing is truer than the incomprehensible, because the sum total of our knowledge consists of the fact that we know nothing. Our reality is an illusion. Thus, illusion is reality.
>
> This is not just a trick with words. And because I believe this, I also believe that I can use the art of illusion to lift a corner of the veil that

conceals the world of my longing—the world beyond the physical.[1]

What a powerful vision of re-enchantment! Yet, I do not really know what to make of it. How can anyone really claim seriously that we "know nothing"? The meaning of "our reality is an illusion" totally escapes me. And besides, how unreachable such a vision is for most of us!

Is re-enchantment possible? If so, is it advisable? Possibly some enchanted magic occurs in gospel magic. At least, it is performed with reference to the mystery of another reality. Some bizarre magic attempts this with evocation of entities from other worlds, as does some of Jeff McBride's stage magic that relies, in intention, structure, and effect, upon western occult magic as well as shamanistic traditions. But the vast majority of magic performed is totally disenchanted. Even so, the evocation of wonder occurs here and there, however minimally. Doug Henning clearly sought to achieve this and succeeded more than most, as have performers with varied perspectives such as Peter Samelson, David Copperfield, and Eugene Burger.

In a useful essay, "High Magic: The Art of Re-enchantment," my friend, the sociologist, novelist, and magician, Victor Walter, uses the terms "mystery," "wonder," and "enchantment" seemingly interchangeably.[2] A good magician is defined as one "whose work should lead you to enchantment, wonder, and mystery."³ As his title suggests, he is traveling on the road to re-enchantment. Further, he says, "A magician like me wants to leave the audience with an experience of enchantment, a sense of wonder, the feeling of hidden forces at the edge of our minds. The other kind wants to teach that every trick is a hoax. Conflict rages between the party of mystery and the party of disenchantment."⁴

This is a fine statement of the situation. Quite properly, mystery, enchantment, and hidden forces are linked together. It is also natural to join wonder with these other terms. But is this the only option? Walter elaborates his position in the following statement:

> Transcendental conjuring is experimental metaphysics, if we think of metaphysics as what lies beyond the physical world. Experimental metaphysics is the mental exploration of what lies beyond our sensory experience. Conjuring is a way of inquiry, questioning the senses, questioning the mind and the way the mind uses its assumptions. We are touched by the hidden power of this questioning. Conjurers play with a power, the power to loosen our moorings in the everyday world, the world of commonsense, where utility is boss and organizes all experience around it. For a sudden moment it liberates us from the tyranny of common sense. It pushes our

questing beyond common sense, beyond intellect to mystery expressed in a metaphor.⁵

Although Walter's use of "metaphysics" is somewhat confusing to me, I can agree with everything stated in the above quotation. He isn't obviously referring to some totally other world, but only the physical, mental, and psychological aspects of our daily life. Going beyond common sense is what science does, that is, what the disenchanted do. But then Walter goes on to make clear that re-enchantment is his goal, adding what he terms a "parable of mystic twins":

> One is called "Magic." Her twin brother is named "Sacred." In the archaic world, they have only one character, sacromagical unity. Eventually, historic changes and secular enlightenment separate them, and the twins go in different directions. Now, in our disenchanted, desacralized world they vanish.
>
> We know how to recall the Sacred by communal worship and private devotions. We can also invoke Magic. When a magician tricks us out of disenchantment, we acknowledge the fragility of our perceptions. That burst of wonder frees us to reunite with spirit, and Magic prowls the marketplace, searching for her lost brother.⁶

In this passage wonder abounds, to be sure. But enchantment is back, fully ensconced along with it. Yet however wonderful, is this trip necessary? Especially when some of us cannot actually "recall the Sacred"?

Enchantment, disenchantment, and re-enchantment. I have spent a good part of my adult life in the quest for re-enchantment. This was done not only by means of traditional religions, such as Christianity and Zen Buddhism, but also modern alternatives, such as depth psychology. So the search for transcendence, for another reality, especially in depth, has occupied me for years. But close attention to experience has also led me to slowly realize that such baggage, however helpful as a guide, is hardly necessary as a belief system. At present, re-enchantment is the last goal I can imagine. My earlier forays into the theory of magic were loaded with implicit assumptions that sponsored depth, mystery, and meaning. I do not dismiss meaning, but depth and mystery are not of interest to me insofar as they include some hidden other reality.

At the same time, I can scarcely tolerate the usual kind of disenchantment expressed in performance magic. Where can one go from here? Maybe the only trip possible is that of falling on one's face. Even that is worth a try. Because a "trip" such as that can be wondered about.

C. Magic as Education

If performance magic is a central and crucial part of our lives, which I believe and explore elsewhere,[7] a decision on this matter is significant. It is not just a matter of how to think but of how to live. As the philosopher of science Paul Roth puts it, ". . . the debate on choice of frameworks is not a matter of appealing to some higher standard of rationality, some algorithm for choosing the most rational from among competing systems of beliefs; it is a choice of how one wants to live one's life."[8]

So, how are we to conceive of ourselves as magicians? How are we to live? As I have written about elsewhere,[9] Orson Welles—truly a wonder-worker—has a suggestion about how to cope with this contemporary dilemma. Recall how he reminds and advises us:

> Before they were painting beasts on the walls of the first caves, there appeared, out of some unfathomable murk, the "Man of Magic."
>
> Because he was an actor (and all magicians are) he cast a spell. He quickened the heartbeats under those shaggy chests with the thrills of poetry and the sense of awe. For all those thousands of years, that's what we've all been after, and making it a kind of entertainment free of lugubrious solemnities of mystic ritual is exactly what raised it into an art. However, to neglect our ancient obligation to the sense of

wonder is to turn the whole edifice of magic into a mere toy shop . . . .

We must command attention. The tricks won't do that for us. From indifference we must charm up collaboration. It is our task to parody something mysteriously real and as old as time. Laughter is a legitimate tool, but we must never lose our sense of obligation to the presence looming over our shoulder; the ancient cause and wonder with awe.[10]

Yes, but the challenge is complicated. Wells advises us to eliminate "mystic ritual" and "to parody something mysteriously real." If we are to be wonder-workers, we are advised to be fake miracle-workers. This does not sit well with me. I do not want to present something that I do not believe in. I do not want to kindle a response from the audience that is unjustified. And I do not want to foster sentimental nostalgia for ancient mysteries. In sum: for me, wonder is real, miracle is not, and a fake miracle is unworthy of wonder. Besides, I am no longer interested in mysteries for all the reasons I offered in the previous chapter.

I do have a solution—at least a response that satisfies me. Miracle is a problem. Recall that miracle comes from the Latin verb meaning to wonder. But a miracle is usually defined as an event or effect in the physical world beyond or out of the ordinary course of things, deviating from the known laws of nature, or transcending our knowledge of these laws. It can also be defined as an extraordinary, anomalous, or abnormal event brought about by superhuman agency as a manifestation of its power, or for the purpose of revealing or manifesting spiritual force. Surely, a miracle is a wonder. But does all the understanding from long past centuries need to be attached? I believe not.

As I have argued, wonder is an experience of respect for the presence of an object, person, or event. It is a meeting with an extraordinary presence and a fulfillment of this meeting with celebration. While previously I felt comfortable with labeling wonder as holy or sacred, I no longer do. For me, paying full respect to something does not require making up or adopting all sorts of understandings about some supernatural reality. Such creativity may well please us, but it is not necessary and it is likely to mislead us. And it is important to acknowledge that we are making up the theologies in response to the prior experience of wonder. Carl Jung once remarked that collecting examples of religious experience was his profession, while making up theories about it was his hobby. That is a wise distinction. As has been said in the Buddhist tradition, we should not mistake the finger pointing at the moon for the moon itself. The wonder experience occurs. For me, that is sufficient.

Mystery, too, is a problem for which I have found a solution. There was a time as a young adult when I dwelt upon a traditional mystical understanding of ultimate reality. It is an understanding in classical Hinduism and in mystics everywhere. It is about a connection between the individual and the universe. Here it is in three words: "Thou art that." To elaborate with a few more words: the very essence of you and the very essence of the universe are one and the same. Taken literally, there are no hidden realities or dualities, although many mystics apparently can't help themselves from imputing one or several.

Here is this understanding of the primal situation stated more fully and in connection with wonder. John Gardner writes:

> Wonder is based upon the feeling that at the deepest levels the world and man's true self are one. This means that the aspirations and ideals, the beauty and goodness, which are natural to the human heart, lie somehow also at the center of the physical universe; that therefore standards of beauty and goodness are not irrelevant to the realities of an indifferent world, but are quite as pertinent to the study of universal events as are the quantitative standards of physical science.[11]

This quote gives us an idea of the size of the basic idea. I do enjoy such intellectual whoppers. It is fun to proclaim what it is "all about" in a few words. Some of us cannot resist, nor should we, and the words can be understood as a celebration of wonder. More importantly, Gardner's thinking reminds us about an important aspect of it. "Wonder," he writes, "is based upon the feeling that at the deepest levels the world and man's true self are one." Just so. For me, wonder is the making of a connection between us and the thing we meet. It breaks down the separation we have, and generally need, between ourselves and our environment. The subject-object distinction is reduced and a primary relationship is restored. There is an experience of a most "mysterious reality," but note that Gardner is talking about an experience, a "feeling," not a metaphysical conclusion. Gabriel Marcel expresses it this way, "A mystery is something in which I am myself involved, and it can therefore only be thought of as a sphere where the distinction between what is in me and what is before me loses its meaning and its initial validity."[12]

If I were forced to use the term I now prefer to set aside, I could agree that mystery is a sign of "another reality," but it is not a metaphysical or supernatural one. It is a psychological one in which subject-object oppositional thinking is relaxed or suspended. But please note: since this is just everyday life in the world, it is not "another reality". In the world, as we live it, the other remains the other and yet, simultaneously, is intimately related to me, and thereby transforms me. This interactional transformation is going on all the time with other people, things, and events, but there is a special sphere of activity in which it especially occurs: the sphere of play. This sphere is far larger than we tend to realize; it encompasses not only the beginning relationship between parent and child, but also the arts, sciences, and religion. And the world of play *is* the real world. It is already here for us without the need of traditional mysteries and additional realities. An experience within it is all the "mystery" we need because here wonder occurs.

So what is a magician? As I stated in chapter 1, the Greeks had a word for it: thaumaturgy—the performance of miracles or wonders, specifically, magic. What is important is the root meaning of the Greek combining form, thaumato-, thaumat-. It is from thauma, thaumatos, meaning *a thing exciting wonder*, and used for *miracle, miraculous*, and *magic*. The Greek word for wonder, then, is inseparable from magic and miracle. The magician is a wonder-worker, a performer of wonders. And wonder is prior to, and more fundamental than, the understandings we create of miracles and mystery. But what are the implications of this intimacy between magic and wonder? Especially if the modern magician is not going to simply imitate or parody the magician as miracle-worker and mystery-monger? Well, I say *we can be edifiers*.

In previous chapters, I drew upon Mark A. Schneider's book *Culture and Enchantment*. His conclusion to the book is suggestive. After having shown that disenchantment is crucial to science and that enchantment is unlikely to be permanently removed, Schneider suggests that there are three options available that will undoubtedly be decided by the individual, mostly on the grounds of taste rather than anything else. These are the roles of scientist, virtuoso, and edifier.[13]

The scientist, he says, is thoroughly disenchanted by intention. *The virtuosos*, like those old collectors of wonders in cabinets who functioned with little discrimination between fact and fancy, are contemporary thinkers who posit other worlds with abandon. *The edifiers*, those who supply edification, fall somewhere and somewhat vaguely in-between. Science considers what it can, data that is amenable to the demands for repeatability and making predictions that are intrinsic to the scientific method. But there are phenomena for which these demands seem limited and perhaps even inappropriate, for example, moral or aesthetic phenomena. And further, the realm of the imagination is quite distinct from the instrumental one. Label the former "edifying." It involves claims upon the individual and society that are not "scientific" in a narrow sense, but still very important. Such claims and data can be organized, explored, and challenged as perverse, trite, inconsistent, and so forth, even though they are not subject to the warrant of scientific method. It is easy to leap from this edification to the realm of marvel that is so appreciated by the virtuoso. Perhaps this kind of edifying exploration is especially true in the fields of philosophy and religion, and in psychology and anthropology. Edification serves as an important reminder to science of its natural limits (indeed, every method has limits), but it is probably also the impetus that leads people to leap to presumptions about "wider" and "deeper" worlds, or some other, hidden reality. Even so, because it is so, it is important to continually remember the great breadth, richness, and complexity of our experiences as human beings in *this* world.

And so I believe that it is possible and worthy for a performance magician to be an edifier rather than a scientist or virtuoso. Rather than limiting oneself to disenchantment or re-enchantment, a magician can focus on wonder. The scientist does wonder, however constraining may be the rigors of the method. The virtuoso does wonder also, but by adding another world. But an edifier can elicit the breadth and depth of wonder without mystery.

Perhaps this is easier than we are inclined to believe. I have speculations about both disenchanted and enchanted magicians. Disenchanted magicians (quasi-scientists) may well possess and inspire wonder, in precisely those realms of behavior that are denigrated by some—cleverness, deception, and trickery. These are extraordinary human phenomena worthy of wonder indeed. Enchanted or re-enchanted magicians may be promoting mystery and other realities because they know no other way to experience and express wonder. As I argued above, magic is primarily about wonder, and only secondarily about either deception or mystery. So my suggestion is that wonder may be what is hidden from magicians in either camp. If so, exploring wonder—what it is and isn't—is useful as a first step. Only then should those possible applications and extensions be considered.

So I conclude that everything hinges on wonder. Let us hope that it is neither a mysterious apparition nor an ultimate marvel.

D. Wonder Performance

Performance magic is symbolic. But symbolic of what? Symbols point toward realities beyond themselves. If magic is not to direct our attention to miracles and mystery, then it occurs to focus our gaze on wonder itself. Magic does not happen simply to entertain people by distracting them from everyday life. Nor does it occur simply to fool people by exhibiting our cleverness. Magic can and, I believe, should be performed to focus the gaze of the audience on their own wonder. To express it more fully: the goal is performances of magic that both remind the audience of the wonders they have experienced and initiate them into further possibilities of experiencing wonder.

Wonder performance requires full experience of wonder, mastery of magic technology, and a creative union of the wonder and magic. Although hardly an easy goal to reach, it is an easy goal to begin striving toward. I suspect that this goal is reached more by attitude than through intellectual suggestions. The legacy of Doug Henning is an illustration of that. But it is possible that some pointers might stimulate the attitude in some readers. What follows, then, are a half-dozen of these to help readers get started. {*Editor's note: in the performance section of this chapter below, you will find some performance examples of each of these different orientations to wonder.*}

The Uncommon

We are reminded rightfully of our enjoyment of novelty. Allow an academic, Philip Garrison, to do so:

> We honor folk notions. But not because we believe in them. No, folk notions represent our collective, half-conscious effort to vivify the drab dailiness of our existence: they have a way of intensifying, of making more thrilling whatever regularity we count on in order to plan our lives....
>
> The landscape of belief and that of fact are not opposed, or not diametrically, at least. No, they lie at some oblique angle to each other. Tired of the predictabilities that nourish, we long for that other world, the one we keep extrapolating, collectively, from scraps of belief. The landscape of belief relates to that of fact in rather the way the planet Pluto related, once, to Neptune. The

> orbit of the latter, or certain irregularities in it, let astronomers infer both the existence and location of a presence they'd never see....
>
> The older I get, the more folk beliefs stick in my mind. They arrange themselves all around the periphery of my thinking. I admire how they hover between life and art, these quirky, archaic forms of behavior....
>
> We do dwell in the landscape of fact. But we never escape the tug a certain counterpart to it exerts.[14]

This is a humble and insightful confession. We enjoy superstitions, Garrison suggests, not so much because we believe them but because we require the thrill of strangeness they provide. Not every one of us who reads the *National Inquirer* is a true believer. Rather, we delight in what is so absurdly different as to be impossible. And there are other ways to engender the experience of strangeness. The performer can focus on the strange, whether it is ancient superstitions, contemporary urban myths, or even the gothic romance material that is so favored by many bizarre magicians. There is so much that is novel to us that we might celebrate in our performances.

The Common

A quite different avenue is opened up when we realize that novelty is not the only form in which we meet the strange and wonderful. The most sophisticated approach is one that perceives them in what is very familiar and highly common. Here is the plea of Charles Beaumont's fictional magician, known to himself as Micah Jackson and to his audience as Dr. Silk:

> Dr. Silk watched and listened and forgot that there lived a lonely, withered old man named Micah Jackson, too tired to care, too old to run, ready for death to catch up.
>
> The men in the bar had their eyes fastened on him. As they would if he were the President: more than that, though, more than mere respect. These were adults, some of them with years painted into their faces, tottering grandfathers; and still, were their eyes much different from children's, now? He studied their eyes in the big bar mirror.
>
> There was respect, yes; a little fear, perhaps; and love—certainly there was that, abundantly.
>
> Why? he wondered, as he always did. Was it because he was a man who could fool them with illusions? Only because he knew how to make pigeons fly out of an ordinary hat?

He threw down the rest of the applejack and hoped this wasn't the answer. The liquid warmed a path. Perhaps, he thought, it was because he brought a little honest wonder into their lives one night out of the year. . . .

Then he remembered the prairie that surrounded this small and weary town. And the applejack made him want to turn and say something to the men. You don't have to wait for me, he wanted to say. Just open your eyes: there's magic in the air. Show me a tree, I'll show you a trick no magician alive could ever do. The dust underneath your boots is a riddle to keep you up nights: What did it used to be before it was dust? Mountains? And the sun! Hey, keep your eyes on the yellow ball—now, it's there, now it isn't. Where does it go to? And why? A stone, a hill, a lake—now there's tricks that are tricks, gentlemen! There is magic for you. And I'd give a lot to figure out how they're done, yes, sir, a lot. . . .[15]

"A little honest wonder. . . . A stone, a hill, a lake . . . . There is magic for you." I like this phrase, "honest wonder." I suppose it expresses a bias; most likely, any wonder is better than none. But an experience of actually meeting any object, any person, any event, can be an occasion for wonder. We can be shocked into wonder by a chair or a book, a casual acquaintance or a handshake, an old movie or a habitual attitude. Magicians have a tendency to focus on the exotic for good reason—cheap wonder. But this need not be so; there is quite a lot to wonder about in our own daily lives. A pulse, heartbeat, breath, being alive this minute. Friends, strangers, lovers. That other people are. That this particular person is. Feelings, ideas, actions. War. Peace. Tricks! Indeed, what is there not to wonder about?

Our Own Experiences

We can also attend to our own experiences of wonder. How aware of wonder are we? Where do we find it in our lives? What gets our own attention, overcomes us with awe, and moves us to celebrate it? What is our response to it? If we have no respect off stage, how can we possibly show respect on stage?

A number of my tricks are about death. This does not surprise me because I have been wondering about death since early middle age. The beginning of this wonder was the long dying of my older brother with ALS and some symbolic dying in the domestic area. This led me to work in a London hospice for half a year. There I met a young man with ALS who told me to read Albert Camus's novel *The Plague* to understand how he felt about life and death. I read it. My brother died. When I returned to the hospice from his funeral in the United States, my friend wanted to know all the concrete details of my brother's death. I wanted to know all the details of his understanding of Camus. We exchanged reactions until he died, too. Out of all this wondering came my card trick, "Sole Survivor."[16] When I perform it, I remember my brother and my friend. And I wonder again about death.

But it is equally true that I wonder about life and so many of the experiences that are possible there.

Our Own Performances

We can also look at our own performances of magic. What do they mean to us? Do they have anything at all to do with our own experience of wonder? We might consider any single trick we perform and ask ourselves what it means to us. This might not be easy, but it would be interesting. What is the history of our association with the trick? Do we still perform it for the same reasons we did at the beginning? I assume that we enjoy a trick for many reasons and that our relationship to it is complex. But is wonder an element in it? Wouldn't it be interesting to discover that our own experiences of wonder were totally disconnected from our performances of magic? And wouldn't it be equally interesting to discover the wonder we have hidden from ourselves in our tricks? How hidden is it from our audience?

As I look back on my own tricks, I see a theme that keeps coming up again and again. It has to do with spatial orientation, especially the idea of up and down and the idea of inside and outside. The tricks involve some seemingly impossible change from one to the other. For example, "State Sign" involves a name that is twisted ninety degrees and yet remains the same, whereas "Real Jokers" involves a card turning inside out. My favorite puzzle creation, "Sheep and Goats," involves changing a folded square of cardboard to intermingle separated colors by a series of steps to turn the model inside out. My favorite magical novelty, which appeared in chapter 3, is "Arrow of Good Fortune," a shape that is turned upside down and yet remains right side up.[17]

It does not require much thought to realize that I have a strong preoccupation with spatial direction. And it is no surprise because I am dyslexic. Such people typically view things in more than one way and take delight in seeing the other ways. This is both a weakness and a strength. I still reverse numbers and letters and mispronounce words accordingly. But I also create oddities that draw upon this personal oddity. The presentation for "State Sign" is an obvious testimony to my ambivalence. And "Real Jokers" presents the theme as a heroic tragedy with religious overtones. Yet it was only recently that I realized how frequently this theme occurred. One of my tricks is a cardboard tube that seems to turn inside out. Fittingly, I title it a "Mystery Tube" and present it as a great mystery, not because it does something unusual or impossible, but because why anyone would invent it is a great mystery.[18] I still feel that way about this theme. Writing about it now, I am still wondering about it, even though I understand it intellectually. Perhaps as I dwell more on this aspect of my creating and performing, I will be able to better communicate this wonder to the audience as I reveal the personal nonsense that so captivates me. Yes, I am prone to label it "nonsense" and present it that way. Of course it is nonsense, but I am defensive about it and insist on exposing it to others. Surely it is very important nonsense for me.

What other forms of nonsense do we perform and feel ambivalent about?

Our Own Audience

We can look at our audience. Maybe they are not open to wonder very much or at all. But if they are, where? Comedians constantly explore what people find to be funny. Can magicians explore what people find to be wonderful? And do we really care about the wonder of others? Maybe we care only about our own, and so the audience responds to our diversion and cleverness but isn't stimulated to explore their own wonder. They can be led to the false impression that wonder is only for the magician. Can our own wonder be expanded to acknowledge the wonder experienced by others? It is one thing to celebrate our own wonder, quite another to celebrate wonder itself, and still more challenging to celebrate the wonder of others.

Audiences differ. On the rare occasions I perform, I do so in the living rooms of friends rather than on the stages of Las Vegas or the furnished basements of children's birthday parties. Even so, my audiences seem to expect tricks that dazzle and are suitable for children. This is how they have come to define magic. Presentations that lead them to wonder about themselves are not expected. But they are open to it in many realms because they are interested and involved in current issues. So I can, and do, offer magical meditations on sex, death, politics, and religion. That they expect such topics from stand up comedians and not from magicians is a sad fact I wish to change. My audiences are interested in what is going on in their lives.

So I often choose to do a card trick called "Perfected Segregation."[19] Couples of mixed race meet to increase solidarity and foster acceptance, but then they become upset by a homosexual couple. The outcome is a complete and perfect segregation by sex, race, and age. The trick acknowledges and lightly makes fun of our contemporary concerns. In "Jack's Veto" (which is included below), a participant is invited to imagine that he is dreaming. He finds himself in a most impressive oval office, seated in front of flags, behind his desk, and looking across it and upward at a most august old man with a long, white beard. I play the role of this old man, holding pieces of stone, actually cardboard, with writing on them. The old man speaks. "I have shattered these, my commandments, in a fit of rage. But you are my most favored son. So I'll give you a line-item veto . . . only one." A process of elimination occurs until only one commandment remains—the one commandment the President may ignore, the seventh one about adultery. The performer concludes, "Be grateful and prosper in your office, Jack." The contemporary concern about role models and adultery in high office is acknowledged, but somewhat delicately because it refers back in time to Kennedy, rather than any recent one.

I do not suggest that all our effects be presented in this way, only that an occasional venture into everyday reality might be interesting, even captivating. Audiences have concerns and conclusions about their experiences of interest to them. Why not wonder along with them?

Wonder Itself

Finally, looking at our own wonder, magic performances, and the wonder of others can be assisted by a sustained focus on wonder itself. My outline on the dynamics of wonder in chapter 2—all the stages, elements, and outcomes of respect—is not so much to be "believed" but rather to be used as a tool to help us tease out possibilities. Please review the three different stages, three different elements within each stage, and three different outcomes. Then look at what we magicians tend to focus on.

Many magicians today focus mostly on the first two elements in the first stage of attention—witness and shock. We make sure the audience knows that something has happened and that they are surprised. And that's about all. It is hardly enough. How rare to experience a trick that includes the third element of that first stage: that is a presence and is received as a gift, and which yields the respect of what I call "simple greeting." Gift? Are we not giving a gift when we perform? Please consider the magic of René Lavand. He and his audiences experience a gift exchange, and both parties know it.

Or consider the second stage, that of awe. We magicians do like to puzzle and dumbfound people (elements one and two). So many of us speak of "killer effects" that "blow away" an audience. But where is that third element of empowerment in our performances? It might be that we are mostly concerned with our own power as magicians; our power performances may be focused mostly on exhibiting our own power.

A quite different direction is possible. Jeff McBride's performances focus on the power of the magus, but also exhibit a concern for empowering others by stressing the need to pass on the heritage to an apprentice. Some lecture demonstrations by mentalists offer possibilities along this line, not simply making false suggestions about how psychic members of the audience are, but showing how they can protect themselves and counter the outright charlatans and deviousness of cults.

(In this regard, James Randi and Bob Fellows come to mind.) Even so, how often do we see performance magic that moves the audience to the outcome of ambivalent greeting? If awe occurs, so does ambiguity, and ambivalence is sure to follow. Indeed, magicians who are wonder-workers are not un-ambivalently enjoyed. Rather, they are provocateurs. Ricky Jay stimulates this reaction at times in his evocation of a confidence artist. Penn & Teller are superbly ambiguous and generate ambivalent greeting unparalleled in contemporary performances. But how rare this is.

Perhaps, too, performance of magic can be seen as a special version of the third stage, the stage of action. The elements of exploration, expression, and celebration all occur in our learning and doing tricks. If so, then our goals could be to exhibit and inspire curiosity; show and sponsor aesthetic elaboration in image, sound, movement, and story; and offer a celebration in which the admirations of performer and audience are remembered and shared. Ideally, then, a performance could involve the outcome of sustained greeting in the mode of play.

E. A Cautionary Wonder

How else to conclude but with a caution about wonder? There can be too much of this good thing. Wonder is not the only value, and it is at cross-purposes with other values such as stability, comfort, safety, satisfaction, and harmony. Further, restoring, refreshing, and revitalizing the intimate link between magic and wonder is not without its own dangers such as the extremes of sentimental gushing and brutalizing dumbfounderment.

Even so, I do conclude that magic can be a creative assistant to wonder. But please note: this means that wonder is more fundamental than magic, and it is quite crucial to magic, as it is to so much else in our lives.

To underscore both of these points—the essential importance of wonder and our need to be cautious about it—I close with two passages that I have used in other contexts. The first is by poet Peter Viereck:

> Being absurd as well as beautiful,
> Magic—like art—is hoax redeemed by awe.
> (Not priest but clown, the shuddering sorcerer
> Is more astounded than his rapt applauders:
> "Then all those props and Easters of my stage
> Came true? But I was joking all the time!")
> Art, being bartender, is never drunk;
> And magic that believes itself, must die.[20]

Hoax unredeemed by awe is not magic; it is mere jugglery. Even so, "magic that believes itself, must die." Again, charting a course for life and magic between jugglery and enchantment has been a primary purpose of this book.

Chapter 4: Wonderwork

But the caution required of us is well expressed in this subtle variation of the story I used at the close of chapter 2:

> One day a demon was traveling through the villages with his attendants. They saw a magician walking who stopped to stare at something he had discovered on the ground in front of him. The attendants asked their master what was happening. He replied, "He is wondering." "Doesn't this bother you when someone wonders, o' evil one?" his attendants asked. "No," the demon replied. "Right after this they usually make a puzzle out of it, and eventually, it may even become a trick."

Notes

1. Punx, "Eternal Longing—a Very Short Biography," in *Farewell Performance*, translated by Bill Palmer (Houston: Exclusive Magical Publications, 1991), pages 4–5.

2. Victor Walter, "High Magic: The Art of Re-enchantment," *Convergence* (Deep Winter, 1997), pages 22-25.

3. "High Magic," page 22.

4. "High Magic," page 22.

5. "High Magic," page 24.

6. "High Magic," page 25.

7. Editor's note: this is the central project of Bob's *An Essay on Magic*, which will be published in 2015 by Theory and Art of Magic Press. The "essay" part of that book, consisting of three chapters, was written before *The Sense of Wonder*.

8. Paul A. Roth, quoted by Schneider, *Culture and Enchantment*, page 202.

9. Editor's note: in *An Essay on Magic*, chapter 1.

10. Orson Welles, "Citizen Abner." From the special Abb Dickson issue of *Genii: The International Conjurors' Magazine*, Volume 52, Number 7 (January, 1989), page. 45.

11. John Gardner, *N. E. A. Journal 46* (February, 1957), page 73.

12. Gabriel Marcel, *Metaphysical Journal* (Chicago: Henry Regnery Co., 1952), page 233.

13. Schneider, *Culture and Enchantment*, page 194.

14. Philip Garrison, *Augury* (Athens, GA: University of Georgia Press, 1991), page 91.

15. Charles Beaumont, "The Magic Man," in *The Magic Man and Other Science-Fantasy Stories* (Greenwich, CT: Fawcett Publications, 1965), pages 81-102.

16. "Sole Survivor," in *Magic and Meaning*, expanded edition, by Eugene Burger and Robert E. Neale (Seattle: Hermetic Press, 2009) pages 133-136.

17. "State Sign," in *Tricks of the Imagination* (Seattle: Hermetic Press, 1991), pages 3-7; "Real Jokers," in *Magic and Meaning*, pages 106-120; "Sheep and Goats," in Martin Gardner's *Wheels, Life and Other Mathematical Amusements* (New York: W. H. Freeman and Company, 1983), page 66; "Arrow of Good Fortune," in this book, performance piece 3.2.

18. "Mystery Tube," *The Magic of Celebrating Illusions* (Sherman, TX: Theory and Art of Magic Press, 2013), pages 311-319. For an early version of the basic effect, see "Inside-Out" in *Self-Working Paper Magic*, edited by Karl Fulves (New York: Dover Publications, Inc., 1985), page 116.

19. "Perfected Segregation" in *Life, Death & Other Card Tricks* (Seattle: Hermetic Press, 2000), pages 147-152.

20. Peter Viereck, "A Walk on Snow," *The Yale Review*, Number 2, 1948, pages 240-241.

Performances for Chapter 4

In this exhilarating chapter, Bob Neale takes his insights and arguments about the nature of wonder to the heart of magic performance itself. If you perform magic at all, I recommend that you study it carefully. It just may rock your world. That is, as with all good philosophy, it may change your views about what you do and why you do it, or it might help you better understand what you do or want to do, even if you end up disagreeing with it.

In brief, carefully reasoning that performance magic is more than distracting trivia, clever puzzles, and re-enchanting mysteries, Bob concludes, "Magic can and, I believe, should be performed to focus the gaze of the audience on their own wonder." Anyone who has read this far understands that "reminding the audience of the wonders they experience" for Bob isn't about getting them to go "ooo" and "ahhh" or become all gooshy and sentimental. Wonder is far too variable for that, both in depth and breadth. It is because of this variety that Bob concludes this chapter by reminding us of five different domains in which people experience wonder, and they are all domains that magicians can, and perhaps should, explore to realize the full potential of their art.

In selecting the performance pieces for this chapter, Bob and I have selected some pieces to exemplify each of those domains. Our interest was to only include unpublished pieces by Bob and to select ones that used a variety of different props and presentation tones. But I also recommend that you flesh out these five domains of wonder—and thereby increase your performing options—by going through all of Bob's publications. You will quickly discover that Bob has been creating material for each of these domains from the very beginning.

To exemplify the domain of *The Uncommon*, we include "Satan's Solitare" (4.1) and "Bizarre Impact" (4.2).

For wonders that touch on *The Common*, you will find "Your Mistakes Were Not Made" (4.3), "Kiddy Trinity" (4.4), and "Money Purse" (4.5).

To explore some wonders of *Our Own Experiences*, there are "Only a Paper Doll" (4.6) and "The Risk Trick" (4.7).

Some of *Our Own Performances* that bring wonder are "Synchronicity Schtick" (4.8) and "Aching Heart Illusion" (4.9).

Finally, to draw attention to our *Audience's Experience of Wonder*, we offer "Upside-Down Man" (4.10), "Jack's Veto" (4.11), and "Twin Towers" (4.12). When you get to that last one, you will understand why I felt it was the way for this book to end.

—Lawrence Hass

Performance 4.1
Satan's Solitaire
(Wondering about The Uncommon)

Script

Would you mind playing the Devil? Right now and for just a moment? You might even gain a little sympathy for him. Please? Thank you.

Suppose that you are Satan. And your mood is bad. What can you, the Lord of Chaos, do to achieve your goals on earth? Nothing. Human beings on their own are doing it all for you. So you have nothing to do but watch our behavior over and over as an insomniac. The only problem is: how can you avoid boredom? The solution? Solitaire. You can play solitaire, a version of your own invention with these nine cards. Satan's Solitaire is all about what stimulates you the most: chaos caused by randomization.

Your game has three parts, after which you will discover whether you win or lose.

The first randomization. Please cut and complete the cut. Deal the cards alternately into two piles. Place either pile on top of the other. Decide whether to cut and deal again or not. Again? Okay, cut the cards, deal them into two piles, and place one pile on top of the other. You have randomized the cards.

The second randomization. Take the top or bottom card and table it. Do this two more times so that you have three cards in a pile. Repeat this action, making a second pile of three cards and taking either the top or bottom card each time. Repeat the action with the remaining three cards to make a third pile. Place any pile on top of another. Place either of the remaining two piles on top of the other. You have randomized the cards again.

The third randomization. Deal the top three cards in a row. If you want, change their order. Place the new top card on top of any one of the first three cards. Place the new top card on top of either one of the two remaining single cards. Place the new top card on the remaining single card. Place the last three cards in the same free manner to form three piles of three cards. Place any pile on top of another. Place either of the remaining two piles on top of the other. You have randomized the cards yet again.

You have randomized the cards three times. Did you win or lose? Deal out three cards face up in a row from left to right. Deal out another row of three below the first row. Deal out the remaining three cards. Now add the three columns to get the total. 666—the Devil's Digits!

It happens every time with no risk, no gamble, and no threat of chaos. It is all so orderly! On Earth chaos rules, but in Hell order prevails. By winning, you lost, just as you always do. There is absolute boredom for the Lord of Chaos. Hell is cursed. So maybe Satan deserves a little sympathy, don't you think?

Routine

As the script indicates, this routine uses nine cards. They are three aces, three twos, and three threes. Stack them in any serial sequence, for one example, ace, two, and three, ace, two, and three, ace, two, and three.

Overhand Shuffle the face-down cards in a way that maintains any such sequence. For one example, run three cards and toss the remainder on top; then repeat that action twice. At the end the cards must be in the same three card sequence repeated three times, whatever that sequence happens to be.

Follow the procedure that is described in the above script. Sufficient order is maintained during each randomization so that the total of the three columns of cards will always be 666.

{*Editor's note: it is not the case that the* rows *will yield that total, only the* columns. *So you might consider dealing out those final cards into three separate face-down piles, and then turning them face up dramatically to reveal the pay-off. Also, when you experiment with this, you will fool yourself because all the free choices make any control feel impossible. Imagine how free it will feel to a participant who has no idea where the piece is heading. And the irony of the final message is both fun and complex.*}

Sources

Shane has a very surprising, shocking, and theologically provocative routine in which the Devil no longer has any work to do and feels unneeded. See "Weeping, An Old Man" in his *Pentalogy* (Orlando, FL: Leaping Lizards Publishing, 2006), pages 249-253. His routine inspired mine, although the trick and mood are different. Poinc would have loved Shane's contribution.

The first randomization: I do not know who first dealt a small packet of cards into two piles, gathered them, and repeated the dealing and gathering, yet maintained some kind of order. Max Maven would know. You will find many uses of the approach in his *Redivider* (Seattle: Hermetic Press, 2002).

{*Editor's Note: I checked with Max, and he says the idea of using a Reverse Faro Shuffle to retain a stack—please note: dealing the cards into two piles is a form of the Reverse Faro—was mentioned by Martin Gardner in his* Mathematics, Magic and Mystery *(Mineola, NY: Dover Publications, Inc., 1956). And Max says, "it was not new then." In* Redivider *Max says the basic idea dates back to at least 1915. For more information on the general history of Faro and Reverse Faro Shuffles and of their use to preserve different stacks, study* Redivider *throughout, but see pages 3-5 in particular.*}

The second randomization uses the Rusduck Principle. See "Outer Space" by J. Russell Duck in the July 1958 issue of his publication, *The Cardiste* (Number 10), pages 3-5.

I believe the third randomization is properly credited to Jack London. Sometime in early 2005, Larry White submitted his fine piece that uses it, "The Power of Fives," to the Shadow Digest. As Larry indicated, this is an old principle. My understanding is that Jack London was the first to employ it. He used borrowed bills. Many other creators, Larry Becker among them, had simplified the approach to nine digits; Larry White got it to five. I have simplified it still further than either Larry. I call my version "The Power of One, Two, and Three."

Performance 4.2
Bizarre Impact
(Wondering about The Uncommon)

Script

[Four cards are removed from four envelopes. The cards portray vampire faces.] **Vampires are universal. So they come in different skin colors—orange, brown, yellow, and pink. Prejudice being what it is, some vampires are considered worse than others. Strangely, this means that some vampires are better than others. Pick one of the colors to indicate which vampire is the best one for you. Ah, the yellow vampire!**

[The envelopes are turned over. They are shaped like coffins, each having a large hole on the front so a face can be seen from inside after it has been inserted.] **All the vampires are ready for their daily sleep. Their coffins have a window, required by law in some places so we can see if the sleeping vampire is a good or bad one. If we see a good one, we may not break open the coffin and stab it with a wooden stake.** *[Each vampire is seen to be face down through the hole in the center of the coffin.]* **Now all of them are at rest.**

[As the coffins are shown again, one of the coffins is upside down.] **But one vampire becomes so restless that it uses its powers to turn its coffin upside down so**

that he is resting face up. How strange! *[All the envelopes are placed face down and shown again as face down.]* **Maybe all four vampires want to rest face up in their coffins like this. Will they stay this way? Not the one who is restless because he is so nice.** *[The selected vampire, in this case the yellow one, is seen to be face up through the hole in the center.]* **He has turned around inside the coffin! The yellow vampire is facing us, hoping that we will not destroy him because he is so nice.**

Construction

Obtain five double-blank, poker size playing cards. You will cut four of them to resemble coffins by cutting off the upper corners at right angles and the bottom corners at a different angle so the bottom of the card is narrower than the top and a portion of each long side has been removed. The completed shape can be seen in figure 46.

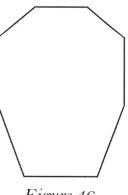

Figure 46

The best way to cut these cards is by creating a template with the fifth card, which you will then use to trace the outline on the four other cards so you can cut them. This procedure will make the cards nicely uniform in shape.

To make the template, fold the fifth card in half with the crease running from the centers of the short edges (figure 47). Then fold both of the long edges back to the center crease you just made (figure 48). Then unfold those flaps, but keep the card folded in half. Cut off a tiny sliver of both long sides, about 1/16 of an inch (figure 49). (This will allow the cards to easily fit in the envelopes.)

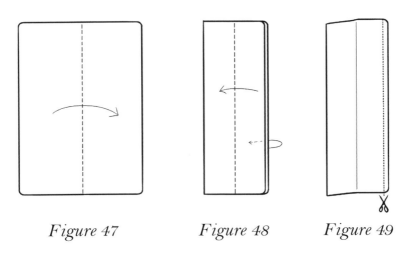

Figure 47   *Figure 48*   *Figure 49*

Now fold a 90-degree dog-ear in both upper corners so the folded part of the top edge falls against the crease; then cut off both dog-ears (figure 50). If the card were unfolded, you would see two uniform upper sides. To cut the bottom, with the card still folded in half, fold both bottom sides so that a diagonal crease runs from the bottom of the crease up to the sides so about 1.5" of the side will be uncut; then cut off both lower corners along this crease (figure 51). This forms two uniform lower sides.

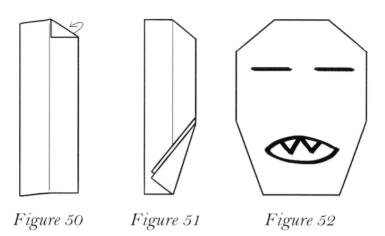

Figure 50 *Figure 51* *Figure 52*

The template is done (see figure 46 again); use it as a template to cut the four other double-blank cards, which you will use for the routine.

On each of those four cards, use a black Sharpie marker to draw a horizontal oval for an open mouth and add two large fangs. Also draw two horizontal lines for the closed eyes. Figure 52 shows the position of these elements.

Now using colored Sharpie markers, color the inside of the mouth red, while leaving the teeth white. Then color the face side (only) of each card, but not the mouth, using four different colors, such as brown, yellow, pink, and orange. I use vertical strokes to color the faces and I try not to obscure the lines for the eyes. It is not necessary to eliminate every speck of white; doing so would make a rather messy product.

Obtain four No. 3 coin envelopes. They are 2.5" x 4.25" in sturdy brown Kraft paper. {*Editor's note: or make your own out of black colored paper so, as you will soon understand, the white backs or color front will visually pop out.*} Use the template to mark them. The envelopes are to be shaped just like the cards, only a little larger. Only the bottom and original parts of the sides remain closed, yet the cards will fit inside easily and remain there when necessary. Cut a 1.25" diameter hole in the center of the face on the plain side of each envelope. When the cards are face up in the envelopes, only the color should show through the circles.

Routine

Begin with the four cards inserted so that only one envelope has a colored face showing (it doesn't matter which one) and the other envelopes have white backs showing through the holes. Position the envelopes so that the one with the face showing through the hole is face up in the second position from the top, while the others are hole side down.

Hold the stack of four envelopes so three of the envelopes are face down (hole side down). Tilt the top ends down and then squeeze the envelopes so all the cards fall out. While the stack of envelopes secretly includes one that is hole side up (the second from the top), the cards will all come out face up.

Turn the stack of envelopes face-up (which leaves the third one from the top hole side down). Ask a participant to name his favorite color. Insert all four cards into the envelopes face down, with the selected card going into the reversed envelope (third from the top). To keep this situation secret, hold the envelopes in a pile with the holes upward and the tops towards you. Squeeze the top envelope open. Insert a card. Slide the envelope to the side, exposing the hole in the second one. Insert another card. Slide both the top and the second envelope to the side to expose just a little of the third envelope without exposing the absence of a hole. Insert the selected card in this envelope. Slide all three away to the side to expose the hole in the fourth envelope and insert the last card. Square up the envelopes.

Elmsley Count the envelopes from hand to hand to show four envelopes with four backs showing through the holes. Then Reverse Count the envelopes from one hand to the other, leaving the last envelope in the hand by itself, to reveal that the envelope is upside down. This is a surprising magical moment.

Replace the three envelopes on the fourth one, turning the three of them face down. Elmsley Count to show that all four envelopes are face down. Turn the packet of envelopes face up and Elmsley Count to show all the envelopes face up with white backs showing through the holes. Reverse Count, leaving the last envelope in the hand by itself to reveal that the selected card is face up inside the envelope. The sudden appearance of the selected color inside is exceptionally magical. Slide the card out a little with the thumb, or shake it out a little, and hand the envelope to a participant for removal. Shake the other cards a bit out of their envelopes and lay them down for examination as well.

Note: if the cards are not totally removed from the envelopes, it is quick and easy to reset the piece. Turn the envelope with the selected card hole side up and locate it in the second position from the top when the other envelopes are hole side down. Otherwise, one must casually pick up and stack the envelopes, getting one of them face down in the third position, and insert the cards face up.

{*Editor's note: these instructions may appear complicated and confusing, but everything will be clear if you make a prototype set of the props and follow along with them in hand. Not only will you understand the various orientations, but you will see how surprising and magical are the two effects.*}

Sources
This is the card and envelope routine by Roy Walton called "Impact," originally in *The Devil's Playthings* and reprinted in *The Complete Walton, Volume One* (London: Lewis Davenport Limited, 1981), pages 23-24. This is an

astonishing card effect and it is my pleasure to remind the reader of it. Walton's original version is superb. My handling modifies Walton's handling a little. More to the point, it changes the props and creates a story to go with them. For an expanded version of the original, see Ed Marlo's "Impact-Collision-Crash" in Jon Racherbaumer's column in the January 1978 issue of *M-U-M* magazine, pages 25-26.

Performance 4.3
Your Mistakes Were Not Made
(Wondering about The Common)

Script

[The performer tables a deck of playing cards.] **With this deck of playing cards and our imaginations, we can do magic. Not just a card trick, but a real and creative miracle of the imagination. And we may discover that it is a miracle we have already experienced. So it will happen again if we allow it to. Let's imagine.**

We have all made mistakes. But what if our universe is only one of an infinite number of universes, so that every event taking place in our universe does not take place in some other universe? Our mistakes in this universe can become, for us, "our mistakes that we did not make" in another universe. Will you be able and willing to imagine such a possibility along with me?

We will be thinking, privately, about three kinds of mistakes we have made as I guide us through the ritual. If you cannot think of an example immediately, one will come to you later today and still will be affected by the ritual.

These cards represent, however abstractly, conditions under which our mistakes occurred. *[The* *performer spreads through the deck and places the Joker on top of a face-down portion.]* **The Joker face up on top of this pile** . . . . *[Three black and three red cards are removed and placed in a face-up pile.]* **A few black cards and a few red cards** . . . . *[The remainder of the deck is spread face down.]* **And a face-down spread of the remaining cards.**

Our first mistake. Think of an example of your behavior when you shirked responsibility. *[The Joker is turned face down and cut into the center of the cards in the pile.]* **Here you were on top as a leader, this Joker, and yet you turned away face down and hid in the center. When did we run away from leadership responsibility, failing to take charge and act? Remember . . . ? I do.**

Our second mistake. Think of an example when you tried to mix together what would not work well together. *[The black and red cards are mixed alternately.]* **Here you were, making a good mix—black, red, black, red, black, red. Recall when we tried to mix people, things, or ideas, but it only made confusion? Remember . . . ? I do.**

Our third mistake. There was an occasion when you were in the middle of a situation that was calm and harmonious. But you were inspired to intervene, creating unnecessary conflict. *[The remaining cards of the deck are reversed haphazardly, face up and face down.]* **Like these cards that face every which way, we made a total mess. Remember . . . ? I do.**

But now let's move into another universe. It is done! This one is exactly like the previous one except we didn't commit those three mistakes. *[The top card of the portion is revealed to be the Joker.]* So here, you and I, the Joker, are back on top where we should have remained! *[The blacks and reds have segregated themselves.]* What we had unwisely mixed is separate again, as they should be! *[The remainder of the deck is spread to reveal them all face down.]* And here, the total chaos we caused has been returned to harmony!

The cards did this trick perfectly. We cannot. We do create new universes in our heads by thoughtfully revising the way we understand our mistakes. But let's not trick ourselves into forgetting our mistakes and failing to learn from them.

Notes on the Routine and Method
The root source of this basic effect is Edward Marlo's "Time Machine," published in issue #7 of *Ibidem* from 1956, which is reprinted in *Ibidem, Volume 1* (no city: Kaufman and Greenberg, 1993), pages 121-123.

My work on this piece was inspired by Ron Bauer's development of Marlo's ideas in *Ed Marlo's Time Machine* (*The Ron Bauer Private Studies Series #16*, Rochester, MI: Electronic Graphic Art Design Studio, 2003). My handling is simplified from Ron's: it requires only a deck of playing cards and a few easy sleights. I will outline my routine below, but because my handling is so indebted to

Ron's and because his book remains for sale, please consult it for the details of the moves and valuable fine points. As with all the Bauer manuscripts, *Ed Marlo's Time Machine* is worth the time and money to study. I have made changes in the handling due to my changes in the presentation.

Unless you are a very good actor, it is best to bring your own mistakes to mind as you ask this of the audience. It is only fair. Besides, you might learn something about yourself. Your attitude will engender a sense of reality about the ritual.

A set-up can provide for smooth handling, but it is far from necessary. Place a Joker (the best card for representing both genders in the audience) about twenty cards from the top. Place three black spot cards on the bottom, with three red spot cards underneath them. Such trivial preparation can be skipped.

Follow Ron Bauer's directions for placing the Ace of Spades face up on the face down portion. In outline: the card is located on top of a packet of about twenty cards. It is face up and has another card hidden face up underneath it. The means for accomplishing this is straightforward and easy.

Bauer handles the red and black cards three separate times to prepare them for the climax: laying out the pile with reds on top of blacks, turning the pile face down and separating it into two piles, and mixing the cards from each pile to apparently alternate the colors. I prefer to combine the second and third steps rather than keep them separated. For the secret move, I use his Method C. In appearance, the reds and blacks are separated into two piles. A card is lifted alternately from each pile and placed together in a new pile between the old ones. Most of these cards are casually shown to the audience as they are alternated.

I have eliminated Bauer's particular use of a face-up court card during the Slop Shuffle, since it adds little to my presentation. But I do use the Slop Shuffle for the remainder of the deck to apparently turn some cards face up and others face down. Bauer has some fine tips on handling of the shuffle convincingly.

Business Card Option

Both the Marlo and Bauer routines employ business cards in addition to playing cards. I found this unnecessary when involving the whole audience in the ritual rather than just a single member of it. For a private showing to one individual, the use of the business cards can still make sense. I would employ three business cards, one being blank on both sides, and follow the Bauer method. I would begin with the business cards and end with them to frame the use of playing cards. Here is the additional script for this handling.

Additional Script When Using Business Cards

[A packet of a few business cards is handed to the participant along with a pen.] **Your need for another universe will be offered up silently. Please write on this card two words: "My Mistakes." They will remain secret, but your writing here certifies them in your mind.** *[The business card is removed and tabled face down.]* **The confession is complete** . . . . *[The script continues as above until the very end.]*

. . . . **Yes, this travel can be real in your life. You wrote "My Mistakes" on this card. Rub it back and forth to remove them. Turn it over.** *[The face of the card is blank.]* **Your mistakes are erased. Welcome to your new universe!**

Sources on the Presentation

I have been entertained by the thinking of some officials that "mistakes were made." The phrase is accompanied by doubt that they were made and by doubt that one was responsible if they were made. On further thinking, I concluded that all of us probably do the same kind of avoidance tactic. How do we cope with our own mistakes? How would we like to cope with them? Such musing led me to imagine a different approach to the "time machine" theme.

Alan Wassilak, on the Shadow-Digest V8 #039 for February 7, 2005, wrote, "According to Theory of the Omniverse, our Universe is only one of many (perhaps

Performances for Chapter 4

only one of an infinite number of) Universes within one of many Multiverses, all of which consist of many Universes, all existing in the same space but on different dimensional planes. Each Universe represents an alternate series of events. Each Multiverse represents related Universes. Every possible event that *could* take place, even if it *didn't* take place in *our* Universe, *does* take place in some *other* Universe. These alternate events are in fact what cause the other Universes to exist within a single Multiverse."

Performance 4.4
Kiddy Trinity
(Wondering about The Common)

Script

[A packet of cards is shown.] There are three special beings in the religion of the child—the Tooth Fairy, the Easter Bunny, and Santa Claus. Are they real? There comes a time when we want assurance, and we can find it. Maybe even as adults.

[The performer shows images on three cards: an empty stocking, a tooth, and an empty basket.] Here are our needs: the empty stocking needs to be filled with exciting and mysterious presents; the hurt and loss of a tooth needs to be removed and our endurance rewarded; and the empty basket needs to be filled with hope of life. Can these needs be met? Yes! But the child must be asleep, be good, and believe.

[The top card is turned face down.] All three of these beings come at night. Let us focus first on the replacement of the tooth. Is there a Tooth Fairy? *[The top card is slid aside to reveal the image of a coin.]* Yes! There is fifty cents. Is there an Easter Bunny? *[The next card is shown with the Easter Eggs on it.]* Yes! There are eggs. And most important of all, is there a Santa Claus? *[The final card is shown to have the wrapped gift]* Yes! There is a present.

Performances for Chapter 4

Is this a trick for children, adults, or both? At best, it is a trick for all of us, even if we are sleepless, not so good, and disbelieve. It becomes a trick for us when we have moved from literalism to disbelief to metaphor.

(Note: the effect is that the empty stocking, bare tooth, and empty basket are magically transformed into a wrapped gift, a coin, and Easter eggs for the basket.)

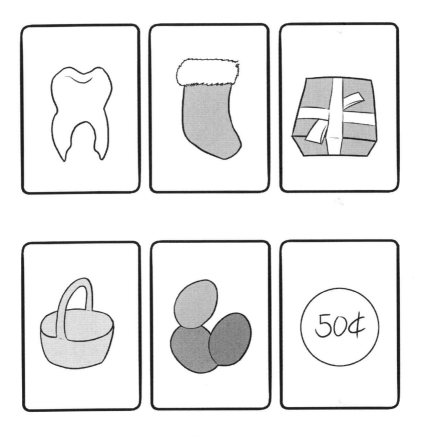

Figure 53

Construction

Obtain two blank-face cards, two double-blank cards, and some Sharpie pens of various colors. On one of the blank-face cards, draw an empty basket. On the other blank-face card, draw a wrapped gift package. On one of the double-blank cards, draw a bare tooth on one side and a fifty-cent coin on the other. On the remaining double-blank card, draw a few brightly colored Easter eggs on one side and an empty Christmas stocking on the other. My drawings are given in figure 53, but remember to color all of them but the tooth.

Routine

Stack the cards face up from the face as follows: stocking, tooth, gift, basket.

Bring forth the packet of cards face down and push over the top card to casually show two backs. Close up the spread and turn the packet face up.

Buckle spread the cards to show the stocking, tooth, and basket. That is, push over the top card, taking it into the right hand, then buckle the bottom card, pushing over the other two cards as one, taking them under the card in the right hand in spread condition, then take the remaining card under those in the right hand in spread condition.

Close up the spread. While appearing to turn over only the top card, Triple Lift the top three cards and turn them face down. (Executing this move end-for-end rather than by side-for-side helps to conceal the minimal sight of the basket, which should be the tooth.)

Push over the top card into the right hand. This reveals the coin card on the face of the cards in the left hand. Push it into the right hand under the first card. This reveals the eggs. Replace the coin card on top of the egg card. Use the face-down card in the right hand to flip all the left-hand cards face down. Two backs are seen. Use the face-down cards in the left hand to flip the single card in the right hand face up, revealing the gift.

Flip the gift-card face down on top of the others. Again, two backs are seen.

Note that a handling for stand-up performance with the packet held chest high is quite feasible.

Discussion

See the book *Flights of Fancy, Leaps of Faith* by Cindy Dell Clark (Chicago: The University of Chicago Press, 1995). What follows are notes from this source.

The Tooth Fairy suggests: loss of body part, pain, limbo period of no tooth, loss of childhood, movement to another stage in development—shift from family to public, school. The fairy is always female. The money is new power to get what you want.

The Easter Bunny suggests: spring, light, heat, and growth—Nature. Children shape this experience more than the other two. The bunny is a cuddly, transitional object, a toy existing between the self and the other. The egg and grass are new life. The child acts, coloring eggs and hunting for eggs.

Santa Claus suggests: Christmas, family bonds, unreciprocated giving, nurturing and generosity. Winter is bleak, but the focus is on excess and indulgence. The adult shapes the holiday for the child. (Holidays may focus and celebrate what is most difficult for them; in this case what has most pressure and conflict is the family.) Santa is grandpa.

Performance 4.5
Money Purse
(Wondering about The Common)

Script

[A folded dollar bill is shown.] **Once upon a time, a dollar bill was folded into a magic money purse. Then it waited . . . and waited . . . for someone to help it do magic.**

[The purse is opened to show a coin through a hole in the bill.] **A mean old man found the folded bill and unfolded it a little. "Ah, a magic purse with a coin inside. If I take the coin out of the purse and spend it, it will come back from the store by magic and I will have gotten what I bought for free." He did not think about the shopkeeper who would lose the money.** *[The performer mimes removing the coin.]* **So the mean man spent the coin.** *[The purse is closed and set aside.]* **The purse remained empty, so he threw it away.**

The magic purse created another coin and waited. *[The purse is opened to show the coin again.]* **A poor widowed woman found the folded bill and opened it up. "Ah, a magic purse with a coin inside. If I take the coin out of the purse and spend it, the purse will create another coin by magic and I will spend them over and over for enough food to last my lifetime."**

She did not think about anyone but herself. *[The performer mimes removing the coin.]* **So the poor widow spent the coin.** *[The purse is closed and set aside.]* **The purse remained empty, so she threw it away.**

The magic purse created another coin and waited. *[The purse is opened to show the coin yet again.]* **Then a little girl found the folded bill and opened it up. "Ah, a purse with a coin inside. Surely, this is magic! Here is just what I need to buy a present for my big sister on her birthday."** *[The coin is removed and given to a participant to keep.]* **So the little girl spent the coin for a gift.** *[The purse is closed and held.]* **She was so pleased by the magical discovery of a coin that helped her help someone else.**

The magic purse no longer waited for someone to help it do magic. It stayed with the little girl quite contentedly. *[The purse is opened to reveal another coin.]* **And she was truly amazed when she found that the magical appearance of the first coin was repeated with a second coin. Such magic! It could be given to someone who needed it.** *[The purse is put away.]* **So the magic purse and the little girl were kept busy doing magic together.**

Notes

This presentation began as intended for a sleight-free routine to accompany Larry White's "Magic Wallet."

This was a make-it-yourself trick he devised for the "Hocus Pocus Cut Out Magic Set" that was an insert in the December 2003 issue of *M-U-M* magazine (Volume 93, Number 7).

I faced this presentational problem: how to vanish a coin prior to its reappearance in the wallet. My solution: remove the requirement by giving the coin to the participant to keep. The rationale: this is the only way that real magic works; something is done for another rather than for oneself.

I thought this idea was sufficient but Larry wanted a story. So I created one. I am bemused by the moralism of my tale. Such surprises are good for me, I suppose. I am not as simply ironic about life as I like to think.

Constructing the Purse

1. Place a new dollar on a surface in front of you with the large "ONE" on the green side visible and right side up. Fold the top long edge down to meet the bottom long edge (figure 54).

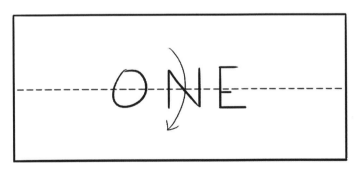

Figure 54

2. Fold the bottom edge of the upper layer only up to the crease just made. Repeat behind (figure 55).

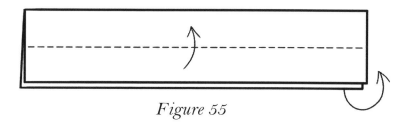
Figure 55

3. Unfold the original crease by bringing the upper two layers to the top, revealing the large "ONE" again (figures 56 and 57).

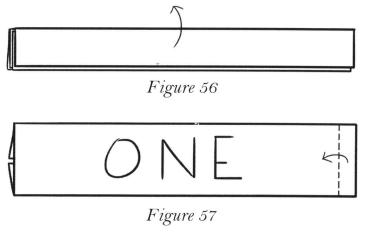
Figure 56

Figure 57

4. Fold the right edge to the left, making a crease along the line forming the white border (figure 58).

Figure 58

5. Turn the bill over, top for bottom (figure 59).

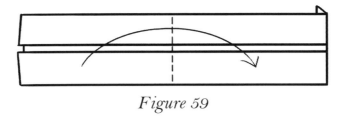

Figure 59

6. Fold the left edge to the right edge, then unfold (figure 60).

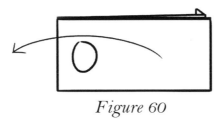

Figure 60

7. Fold the left edge to the center crease. Fold the right edge to meet the left edge at the center crease. Note that the border of the right edge will overlap the left edge (figure 61).

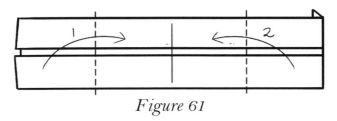

Figure 61

9. Tuck the border area of the right flap inside the left flap (figure 62).

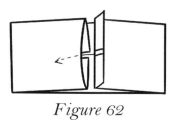

Figure 62

10. Cut a hole, in the upper layer only, in the very center of the left flap. It should be about five-eights of an inch in diameter. A dime is fine as a template (figure 63).

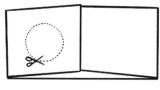

Figure 63

11. Close the right half on top of the left half (figure 64).

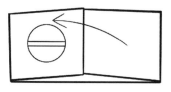

Figure 64

12. The model is completed (figure 65).

Figure 65

Handling the Purse

As you tell the story about the first two people using the purse, simply mime that you remove the coin and spend it with the purse being empty. When the little girl uses the purse, the action is real and the magic unexpected. When the first coin is removed, give it to a member of the audience to keep. As written, the coin should be given to a young woman. If one is not available, change the person in the story so that it is still given to someone who somewhat fits the description—young boy, older boy, young girl, man, or woman. (Indeed, anyone can receive a birthday gift.) It is important that the first coin be given away because this is the whole point of the story. The second one could also be given away, but it need not be since it is consistent with the story that she waits to find someone who especially needs it.

Set-up: load identical quarters face up into each end and join the ends. Close up the purse.

To perform, hold the purse in the left hand with the letters on the green side right side up from the audience view. Rest it on the fingertips with the thumb holding it secure on the top.

Open the purse with the right hand, moving the upper half to your right. Expose the coin in the hole on the left side. Slide it out to the other side. Careful: the coin may be inclined to catch on the inner edge of the right end. To prevent this, squeeze the upper and lower edges of the left side between the left thumb and forefinger, while also pressing down on the right side with the right thumb.

Lift up the coin and show it. Replace on the right side and slide it a little bit into the left side.

The script continues and you will mime that you remove the coin. The handling for this is not intended to fool anyone at all; it simply follows the story line. Pretend to pick up the coin in the right hand and make a fist with it. Actually, slide the coin back fully into the left side. Immediately tilt the left hand so that the inside is hidden and the right end is pointing upward. (This is important for setting up for the final move to load the extra coin.) Press with the left thumb against the left fingers to prevent the extra coin from sliding downward.

Pretend that you hand the coin to the imaginary mean old man. Then open the hand to show it empty. Your hand returns to the purse and close the right end onto the left end.

Repeat all of the above handling with reference to the poor widowed woman: open the purse to show the coin, remove it, replace it, and mime removing it again, ending with the pretense that you hand the coin to the imaginary woman.

Repeat the above handling again, but actually remove the coin and give it to an audience member, duplicating all the movements employed before. As you actually hand over the coin to the person, the right end of the purse is upright. Move the left thumb to the bottom edge and squeeze the left and right edges at the center of the wallet between the right forefinger and thumb. This will open up the hidden compartment and allow the extra coin to fall down into the left end. If necessary, shake the wallet just a little to help it happen. As before, close the purse.

Open the purse and show the coin inside. Remove the coin, return to the purse, close the purse, and put it away.

Performance 4.6
Only a Paper Doll
(Wondering About Our Own Experiences)

Magic grants us symbolic power over life and death by means of hope. Without this celebration of hope, we become demoralized and cannot function. Imagine that theater magic is basically ritual performance with the performer and the audience as partners, each giving the other permission for the ceremony to occur effectively. If so, then some definition should be given to the opening, closing, and to what goes on in between. Why? Because before this ceremony nothing is possible, while after it everything is possible, or at least, *something* is possible—protest, humor, kindness, beauty, and/or illusion.

Magicians tend to open with a flash demonstration and close with a big effect, all witnessing to the great power of the performer. But the opening might be an invocation and the closing a benediction. The opening might not be the usual flash, but an invoking—or this could occur after a flash opening. The ritual then might continue in one or more of the traditional ways: invocation, reassurance, and thanksgiving, followed by the darkness and demand of sacrifice, and then an outcome of glory and hope. On this scheme, one might make the best, most striking trick, not last, but next to last. Finally, the benediction occurs, focusing on the audience and helping it to return to the real world.

The following piece is an example of such a closing benediction. It is a very simple trick. So, too, is the trick by which we live. Both tricks are about our three life and death concerns of connection, movement, and integrity. We experience death as separation from our families and friends, loss of independence, and having our projects and lives being cut short. Life, for us, is the freedom of being able to forge lasting relationships with other people, to choose and control our own behavior, and to grow and develop fully. A trick is about moving from death to life. So a benediction trick aims for a transfer of hope from the theater to everyday life.

Script

We are coming to an end of doing magic together. Our magic—both on stage now and off stage later in our lives—grants us symbolic power over life and death by means of hope. Without this celebration of hope, we become demoralized and cannot function.

[A paper doll is shown.] **But on this return from here to our daily lives, we are reminded of our losses.** *[The legs are torn off.]* **We have suffered loss of movement, becoming unable to go ahead with our plans.** *[The arms are torn off.]* **We have suffered loss of connection, becoming separated from others we have befriended and loved.** *[The head is torn off.]* **And we**

have suffered loss of integrity, not being able to make sense of our lives and ourselves. *[The pieces are folded.]* The losses are real. *[The pieces are wadded into a ball.]* We may believe that we have been crushed to death.

But the heart is left. The beating heart is magic. And it is sufficient. *[The ball is opened.]* So what must be is. *[The ball is opened more.]* The impossible becomes possible. *[The paper is partially unfolded.]* From disillusionment, we enter new illusionment. *[The legs, arms, and head are unfolded.]* Now we can move . . . connect . . . and understand . . . .

[The doll is shown on both sides while being placed over the heart.] Regardless of how we began our time together, may we leave with the magic of hope, empowered to live in the face of death and life. *[The trunk of the doll is wedged into the breast pocket.]* We may be wrinkled and a little crushed here and there, but we live. Go forth in confidence.

Preparation

Obtain two-ply white cocktail napkins. Fold one in half and cut out a very basic image of paper doll that uses the full height of the paper. (See figure 66 for an example.)

Figure 66

After the doll is cut, separate the layers to form two identical dolls. This is easy to do by examining any area of the edge where the napkin's rim has been entirely removed. The layers become nearly visible.

One doll is folded, head in, arms in, and legs in, and then the body is folded in half vertically, again horizontally, and rolled up into a ball. Squeeze the ball tightly to make it very small. Fold the other doll in quarters, using the original creases of the napkin. Set the ball and doll together in a place suitable for easy access. I use a 6.5" by 3.5" white envelope, resting the ball on top of the doll.

Routine

Pull out the paper and unfold the doll, stealing the ball into a finger palm with the right hand. The envelope provides excellent cover for this steal.

Hold the doll by the head with the thumb and forefinger of the left hand. After this display, place the trunk over the ball in the right hand and hold it there with the right thumb. Tear off the legs, one at a time, and place them together under the right thumb. Repeat with the arms, and conclude with the head. Wad all the torn pieces into a very tight ball, meshing the concealed ball with it at the last moment.

Hold the wad between the thumb and forefinger of the left hand. Display the wad with the ball of pieces toward the audience, clearly revealing the emptiness of both hands. Secretly peel off the ball consisting of torn pieces into a finger palm in the right hand as you begin to open the other ball. Open it slowly, showing the legs first, then the arms, and finally the head. Straighten out the figure, smoothing the creases with the free hand.

Hold the doll by the head between the thumb and forefinger of the left hand. Lay the doll on the fingers of the right hand, covering the ball with the head, holding everything in place with the right thumb. Show the doll casually on both sides. Return it to the envelope, dumping the ball inside as well. The doll can be given away as an afterthought or later, if it is requested.

If it is desirable to place the doll in the jacket breast pocket instead, transfer it to the left hand. Open the top of the pocket with the right hand, dropping the ball inside. Tuck just a little portion of the trunk of the body inside, allowing the head, arms and legs to remain visible.

Alternate Routine and Presentations

Instead of beginning with a doll and a concealed ball, one can begin with two identical balls. Carry two (or more) in a pocket. When reaching into it for one, bring out the other concealed. Open up one ball to reveal the paper doll and go through the tearing and restoration.

Presentations for this alternate routine can consider birth (the egg, division of cells, formation of limbs and head, birth), struggle to survive (tearing off of limbs and head), and rebirth (either that of the "born again" variety or any of the nearly universal rebirth themes).

Performance 4.7
The Risk Trick
(Wondering About Our Own Experiences)

Script

Sometimes it is worth your while to take a risk, even over a matter of life and death.

I use these few playing cards to perform "The Risk Trick." It is risky because if it fails, you are going to be unhappy with me. But if we succeed, you will be very happy indeed, and so will I. Who among you is willing to take this risk?

I spoke about risking a matter of life and death. The images on these cards are symbolic. The color and shape of this ace, taken together, represent a heart—a symbol of life. The color and shape of the image on this other ace? The basic shape of the image is that of the heart, but it is turned upside down. It represents, at least, a troubled heart. And the stem? Is it not the handle of a dagger that has been plunged deep into the heart? No wonder the heart is black. The color represents what has happened to it. It is a decaying heart—a symbol of death. Life and death! Aren't you glad you chose to take a risk?

Here's the deal. After mixing the cards, the location of the spade will tell us when you are due for death. If a heart is here in the first position, you have this day to live for sure. But if the spade is here, you are due for death today. If the spade is here in the second position, you have no more than a week to live. In the third position, no more than a month. In the fourth, no more than a year. The fifth, no more than a decade. Sixth, no more than a score of years. And in the seventh position, you have no more than a century to live.

The cards are face down, and I have been mixing them. Maybe the spade is there at the face in first position, or maybe not. I'll continue mixing the cards until you tell me to stop. Risk a decision.

Let's face the revelation together. Do you have more than a day to live? *[A heart is revealed.]* **Yes.** More than a week? *[A heart is revealed.]* **Yes.** More than a month? *[A heart is revealed.]* **Yes.** More than a year? *[A heart is revealed.]* **Yes.** More than a decade? *[A heart is revealed.]* **Yes.** More than a score of years? *[A heart is revealed.]* **Lucky you! The cards reveal that you have a full century . . . . The Ace of Spades is gone. Death has disappeared!** *[The last card, surprisingly, turns out to be a heart, too.]*

So you are not due for death . . . ever. You must be immortal!

Congratulations! Sometimes it is worth your while to take a risk, even over a matter of life and death.

Method

Use the Ace of Hearts, four other spot heart cards (except the Four of Hearts), and a double-face Ace of Spades/Four of Hearts. {*Editor's note: this is the standard pairing on double-face cards manufactured by the United States Playing Card Company.*} The packet is face down with the Ace of Spades at the face and the Ace of Hearts immediately above it. Orient the aces so that the audience will see them right side up.

Casually spread the packet face down, concealing the bottom, double-faced card. Close up the spread. Turn the packet face up and spread the cards casually to show a bunch of heart cards below the Ace of Spades. Close the spread. Lift off the Ace of Spades and use it to point to the Ace of Hearts while talking about the symbolism of the latter. Replace the Ace of Spades and talk about how it symbolizes death.

Show the cards by using the Norm Osborne Cover Up Count to reveal seven cards. In brief: hold the packet face up in the left hand. Shove the Ace of Spades over to the right with the left thumb. Take it into the right hand at the upper right corner, the right forefinger and second finger on top, the right thumb underneath. Tilt your hand forward toward the audience to show the Ace. Tilt your left hand back toward you and place the card in the right hand on the bottom of the packet, Ace side forward. (This handling conceals the heart card on the other side of the

Ace.) Perform this action as you explain the meaning of the first position.

As you discuss the meaning of each of the other positions, you will repeat those actions exactly as before. That is, remove a heart card from the face-up packet, tilt the card forward to show the face while tilting the left hand cards back, and return the card face-forward to the bottom of the packet. You will do this for each of the heart cards in the packet, and you will also do it with the Four of Hearts, the Ace side of which will remain hidden, just as the Four side remained hidden before. Stop after displaying the Four of Hearts, and turn the packet face down. You have displayed six cards as seven without counting them. The Ace of Spades is face up at the bottom.

Transfer the packet to the right hand and hold it from above at the ends for a Side Glide. (A regular Glide may be used instead.) Glide the bottom card and then transfer the cards one at a time apparently from the bottom to the top until the participant calls stop. Note that this transferring of cards, ostensibly to lose the Ace of Spades, apparently shows all the backs of them. *{Editor's note: instead of this Glide procedure one can Overhand Shuffle the packet by milking the top and bottom card off together, repeatedly, as needed. This will keep the double-faced card at the bottom. However to keep it from flashing, one must do so in a tight and controlled way.}*

For the sequence of revelations, turn the packet face up, point to the heart card on the face, and Reverse Count the cards (slowly and one by one), to show they are all hearts. Spread the packet casually, close it, and put it away.

Note
Here is an optional handling for the sequence of revelations. Tilt the packet vertically so that the bottom card faces the audience. Deal it off the face and place it on back, which hides the Ace of Spades. Repeat this movement for the remaining cards, gradually lowering the packet down so backs are seen. Casually spread the face-down cards so only backs are seen, then turn the packet face up and Reverse Count the cards. Spread the face-up packet again, close it and put it away.

Sources
The brilliant idea of defining an absent card as a signal of immortality belongs to Gaetan Bloom. His routine is titled "Immortal" and can be viewed on *Tales From the Planet of Bloom, Volume 2* (Rancho Cordova, CA: A-1 Magical Media, 1999). Inspired by Bloom's routine, Christian Chelman published "The Immortal" in *Capricornian Tales: The Magic of Christian Chelman* (Tahoma, CA: L & L Publishing, 1993), pages 77-80.

For another use of this plot, see my "Immortal" in *Life, Death & Other Card Tricks* (Seattle: Hermetic Press, 2000), pages 294-300.

The idea of counting a double-faced card twice belongs to Norm Osborn. See *Unlimited*, second edition, by Norm Osborn and Edward Marlo, revised and edited by Jon Racherbaumer (no city: 1983).

The symbolism developed for the Ace of Spades is my contribution.

Performance 4.8
Synchronicity Schtick
[Wondering About Our Own Performances]

This is a presentation and routine for the Pom Pom Prayer Stick, an apparatus invented by Louis S. Histed and marketed by Kovari in a version that can be pulled apart at the center and put together again. Figure 67 shows the prop.

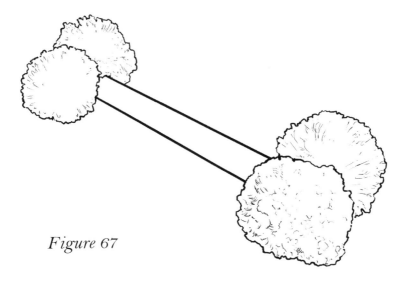

Figure 67

Script

[Please note: the numbers and letters in brackets refers to the specific moves that will be explained in the "Routine" section below.]

The Sense of Wonder

This Sanctuary for Synchronicity allows us to worship our experience of meaningful coincidence. And this relic in the very center of our space and time retells of the tale of our origins—the dialogue between our Founder and a Disbeliever.

    Founder showed a stick with four pom poms and spoke, "This is a symbol of both causality and a-causality. Causality is that kind of connection that commonsense believes in. These two pom poms are connected by a long string, which symbolizes two events connected by a string of events. The other two pom poms are connected by a short string of events. But these two pom poms on top are not connected by any string, nor are these two on the bottom. Their connection is a-causal. See? *[Move 1a]* One moves the other even though there is no causal connection whatsoever." *[Move 1b]*

    Disbeliever was not about to believe. Disbeliever said, "That is nonsense. There is only the connection of causality. In this case, you just refuse to see it. This pom pom is connected by a causal string that runs up to the stick and through it over to the other pom pom. This is perfectly obvious and you are manufacturing an unnecessary mystery."

    Founder responded, "How could that be? *[Move 2a]* These two pom poms have their own long chain of events, as this long string reveals. *[Move 2b]* Yet these two bottom pom poms are connected. *[Move 2c]*

And now you see that these other two pom poms are connected by their own long chain of events. Each set is connected by causality, but between the sets, there is the a-causality of synchronicity. *[Move 2d]* This is a mystery, and you cannot explain it."

Disbeliever was unhappily mystified. "I do not allow any connection between these two pom poms whatsoever. *[Move 3a]* See what I have revealed! *[Move 3b&c]* There is a causal relationship between these two pom poms and between these two pom poms, but no connection whatsoever between the top pom poms or the bottom pom poms. There is no mystery, only causality. Look again. *[Move 4a]* Inside this stick there is nothing—no connections, causal or a-causal. There is no mystery inside the stick and no mystery outside. *[Move 4b]* There is only causality and the nonsense of your belief."

Founder was moved to have pity on Disbeliever. So he instructed him, "Everything is related to everything. But this harmonious complexity is beyond your vision. *[Move 5a&b]* You see only what you can bear to see. I will show you how to increase your seeing of relationship. Do not try to see all four of these pom poms as related to each other. That is too difficult for you. Begin by trying to see just this one pom pom connected to the others. *[Move 5cde]* See it connected to this one, to this one, too, and also connected to this one? *[Move 5fgh]* Once you are able

The Sense of Wonder

to see this, you can see both causality and a-causality. Both kinds of connection are real. And when you can see both as real you will soon be able to see a new and marvelous complexity of relationship. *[Move 6]* **Look. Everything is connected to everything!**

And so it is for we who worship in the Sanctuary of Synchronicity.

Routine

Consider the four pom poms to be Top Left (TL), Bottom Left (BL), Top Right (TR), and Bottom Right (BR). Begin with BR extended all the way down. Grasp the stick in the middle with the left hand.

Move 1: a. Pull the BL down with the free right hand. b. Pull the BR down so you are back to where you began. This suggests a mystery.

Move 2: a. Pull the TR up and let the TR and BR drop back down. b. Pull the BL down. c. Pull the TL up and let the TL and BL drop back down. d. Pull the BR back down. This deepens the mystery.

Move 3: a. Hold onto the BR and with the same hand grab the BL as well and pull them down gently so that both are fully extended. b. Pull the TL up and let the TL and BL drop back down. c. Repeat this action with the TR and BR. The mystery has been disrupted.

Move 4: a. Hold the stick in both hands and pull it apart at the center. b. Pause and replace the two parts.

The disruption is more complete, but the former mystery is deepened.

Move 5: a. Grasp the stick again with the left hand; pull the TL up and let the TL and BL drop back down. b. Repeat this action with the TR and BR. c. Grab the BR with the free right hand and touch the BL with it; turn the stick to a vertical position so that the right end is on top. d. Raise the BR to touch the TL. e. Continue moving it upward and touch it to the TR (this procedure reconnects the strings); restore the stick to the usual horizontal position. f. Pull the TR up and let the TR and BR drop back down. g. Pull the BL down. h. Pull the TL up and let the TL and BL drop back down. The disruption has been surmounted and the mystery deepened as well.

Move 6. Pull the TL up and let the TL and BL drop back down. Pull the TR up and let the TR and BR drop back down. Repeat these moves at a more rapid pace. The mystery is deepened again for a conclusion.

Performance 4.9
Aching Heart Illusion
[Wondering About Our Own Performances]

Script

"Illusion" means to be "in play." Remember the saying, "All work and no play makes Jack a dull boy?" It is also the case that "All play and no work makes no Jack." Illusion is that form of play we cannot live happily without or safely with. *[A deck of playing cards is spread face up.]* Here is a story about it, "The Aching Heart Illusion." *[The performer points to a few heart cards.]* Hearts, like these, will represent the world of play. *[The performer separates the spread into two portions with spade cards at the face of each.]* And spades, like these, will illustrate the world of work. *[The portions are placed face-to-face with the top portion injogged. The top portion is raised and lowered so the faces of both portions are seen again as showing spades.]* Work, work, work.

[The upper portion is slid over the lower and then jogged again, revealing the King of Hearts.] There was a person who wandered throughout the world of work, a MAN WITH AN ACHING HEART. He was looking for fulfillment and happiness, but never came to it. Finally one day he sat down exhausted underneath a great tree. *[The upper portion is raised to reveal the Three*

of Hearts.] **What he did not know is that this was a magic tree, the** TREE OF HEARTFELT ILLUSION. **Whatever one hopes or fears when seated underneath it immediately appears.**

As he rested, he thought to himself, "What a beautiful spot this is. I wish I had a home here." Instantly before his eyes a lovely home appeared. Surprised and delighted, he thought further, "If only I had a partner to be here with me, then my happiness would be complete." A beautiful woman appeared calling him "husband" and beckoning to him. "Well, first, I am hungry," he thought. "I wish there was food to eat." Immediately a banquet table appeared covered with every wonderful kind of food and drink, main courses, pastries and sweets of every variety. The man sat down and began to feed himself hungrily.

[The two portions are placed back face-to-face and outjogged.] **Finishing the meal, the** MAN WITH AN ACHING HEART **sat back down to lean against the** TREE OF HEARTFELT ILLUSION **and began to reflect, "How amazing it is that everything I wish has come true. There is some mysterious force about this tree. I wonder if there is a demon who lives in it." No sooner did he think this than a great demon appeared. "Oh my," he thought, "this demon will probably eat everything up." That is just what it did. It ate up the house, the wife, and the food.** *[The upper portion is slid*

over the lower and then jogged again, revealing a spade card.] **It also ate up the** Man with an Aching Heart. *[The upper portion is raised to reveal a spade card.]* **And it even ate up the** Tree of Heartfelt Illusion **itself!** *[Both portions are turned face up and the face cards spread to reveal only spade cards.]* **Nothing remained but the world of work.**

[The pack is reassembled face down.] **What happens next is a great mystery.** *[The face down pack is spread to reveal the King of Hearts face up.]* **But some say that the** Man with an Aching Heart **will reappear . . .** *[The King of Hearts is cut to the top, and with a quick gesture of the hand, separates itself and the Three of Hearts from the deck]* **. . . and that he will find again the** Tree of Heartfelt Illusion. **If so, will the outcome differ?**

Sources

I found this story from the Hindu tradition in the anthology *Stories of the Spirit, Stories of the Heart*, edited by Christina Feldman and Jack Kornfield (New York: HarperCollins, Publishers, 1991), pages 292-293. I have modified the original text by strengthening the focus on illusion, shortening the text, and adding the puns and the disappearance of the tree.

Ed Marlo's "Double Vanish and Recovery" first appeared in Martin Gardner's *Cut the Cards* (reprinted in *Martin Gardner Presents*, Silver Spring, MD: Kaufman and Greenberg, 1993), pages 379-397; Marlo's routine is on pages 383-384. Marlo's own versions, "Marlo's Double Vanish and Recovery" and "Casanova Card Trick," appeared in his *Deck Deception* (Chicago: Magic, Inc., 1942). See both sources for details of the three different versions.

The basic effect is this: when two halves of the deck are faced, the face cards disappear; then one appears face up, and it is used to find the other. I have changed the handling somewhat so that the two cards first appear and then disappear on the faces of the two packets. Inserting the King to find the Three is too slow a process for my presentation, so a simple flourish is substituted. A change in the stack allows the faces of the packets to be shown freely.

My original version for telling this tale in a packet trick employed the specially printed Tree of Hearts card and blank cards.

For another use of the Double Vanish and Recovery, see my routine "Maya" in *The Magic of Celebrating Illusion* (Sherman, TX: Theory and Art of Magic Press, 2013), pages 234-237.

Handling

Cut the Three of Hearts to the face of the deck. Locate the King of Hearts and place it face-to-face with the Three. Place two spade spot cards at the face of the deck. Either place another two spade spot cards together in the center of the deck or situate them there openly during the following spread at the beginning of the performance.

In performance, spread the cards face up, concealing the Three and face-down King. Point to a few heart cards. Locate (or look for and relocate) two spade spot cards together near the middle of the deck. Point to them and to the spade card at the face. Cut the deck so the two spade cards in the center become the face cards of one half of the deck in the left hand. Gesture with the portions so that the appearance of the spades at the faces is clear and noted. Turn the other half in the right hand face down and place it highly injogged on top of the face-up portion.

While talking, do a Thumb Count to get a thumb break above three cards in the upper packet. Raise the upper packet so the audience can see the face of both packets again, spade spot cards being shown. Lower the upper packet to the face of the other packet and slide it forward. Drop the three cards onto the lower packet, keeping a break under them with the left little finger, and slide the upper packet back again. This exposes the King on the face of the lower packet. Raise the upper packet to expose the Three.

Lower the upper packet and slide it forward, picking up the three cards at the face of the lower packet. Slide the upper packet back again. This exposes a spade spot card. Maneuver the hand about the upper packet so that it is face up in the palm-up hand. Use the thumbs to push over the face card of each packet, showing two spade cards at their faces.

Place the left packet on top of the right packet and turn the deck face down. Fan or spread the cards to reveal the face-up King. Cut the deck to bring the King to the top. Holding the deck with the thumb on top and the fingers underneath, toss it into the other hand, retaining the top and bottom cards in the hand. Twist the wrist to reveal the face-down card to be the Three.

The Sense of Wonder

Performance 4.10
Upside Down Man
[Wondering About Our Audience's Experience of Wonder]

The prop is a human figure suspended in a frame (see figure 68). It may be made out of paper or some other flexible material.

In performance, holding the prop right side up, the participant encloses each arm in the prop between the thumb and forefinger of each hand, thus allowing the arms to revolve freely, but not to escape the hold. The performer manipulates the prop and the figure is turned upside down. With a larger prop, two participants can be used, each one holding onto an arm, perhaps even with their fists. I provide two presentations.

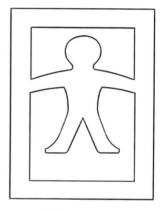

Figure 68

{*Editor's note: as with so many of Bob Neale's routines, this piece is a great playground for further thought and other ideas. For instance, an alternate presentation could revolve around the important lessons of "The Hanging Man" card in the tarot deck. Have fun!*}

Presentation 1: The Upside Down Artist

Have you ever noticed how we tilt our heads sideways when we question something we have heard or seen? Our body automatically helps us seek an alternative perspective.

    Visual artists go further. *[The performer does what he says.]* **To get a fresh view of what is in front of them, they do this: turn around, spread the legs, bend over with hands on knees, and look out through the legs.** *[Perform the action with either your back or your side to the audience.]* **Like this. Try it sometime. Perhaps in private? It works! Everything looks quite different.**

    [Show the prop.] **Here is my portrait, so very nicely framed, created in memory of the Upside Down Artist who carried his mission to an extreme. To curtail his bad habit, we need someone to be his friend, keeping him upright by holding his arms. Enclose each arm between your thumb and forefinger. Like this. Fine. You are holding him just right. It means that he cannot turn from side to side or up to down or any way at all.**

    I will be his friend, too, reminding him of the danger. Maybe we will keep him upright. Or maybe not. Do not let go, even though he may struggle. Okay:

> An artist was filled with ambition
> To see the real fact of his vision.

**To prove what he said
He stood on his head
And drew the new view with precision.**

He is upside down again! Artists can be odd. But we might try it ourselves now and then.

[*An alternate limerick:*

> *There once was an artist I knew*
> *Who sought to enhance his own view.*
> *He stood on his head*
> *Until he was dead.*
> *By then he'd seen something quite new.*]

Method

As stated at the outset, the prop may be cut from paper or index card stock. For totally impromptu use, fold a sheet of copy paper in half and tear out two sections to form the prop. For more enduring material, use the very light and flexible vinyl material from file folders, foam material such as Foamtastic that is sold in Michaels and other craft stores, or Tyvek paper (known to magicians as "no tear paper," which is obtainable on the Internet.)

Basically, the prop is turned inside out; all the edges are moved through either one of the holes from one side to the other side. The bigger the hole, the easier the manipulation. With the human figure model, be sure to push all the edges through the larger hole. Remember to require the participant to allow the arms to revolve.

Here is the procedure in brief, with the participant facing you and his thumbs and forefingers extending around the arms toward you: 1) pull the upper short edge toward you and down and away from you through the large hole, the man turning upside down, 2) allow and encourage both long edges to follow into and away from you through the hole as well, and 3) allow and encourage the remaining lower short edge to do the same. The prop has been both turned from one face to the other and upside down.

For the following presentation, make a simple smile on both sides of the head.

Presentation 2: The Upside Down Performer

[The prop is shown.] **Here is the Upside Down Man. To experience his street act, we need someone to keep him upright by holding his arms. Enclose each arm between your thumb and forefinger. Like this. Fine. You are holding him just right. It means that he cannot turn from side to side or up to down or any way at all. Even so, see the smile on his face. He likes you!**

He performs his trick while reciting a limerick. I'll say it for him and hope that his trick occurs. Ready for the impossible? Okay:

> There once was a man who did tricks
> With arms that were held tightly fixed.
> He turned upside down
> A smile turn'd frown
> His feet were then bowed for his tips.

He is upside down! And he is frowning now for you to let go so he can gather tips with the hands.

Sources

> "You are old, Father William," the young man said,
> "And your hair has become very white;
> And yet you incessantly stand on your head—
> Do you think, at your age, it is right?"

These are the opening lines to the poem Alice recites to the Caterpillar in Lewis Carroll's *Alice's Adventures in Wonderland*. I suspect that Lewis Carroll thought it was right to stand on your head at any age, and so do I. For the full poem, see *The Annotated Alice*, with an introduction and notes by Martin Gardner (New York: New American Library, 1960), pages 70-71.

This is a version of my topological effect, "Get Out of Jail Free" in my book with David Parr, *The Magic Mirror* (Seattle: Hermetic Press, 2002), pages 131-134. For yet another version, see "To the Other Side of No" in *This is Not a Book* (Seattle: Hermetic Press, 2008), pages 151-159. And for still another version, see "Reversal of

Performances for Chapter 4

Fortune" in *Magic Matters* (Sherman, TX: Theory and Art of Magic Press, 2009), pages 228-230. The previous effects focus on a seemingly impossible movement from one face to the other, while this one presents the impossible movement from top to bottom.

Performance 4.11
Jack's Veto
[Wondering About Our Audience's Experience of Wonder]

Script

Imagine that you have had a dream. You find yourself in a most impressive oval office, seated in front of flags, behind your desk, and looking across it and upward at a most august old man with a long, white beard. He holds pieces of stone with writing on them. He is me in disguise.

[Heart spot cards are removed from the deck and displayed.] **"I have shattered these, my commandments, in a fit of rage.** *[The cards are placed face down on the table and scattered about.]* **But you are my most favored son. So I'll give you a line-item veto . . . only one. Mix them up here on your desk. Now touch any four commandments you might want to veto. Use your thumbs and forefingers. I will touch three of these that you must keep. Let's see what they are . . . . Number three, 'You shall not take the name of the Lord your god in vain,' number six, 'you shall not kill,' and number eight, 'you shall not steal.'"** *[Proceed to reveal and read six more as described below.]*

"All nine of these commandments you must keep. But you are my most favored son. One

commandment remains. Already, I have removed it from the ten. *[The card is turned only so that the spectator can see it.]* **I will turn it over now, but surely you know which one it is. Can you recite it aloud? Yes, it is the seventh commandment, 'You shall not commit adultery.'"**

[The card is shown to the audience. It is the Jack of Hearts.] **"Be grateful and prosper in your office, Jack."**

Simple Method

Use the Ace through Ten of Hearts, but substitute a Jack of Hearts for the Seven, the commandment about adultery. Mark the back of the Jack.

Learn the following commandments (or display a list for use by you and your audience):

1. You shall have no other gods before me.
2. You shall not make yourself a graven image.
3. You shall not take the name of the Lord your God in vain.
4. Remember the Sabbath day, to keep it holy.
5. Honor your father and your mother.
6. You shall not kill.
7. You shall not commit adultery.
8. You shall not steal.
9. You shall not bear false witness against your neighbor.
10. You shall not covet your neighbor's house.

Process

Remove the required hearts in any order with the Jack at the back of the face-up packet.

Keeping the Jack concealed at the back, spread the face-up packet casually to reveal the hearts. (Or don't bother to show the cards at all.)

Allow the participant to mix the cards on the table before each of the three elimination processes.

The participant extends the thumbs and forefingers in order to touch four cards; the performer turns three of them face up, defines them, and sets them aside. Seven cards remain. The performer touches four cards and the participant turns three of them face up. The performer defines them and sets them aside. Four cards remain. The participant touches these four cards, and the performer eliminates three of them, turning them face up, defining them, and setting them aside.

To end with the Jack, simply avoid selecting it yourself throughout the selection process. That is, do not remove it as one of the three if the participant selects it, and do not make it one of the four you select.

Turn the remaining card face up, showing it to the participant only. He sees the Jack of Hearts and can try to state the commandment. Show the Jack to the audience.

Advanced Method

Remove the thirteen hearts. Hold the packet face up. Cut the Seven to the back. Upjog the three face cards and place them to the back, being sure that the Jack is situated next to the Seven.

Spread the packet face up so that the audience can see them. As you come to the last four cards, spread them widely. Now appear to remove and discard the picture cards, but actually remove the King, Queen and Seven, leaving the Jack at the back of the deck. That is, perform Howard Lyon's "Slipduc." What happens during this move is that while you separate the picture cards from the others and turn both groups face down, the Jack and the Seven are switched. In brief: spread the three picture cards and the Seven widely. The thumbs are on the faces and the fingers on the backs. The left thumb rests on the face of the Seven. The right fingers press against the back of the Jack. As you twist the wrists to turn the cards face down, separate them so that the Seven is stolen with the two picture cards and the Jack is stolen with the number cards. All the cards have been turned face down. This sleight is easy and natural. The larger movement hides the smaller one. Place the packet of three cards face down on the deck and overhand shuffle the remainder.

While showing the cards in the spread, make an opening comment as follows, "These number cards are abstractions, but we will give them a very concrete meaning, while these picture cards will come into play more concretely later on."

Proceed from the very beginning of the presentation for the first routine and perform the routine as written.

Source

This is one of my versions of "Sole Survivor." It uses one of my several variations on the P-A-T-E-O Force by Roy Baker. Howard Lyon's "Slipduc" appeared in *Ibidem #9*, which is reprinted in *Ibidem, Volume 1* (no city: Kaufman and Greenberg, 1993), page 181.

Performance 4.12
Twin Towers
[Wondering About Our Audience's Experience of Wonder]

Editor's Preface
Bob sent me this performance idea in an email dated September 17, 2001—that is, six days after the World Trade Center was destroyed in a terrorist attack, the event we now call "9/11." This performance, this idea, is a perfect example of a piece that focuses on the audience's experience of wonder. But even more, I cannot think of a better, more fitting way to conclude this book in which the experience of wonder means respect. That is, really seeing and acknowledging something or someone in its being.

Here is the context in which Bob sent this piece to me. Three days after the event, Bob sent me a few short magical tales as "Responses." I wrote back, thanking him for offering artistic responses, rather than the hyper-intellectual yet thoughtless reactions I was hearing from some of my academic colleagues and the talking heads on television. I said to Bob that, as a philosopher, I was trying for a different response: actually feeling my sadness and shock, really looking at people in the eyes, touching them or hugging them, and supporting our students who lost family or friends. (Indeed, my college at the time—Muhlenberg College—is just 90 minutes from Manhattan.)

Here, then, was Bob's reply (in part): "Larry, you did as my wife did: touch people and hug them. But please be kind to those of us who rely—actually *over-rely*—on other strengths. We use what we can, but oh boy, how not to be stupid? I suspect only by not saying anything. Me? I have to continue responding in the world of magic. Here is one more response. Love, Bob."

Here is what immediately followed in the email.

Twin Towers

Within a day after the tragedy, my recent preoccupation with burning tea bags gave rise to a realization that two tea bags could be opened up and emptied, and their tubes placed side-by-side and burned. For me, the tubes were the Two Towers.

But what could I say? No words came. Then I recalled the observation by a poet who survived an earlier event in the last century. In response to a discussion about the arts and the Holocaust, he said that one must write as if keeping silent. Yes, but I could not write that well. So I must actually keep silent.

Such silence requires a ceremony. So I imagined a table on which resided two large lit candles in their candlesticks and two smaller tables on opposite sides filled with small votive candles. In my imagination, the celebrant behind the table would open up and balance the two tubes on the table and then light them, each with one of the large candle flames. The tubes would burn and ashes ascend and descend. The participants would stand and proceed in two orderly lines to the small tables, pick up a votive candle, light it from one of the large candles, place it on a large table where the tubes had been, and return to their seats. The celebrant would blow out the flames of the large candles to conclude the ceremony.

Only in my imagination did this happen. I hope that this amounts to something, however so very little.

Editor's Note on Sources

It turns out that there were important roots behind Bob's vision. Previously, Bob had been exploring different versions of the old magic effect known by various titles such as "Red Ash" or "Phoenix Ashes." It appears as "Ashes of the Phoenix" in *Scarne's Magic Tricks* (Mineola, NY: Dover Publications, Inc., 2003), pages 192-193. In the classic effect, a piece of red tissue paper is lit on fire in the magician's hand. As it burns down, the magician releases what is left, and it floats up in the air and then slowly floats down as ashes. The performer then reaches into the falling ashes and pulls out the strip of tissue paper, fully restored.

After working with Karl Norman's routine "The Polish Rocket," which is included in his booklet, *Here's How: The Close-Up Magic of Karl Norman* (Washington,

D.C.: Collector's Workshop, 1985, page 24), Bob had been informed by various people on Electronic Grimoire about the then-recent development of using paper from a tea bag for the effect. Also, Jeff Hass told him about Andrew Mayne's version of the tea bag approach. Andrew's routine is titled "Tea Ceremony," and it was published in *Mad Mojo* (no city: self-published, 1998), pages 23-26.

So this was all in the background of Bob's insight on the day after September 11, 2001, that two tea bags could be opened up, placed next to each other, and lit on fire (with floating ashes) as a symbol of the Twin Towers.

If you are inclined to try to perform this memorial ritual, Bob's experimentation has yielded some helpful insights about the materials. Bob says:

> Twining's Earl Gray tea bags, or others of this brand, works well. So also does the bag from Bigelow's Lemon Lift. Despite several opinions I have heard to the contrary, some other brands do not work. For example, several varieties of Lipton tea bags that I have tried leave no ash to rise. Needless to say, explore only flow-through bags!
>
> I prefer the use of tea bags rather than tissue paper since they are already formed into perfect tubes and easily available. Carefully remove the staple, straighten out the long rectangle and dump out the tea. (A staple remover works well and prevents damaging the

Performances for Chapter 4

fingernails.) The flattened tube is about 1.5" wide and 6" long. It is already folded in one long direction with the two creases going from open end to open end. Fold it in opposite long direction, the two new creases also going from open end to open end, so that a square tube is formed.

Bob's exploration of the ashes effect did not stop with "Twin Towers." He has created at least two other presentations, which currently remain unpublished.

Bibliography

Books

Anonymous, *The Devil of a Bar & Pub*. Orlando, FL: Leaping Lizards Publishing Company, 2007.

Anonymous. *Webster's New International Dictionary, Second Edition*, Unabridged. Springfield, MA: G. & G. Merriam Company, 1955.

Beaumont, Charles. "The Magic Man." *The Magic Man and Other Science-Fantasy Stories*. Greenwich, CT: Fawcett Publications, 1965, pages 81-102.

Benjamin, Walter. "The Storyteller: Reflections on the Works of Nikolai Leskov." *Illuminations: Essays and Reflections*, New York: Schocken Books, 1969, pages 83-110.

Borges, Jorge Luis. "The End." *Ficciones*. New York: Alfred A. Knopf, 1993, pages 127-130.

-------. "The Flower of Coleridge," *Borges: A Reader*. Emir Rodriguez Monegal and Alastair Reid (translators). New York: E. P. Dutton, 1981, pages 163-165.

Burgin, Richard (editor). *Conversations with Jorge Luis Borges.* Jackson, MS: University Press of Mississippi, 1998.

Carroll, Lewis. *The Annotated Alice.* Martin Gardner (introduction and notes). New York: New American Library, 1960.

Cervon, Bruce. *The Black and White Trick and Other Assorted Mysteries.* Tahoma, CA: L & L Publishing, 1989.

Chesteron, Gilbert Keith. *Orthodoxy.* London: Bodley Head, 1949.

-------. *Tremendous Trifles.* New York: Dodd, Mead and Company, 1920.

Clark, Cindy Dell. *Flights of Fancy, Leaps of Faith.* Chicago: The University of Chicago Press, 1995.

Conan Doyle, Arthur. "A Study in Scarlet," in *Sherlock Holmes: The Complete Novels and Stories, Volume 1,* New York: Bantam Books, 1986, pages 1-103.

Crossan, John Dominic. *Raid on the Articulate.* New York: Harper & Row, Publishers, 1976.

Feldman, Christina & Jack Kornfield (editors). *Stories of the Spirit, Stories of the Heart.* New York: HarperCollins Publishers, 1991.

Feynman, Richard P. *The Feynman Lectures on Physics, Volume 1.* Reading, MA: Addison-Wesley, 1963, pages 3-6.

-------. *"What Do You Care What Other People Think?": Further Adventures of a Curious Character.* New York: W. W. Norton and Company, Inc., 1988.

Fulghum, Robert. *True Love: Stories Told to and by Robert Fulghum.* New York: HarperCollins Publishers, 1997.

Fulves, Karl. *Robert Neale's Trapdoor Card.* Teaneck, NJ: Karl Fulves, 1983.

Gardner, John. *N. E. A. Journal.* Volume 46, February, 1957.

Gardner, Martin. *Mathematics, Magic and Mystery.* Mineola, NY: Dover Publications, Inc., 1956.

-------. "Order and Surprise." *Order and Surprise.* Buffalo NY: Prometheus Books, 1983, pages 57-67.

-------. "Science vs. Beauty," in *The Skeptical Inquirer,* Volume 19, Number 2, March-April 1995, pages 14-16, 55.

-------. "Surprise" in *The Night is Large: Collected Essays 1938-1995.* New York: St. Martin's Press, 1996, pages 551-565.

-------. *Wheels, Life and Other Mathematical Amusements.* New York: W. H. Freeman and Company, 1983.

Garrison, Garrison. *Augury.* Athens, GA: University of Georgia Press, 1991.

Geertz, Clifford. "Religion as a Cultural System." *Anthropological Approaches to the Study of Religion*, Michael Banton (editor). London: Tavistock Publications, 1965, pages 1-46.

Giobbi, Roberto. *Card College, Volume 2.* Richard Hatch (translator). Seattle: Hermetic Press, 1996.

Goldstein, Phil. *Redivider: Adventures with a Fascinating Principle.* Seattle: Hermetic Press, 2002.

Guiley Rosemary Ellen. *The Encyclopedia of Witches & Witchcraft, Second Edition.* New York: Facts On File, Inc., 1989.

Halberstam, Yitta & Judith Leventhal. *Small Miracles: Extraordinary Coincidences from Everyday Life.* Holbrook, MA: Adams Media Corporation, 1997.

Harris, Paul. *The Art of Astonishment, Book 1.* Rancho Cordova, CA: A-1 Multimedia, 1996.

Hitchens, Christopher. *The Missionary Position: Mother Theresa in Theory and Practice.* London: Verso Books, 1995.

Hudson, Charles M. "Norman Gilbreath's Second Principle." *The Linking Ring*, Volume 46, Number 8, August 1996, pages 63-69.

James, Stewart. *Stewart James In Print: The First Fifty Years*. P. Howard Lyons and Allan Slaight (editors). Toronto: Jogestja Ltd., 1989.

James, William. "Sentimentality of Rationality." *The Will to Believe and Other Essays in Popular Philosophy*. Mineola, NY: Dover Publications, 1956, pages 63-110.

Jenkyns, Richard. "Child's Play" in *The New York Review*, July 17, 1997, pages 42-44.

Kazantzakis, Nikos. *Zorba the Greek*. New York: Simon & Schuster, 1965.

Keen, Sam. *Apology for Wonder*. New York: Harper & Row, Publishers, 1969.

Kenyon, Jane. *Collected Poems*. Graywolf Press, Saint Paul, Minnesota, 1996.

Lawrence, D. H. *The Later D. H. Lawrence*. New York: Alfred A. Knopf, 1959.

Marcel, Gabriel. *Metaphysical Journal*. Chicago: Henry Regnery Co., 1952.

Marlo, Edward. *Deck Deception*. Chicago: Magic, Inc., 1942.

Maven, Max. "Ennui Are The World." *MAGIC Magazine*, Volume 1, Number 3, November 1991, page 15.

Millhauser, Stephen. "The Barnum Museum." *The Barnum Museum*. Normal, IL: Dalkey Archive Press, 1997, pages 89-90.

Neale, Robert E. *Life, Death & Other Card Tricks*. Seattle: Hermetic Press, 2000.

-------. *The Magic of Celebrating Illusion*. Sherman, TX: Theory and Art of Magic Press, 2013.

-------. *Three Magic Arrows*. Leeds, MA: self-published, 1991.

Neale, Robert E. and David Parr. *The Magic Mirror*. Seattle: Hermetic Press, 2002.

O'Neill, David P. *What Do You Say To A Child When You Meet A Flower?: A Book for Parents of Preschool Children*. St. Meinrad, Indiana: Abbey Press, 1975.

Osborn, Norm, and Edward Marlo. *Unlimited*, second revised edition. Jon Racherbaumer (editor). No city: 1983.

Penner, Dick (editor). *Fiction of the Absurd: Pratfalls in the Void*. New York: New American Library, 1980.

Pollack, Rachel. *78 Degrees of Wisdom: A Book of Tarot, Revised Edition*. Newbury Port, MA: Weiser Books, 2007.

Punx. "Eternal Longing—a Very Short Biography." *Farewell Performance*. Bill Palmer (translator). Houston: Exclusive Magical Publications, 1991, pages 4-5.

Schneider, Mark A. *Culture and Enchantment.* Chicago: University of Chicago Press, 1993.

Sharpe, S. H. *A Thousand Thoughts on Art & Magic,* in *Art and Magic.* Todd Karr and Vito Lupo (editors). No city: The Miracle Factory, 2003, pages 29-178.

-------. *Neo Magic,* Part 1 of *Neo-Magic Artistry.* Todd Karr (editor). No city: The Miracle Factory, 2000, pages 5-166.

-------. *Words on Wonder,* second edition. In *Art and Magic,* Todd Karr and Vito Lupo (editors). No city: The Miracle Factory, 2003, pages 179-226.

Solzhenitsyn, Alexander. *The Gulag Archipelago.* New York: Harper & Row, 1973.

Spence, Lewis. *An Encyclopaedia of Occultism.* Mineola, NY: Dover Publications, Inc., 2003. Originally published in 1920.

Szymborska, Wislawa. *View with a Grain of Sand: Selected Poems.* New York: Harcourt Brace & Company, 1995.

Taylor, Charles. *Sources of the Self: The Making of the Modern Identity.* Cambridge, MA: Harvard University Press, 1989.

Viereck, Peter. "A Walk on Snow." *The Yale Review,* Number 2, 1948, pages 240-241.

Walter, Victor. "High Magic: The Art of Re-enchantment," *Convergence*. Deep Winter, 1997, pages 22-25.

Weber, Max. *Economy and Society: An Outline of Interpretive Sociology* (in three volumes). Guenther Roth and Claus Wittich (editors). New York: Bedminster Press, 1968.

Wells, Orson. "Citizen Abner." *Genii: The International Conjurors' Magazine*, Volume 52, Number 7, January, 1989, page 435.

Weschler, Lawrence. *Mr. Wilson's Cabinet of Wonder*. New York, Pantheon Books, 1995.

Wiesel, Elie. *The Gates of the Forest*. Francis Frenaye (translator). New York: Holt, Rinehart, and Winston, 1966.

Wittgenstein, Ludwig. *Tractatus Logico-Philosphicus*. London: Routledge & Kegan Paul, 1961.

Wordsworth, William. "My Heart Leaps Up When I Behold." *Poems in Two Volumes*. London: Longman, Hurst, Rees and Orms, 1807, page 246.

--------. "The Daffodils." *Poems in Two Volumes*. London: Longman, Hurst, Rees and Orms, 1807, page 303.

Zimbardo, Philip. *The Lucifer Effect: Understanding How Good People Turn Evil* (New York: Random House, 2007.

DVDs, Tricks, and Other Media

Bauer, Ron. *Ed Marlo's Time Machine. The Ron Bauer's Private Studies Series #16.* Rochester, MI: Electronic Graphic Art Design Studio, 2003.

Bloom, Gaetan. "Immortal" (trick). *Tales From the Planet of Bloom, Volume 2* (DVD). Rancho Cordova, CA: A-1 Magical Media, 1999.

Chelman, Christian. "The Immortal" (trick). *Capricornian Tales: The Magic of Christian Chelman.* Tahoma, CA: L & L Publishing, 1993, pages 77-80.

Chesbro, Verne. *Ultimate Color Separation, No. 1.* No city: self-published, 1963.

-------. *Ultimate Color Separation, No. 2.* No city: self-published, 1965.

Duck, J. Russell. "Outer Space" (trick). *The Cardiste.* Number 10, July 1958, pages 3-5.

Gardner, Martin. "The Tic-Tat-Toe Trick" (trick). *Mathematics, Magic and Mystery.* Mineola, NY: Dover Publications, Inc., 1956, pages 28-31.

Gibson, Walter B. "Like Seeks Like" (trick). *The Jinx.* Number 91, 1940, page 569.

Gilbreath, Norman. "Magnetic Colors." *The Linking Ring*, Volume 38, Number 7, page 60.

Hartman, J. K. "Deep Voodoo." *Genii: The Conjuror's Magazine*, Volume 62, Number 6, June 15, 1999, pages 48-49.

-------. "Fixit Mixer." *Card Craft* (no city: Kaufman and Greenberg, 1991), pages 376-378.

Lorayne, Harry. Harry "Any-Deck Tally-Ho Extended." *Genii: The Conjurors' Magazine*, Volume 66, Number 2, February 2003, pages 58-59.

Lyons, Howard. "Slipduc" (sleight). *Ibidem, Volume 1* No city: Kaufman and Greenberg, 1993, page 181.

Marlo, Edward. "Double Vanish and Recovery" (trick). *Martin Gardner Presents*. Silver Spring, MD: Kaufman and Greenberg, 1993, pages 383-384.

-------. "Impact-Collision-Crash" (trick). *M-U-M* magazine, Volume 67, Number 8, January 1978, pages 25-26.

-------. "Oil and Water" (trick). *The Cardician*. Chicago, IL: The Ireland Magic Company, 1953, pages 111-117.

-------. "Time Machine" (trick). *Ibidem, Volume 1*. No city: Kaufman and Greenberg, 1993, pages 121-123.

Mayne, Andrew. "Tea Ceremony" (trick). *Mad Mojo*. No city: self-published, 1998, pages 23-26.

Neale, Robert E. "Get Out of Jail Free" (trick). *The Magic Mirror.* Robert E. Neale and David Parr (authors). Seattle: Hermetic Press, 2002, pages 131-134.

———. "Immortal" (trick). *Life, Death & Other Card Tricks.* Seattle: Hermetic Press, 2000, pages 294-300.

———. "Inside-Out" (trick). *Self-Working Paper Magic.* Karl Fulves (editor). New York: Dover Publications, Inc., 1985, page 116.

———. "Maya" (trick). *The Magic of Celebrating Illusion.* Sherman, TX: Theory and Art of Magic Press, 2013, pages 234-237.

———. "Mystery Tube" (trick). *The Magic of Celebrating Illusion.* Sherman, TX: Theory and Art of Magic Press, 2013, pages 311-319.

———. "Perfected Segregation" (trick). *Life, Death & Other Card Tricks.* Seattle: Hermetic Press, 2000, pages 147-152.

———. "The Probability Pack." *Life, Death & Other Card Tricks.* Seattle: Hermetic Press, 2000, pages 213-220.

———. "Real Jokers" (trick). *Magic and Meaning*, expanded edition. Eugene Burger and Robert E. Neale (authors). Seattle: Hermetic Press, 2009 pages 106-120.

———. "Reversal of Fortune" (trick). *Magic Matters.* Sherman, TX: Theory and Art of Magic Press, 2009, pages 228-230.

--------. "Sole Survivor" (trick). *Magic and Meaning*, expanded edition. Eugene Burger and Robert E. Neale (authors). Seattle: Hermetic Press, 2009, pages 133-136.

--------. "Sheep and Goats" (trick). In Martin Gardner's *Wheels, Life and Other Mathematical Amusements*. New York: W. H. Freeman and Company, 1983, page 66.

--------. "State Sign." *Tricks of the Imagination*. Seattle: Hermetic Press, 1991, pages 3-7.

--------. "To the Other Side of No" (trick). *This is Not a Book*. Seattle: Hermetic Press, 2008, pages 151-159.

Neale, Robert E. and David Parr. "The Last Dream." *The Magic Mirror*. Seattle: Hermetic Press, 2002, pages 119-126.

Norman, Karl. "The Polish Rocket" (trick). *Here's How: The Close-Up Magic of Karl Norman*. Washington, D.C.: Collector's Workshop, 1985, page 24.

Ostin, Bob. "Romantic Card Trick." *The Linking Ring*, Volume 79, Number 7, July 1999, pages 74-76.

Racherbaumer, Jon. "Oil Slick and Water Wonderful" (trick). *Kabbala, Volume 3*. New York: Louis Tannen, Inc., 1976, pages 46-48.

Rogers, Terri. "The Pirish Compass" (trick). In *Secrets: The Original Magic* of Terri Rogers. London: Martin Breese Publishing, 1986, pages 15-25.

Scarne, John. "Ashes of the Phoenix" (trick). In *Scarne's Magic Tricks*. Mineola, NY: Dover Publications, Inc., 2003, pages 192-193.

Shane. "Weeping, An Old Man" (trick). *Pentalogy*. Orlando, FL: Leaping Lizards Publishing, 2006, pages 249-253.

Solomon, David. "Refined Oil and Water." *Sessions*. Simon Aronson and David Solomon (authors). No city, no publisher, 1982, pages 125-131.

Vernon, Dai. "Oil and Water" in *More Inner Secrets of Card Magic*. Lewis Ganson (author). In *Dai Vernon's Inner Card Trilogy*. Tahoma, CA: L & L Publishing, 1996, pages 20-25.

Walton, Roy. "Impact" (trick). *The Complete Walton, Volume One*. London: Lewis Davenport Limited, 1981, pages 23-24.

White, Larry. "Hocus Pocus Cut Out Magic Set." Booklet of tricks inserted in *M-U-M* magazine, Volume 93, Number 7, December 2003, pages 20-forward.

About the Author

Bob Neale is a teacher and writer. Throughout his career, he has exercised his imagination by making up things in the overlapping areas of religion, magic, and the arts. The results have been psychological theories about death and dying, religion as mature play, and the relations of loneliness, solitude, and companionship. An understanding of the place of magic in daily life grew out of these explorations. And the expression of it was facilitated by his creation of origami models, puzzles, and tricks that are frequently presented with social, political, and philosophical meanings. He cares about magic as imagination at play in the expression of truth through illusion.

Bob is an ordained minister in the United Church of Christ with degrees from Amherst College and Union Theological Seminary in New York, where he taught for twenty-four years as Professor of Psychiatry and Religion. His publications during that time include In *Praise of Play* (1969), *The Art of Dying* (1973), and *Loneliness, Solitude, and Companionship: New Dimensions in Relationship* (1984).

Bob is an internationally exhibited and published creator of origami models. In 1964, he delighted many paperfolders and magicians with his "Bunny Bill." In 2009, his impossible object "The Impossi-Bill Braid" gave instruction on construction in both text and DVD. Between these years, he has published *Origami, Plain and Simple* (1994), *Folding Money Fooling* (1997), *Frog Tales*

(2000), and *Which Came First? A Collection of Magical Designs* (2006).

Bob's essays on magic and tricks have appeared in many journals, pamphlets, and books. He was a monthly columnist for *The Linking Ring* for five years. His first book for magicians, *Tricks of the Imagination* (1991), was followed by *Magic and Meaning*, co-authored with Eugene Burger (1995, now in an expanded, second edition from 2009); *Life, Death & Other Card Tricks* (2000); *The Magic Mirror*, co-authored with David Parr (2002); *Celebration of Sides: The Nonsense World of Robert Neale*, with the assistance of Michael Weber (2006, DVD); *This Is Not A Book* (2008); *Magic Matters* (2009); *Gift Magic: Performances that Leave People with a Souvenir*, with Jeff McBride, George Parker, Lawrence Hass, Eugene Burger, and Rich Bloch (2010); *444 and Three More* (2011); and *Nine Uneasy Pieces* (2012).

Bob's ground-breaking *Trilogy of Magic* was launched in 2013 with the publication of *The Magic of Celebrating Illusion*. This book, *The Sense of Wonder* (2014) is the second installment. The Trilogy will conclude with *An Essay on Magic* in 2015.

In 2014, Bob Neale was the recipient of a Special Fellowship from the Academy of Magical Arts in Hollywood, California. He makes his home in Vermont.

About Theory and Art of Magic Press

Lawrence Hass, Ph.D., founded Theory and Art of Magic Press in 2007 as an outgrowth of his internationally-famous Theory and Art of Magic Program, which had an eleven-year run at Muhlenberg College in Allentown, Pennsylvania (1999-2009). During that time the program featured performances, talks, and lectures on the magical arts by such world-leading stars as David Blaine, Eugene Burger, Roberto Giobbi, Max Howard, René Lavand, Max Maven, Jeff McBride, Robert E. Neale, Jim Steinmeyer, Juan Tamariz, and Teller (among many others).

In the same spirit of excellence, the mission of Theory and Art of Magic Press is to publish thought-provoking magic books and professional routines by world-famous performers and wise teachers of the art. Its goal is to produce top-flight materials that will assist people in becoming more effective and knowledgeable performers of magic and mystery.

Publications

Transformations: Creating Magic Out of Tricks
Lawrence Hass, 2007

Magic Matters
Robert E. Neale, 2009

Gift Magic: Performances that Leave People with a Souvenir
Jeff McBride, George Parker, Lawrence Hass, Eugene Burger, Rich Bloch, and Robert E. Neale
Lawrence Hass, editor, 2010

444 and Three More
Robert E. Neale, 2011

The Show Doctor
Jeff McBride
Additional Material by Lawrence Hass, 2012

INDEX-terity: A Revolutionary Approach to a Powerful Tool
George Parker, with Lawrence Hass, 2012

Nine Uneasy Pieces
Robert E. Neale, 2012

Deep Mental Mysteries
Lawrence Hass, 2012

Eugene Burger's Unpublished Secrets: The Spot Card
2013

Eugene Burger's The Paper Hat Mystery
2013

The Magic of Celebrating Illusion
Robert E. Neale, 2013

A Magical Vision: The World of Eugene Burger
A Film by Michael Caplan, 2014

The Sense of Wonder
Robert E. Neale, 2014

Creating Theatrical Magic: A Study of The War Wizard *and the Magician as Actor*
Max Howard, 2014

**To purchase our books and products, go to:
www.TheoryandArtofMagic.com.**

Made in the USA
San Bernardino, CA
24 October 2014